THEOLOGY WITH SPIRIT

HENRY I. LEDERLE

THEOLOGY WITH SPIRIT

The Future of the Pentecostal & Charismatic
Movements in the 21st Century

HENRY I. LEDERLE

Foreword by Jon Mark Ruthven

WORD & SPIRIT PRESS
Tulsa, Oklahoma

Theology with Spirit: The Future of the Pentecostal & Charismatic Movements in the Twenty-first Century

ISBN 978–0–9819526–3–5 (perfect bound)

Published by Word & Spirit Press, Tulsa, Oklahoma.

http://WandSP.com ; <WordSP@gmail.com>

Scripture quotations marked KJV are from the Holy Bible, King James Version, which is in the public domain.

Scripture quotations marked NASB are taken from the NEW AMERICAN STANDARD BIBLE®, Copyright © 1960, 1962, 1963, 1968, 1971, 1973, 1975, 1977, 1995 by The Lockman Foundation. Used by permission.

Scripture quotations marked NIV® are taken from the HOLY BIBLE, NEW INTERNATIONAL VERSION ®. Copyright © 1973, 1978, 1984, Biblica. Used by permission of Zondervan. All rights reserved.

Manufactured in the United States of America if purchased in North America, in the United Kingdom if purchased in Europe.

Printed on acid-free paper that meets the minimum requirements of paper permanence for library materials: ANSI Z39.48—1992

Contents

Foreword

Henry I. Lederle's *Theology with Spirit: the Future of the Pentecostal and Charismatic Movements in the Twenty-first Century* is the first historical theology of the Pentecostal-Charismatic tradition of which I am aware. I taught contemporary theology for many years in a course required for aspiring PhD students. This book would definitely have been a required text for this class and certainly on the reading list for my other theology courses.

Theology with Spirit is a unique and thoroughly reliable historical and theological map of a movement that now probably has the largest share of active members in Christendom. Lederle, as a good historian, traces in detail the relationship of Pentecostal -Charismatic ideas and those who espoused them to the surrounding religious culture at every stage, from the Enlightenment into post-modernism.

Dr. Lederle's work is clear and compelling. For example, he rightly shows that opposition to Pentecostalism was based far less on theological—much less biblical—principles than on the fact that conservative denominations at the turn of the 1900s were in the thrall of Enlightenment rationalism, with its strong (and invalid) schema of "natural" and "supernatural" categories and its "miracle-free" worldview. He points out that people groups uninfected by this rationalism (including our post-modern world) are immediately attracted to this biblical expression of the Spirit's life and power.

Lederle's work is an amazing, rich feast of insights and connections I have never before encountered, prompting many "Ahas!" of recognition and pleasure as I read.

I was with him until his conclusion. He predicts that a certain sub-species of Pentecostalism will come to dominate the world Christian scene (I don't want to spoil the ending). His choice at first suggested to me that he may have put his academic career on a suicide watch. But I had completely forgotten for the moment that I had written an article myself a few years ago, defending this same movement for most of the same reasons! I swung round to the conclusion that he probably was right after all.

Dr. Lederle is no heresy hunter. Just as he identifies the variety of heterodoxies in the Pentecostal groups, he also points out (refreshingly) that these same groups tend to correct themselves over time. His insightful balance and clarity express his callings as not only a scholar with academic brilliance but also a pastor with the gift of discerning, Charismatic warmth.

Theology with Spirit is an absolute *must* for every Pentecostal-Charismatic leader's bedside table, classroom, or pastor's study—and for all others, whether friend or critic, who would understand the Spirit movements of today from within their distinctive and developing beliefs. I found it utterly fascinating: works of this caliber and broad scope are rare in our movement, so snap it up and devour it!

Jon Mark Ruthven, PhD
Professor Emeritus, Regent University
Author, *On the Cessation of the Charismata:*
The Protestant Polemic on Post-biblical Miracles

Preface

Theology with Spirit has been about twenty years in the making. The title represents a protest against the *absence* of a developed theology of the Holy Spirit—a phenomenon that has been widespread in mainline and evangelical Christian circles for many centuries. This lack is sometimes called "functional binitarianism" (operating as if there were only *two*, instead of *three*, Persons in the divine Trinity). In the twentieth century, the pendulum swung the other way and the Spirit, or Pentecostal and Charismatic, movements arose and mushroomed to become the largest sector of Protestantism within a century. That is the story of this volume, but it focuses on the *teachings* of these churches and what the future holds for them.

In 1990, I immigrated to the United States with my family from South Africa. Since that time, I have become fascinated by the contours, groupings, and state of Charismatic Christianity. I taught theology at the graduate level at Oral Roberts University for eight years. ORU is a veritable laboratory for research in this area. I also served as an associate pastor for adult education in a downtown Presbyterian church in Tulsa and, more recently, as chaplain, director of missions, and professor of theology at a liberal arts college in rural Kansas. Sterling College graciously granted me a six-month sabbatical in the spring of 2009, which afforded me the opportunity eventually to write this book. I have purposely tried to limit academic documentation because I wrote for the general Christian reader rather than the scholar. Readers may judge whether I succeeded. As a "participant observer," I am experientially part of this Spirit movement and rejoice greatly in the abundant renewal that has come to the Church through it: the blossoming of empowered life in the Spirit that includes the charisms and the fruit of the Christian life under the Lordship of Jesus.

I believe we are now entering a season of *recalibration.* Magazine editorials from within the movement declare that Pentecost has been cheapened and many preachers have become guilty of hype and even charlatanism. The public cries out against some television fundraising methods and moral lapses in high places. Calls for renewed *repentance* are in order and should involve every one of us. May God in His grace sustain us. The fledgling awakening of the last few months at the International House of Prayer University in Kansas City and the widespread renewal of passionate worship from coast to coast are signs of hope in the U.S., and overseas the growth of Independent Charismatic churches continues steadily and unabated.

At this juncture, the Pentecostal and Charismatic segment of Christianity is poised to play an increasing leadership role, and I believe that part of the recalibration needed urgently involves serious *theological reflection.* The younger generation seeks mentoring and guidance, and this includes the clarification of doctrinal teaching and distinctives. This study is one small contribution toward this goal. May the discourse continue.

In conclusion, I thank sincerely Erin Thiessen, a previous student of mine at Sterling College, for the cover design; and I dedicate this book to the four women in my life:

> To Fran, my wife and praying partner in the faith
> for some thirty years,
> and to Stephanie, Christine, and Karin,
> daughters of whom I am so proud,
> all seeking to live their lives with us to the glory of
> God.

May 2010

1

Introduction:

A New Pentecost and Unity

*I*t happened in Los Angeles, California, in the spring of 1906. A one-eyed, black Holiness preacher named William J. Seymour experienced a deep touch of God in his life on the night of April 12. He relates that divine love melted his heart. He heard prophetic words of healing and encouragement in his soul, and out of his innermost being adoration and praise poured forth in a strange and beautiful language he did not know. He was being empowered by the Holy Spirit to pioneer a remarkable move of God in the twentieth century.

Within days, his ragtag group of parishioners had renovated an old livery stable—a two-story building at 312 Azusa Street—and an unprecedented "Holy Ghost" revival began that would last three and a half years, turning the established religious world upside down. Meetings were held at the Apostolic Faith Mission three times a day, often stretching daily from morning until midnight.

This Azusa Street awakening signaled the birth of classical Pentecostalism. People from an amazing variety of ethnic, social, national, and denominational backgrounds experienced loving fellowship and unity as they crowded into the meetings. The building could hold about eight hundred, with several hundred more clamoring at the doors and windows to experience something of this fresh wave of God, to witness the gracious demonstrations of miracles of healing and repentance and dramatic signs of a present-day outpouring of God's Spirit. Remarking on the interracial mingling, most exceptional at the time, a journalist uttered the frequently quoted line: "The color bar was washed away in the blood of Jesus."

Within a few months or years (depending on the case), the first missionaries departed to spread this Pentecostal fire to Norway, England, Sweden, and Germany in Europe, to Brazil and Chile in South America, to India, South Africa, the Soviet Union, and further afield. Under the humble leadership of Seymour, an international movement had started. He sent his newspaper, *The Apostolic Faith,* free of charge to some 50,000 subscribers across the world.

A century later, in the year 2006, demographers estimated the global membership of Seymour's legacy—the various Pentecostal and Charismatic Renewal movements of the twentieth century—at 600 million. Church historian Bruce Shelley projects a membership of one billion by 2040. It is this remarkable tale of the Spirit churches of the twentieth and twenty-first centuries that will be outlined and interpreted in the following pages.

Finding a Name

The new movement was in need of a name. In the first decades, it was described variously as Apostolic Faith, Full Gospel, Latter Rain, and Pentecostal. They all communicated the idea of the power of the Holy Spirit. Let us consider them briefly.

• "Apostolic Faith" laid claim to the fact that the early Pentecostals saw their experience as a reviving of the faith and practice of the first apostles of the New Testament era.

• "Full Gospel" expressed the idea that part of the gospel had been lost over the centuries of the history of Christianity and now was being reclaimed and rediscovered. *The "Full Gospel" restored the neglected supernatural dimension.* The age of miracles and divine healing was not over. God was still pouring out His gifts of grace, or charismatic manifestations, on the Church. This view challenged "cessationism," the belief that all supernatural "signs and wonders" had ceased, an idea accepted in many evangelical circles.

• The term "Latter Rain" used a biblical analogy—the new outpouring of the Spirit at the beginning of the twentieth century. This understanding also anticipated the Second Advent or return of Jesus. (It seems as if, technically, this analogy actually misunderstood the climate patterns of Palestine which, being part of the Mediterranean region, receives its annual rains in the winter and spring. As a result, between the early rains of October and the latter rains of April stretch, not hot and dry summers, but moist winters! As William Faupel points out, this fact, unfortunately, does not fit into a restorationist version of Church history. It traditionally sees the apostolic epoch as the early rains, followed by a steep, arid decline and a long drought and, only then, the latter rains of restoration in the sixteenth, eighteenth, or nineteenth centuries, reaching a pinnacle in the present!)

• However, the term which ultimately gained ascendancy to describe the new movement is "Pentecostal." This term employs another biblical analogy: the comparison with the day of Pentecost described in Acts 2. Regarding this day Luke declared, "You will receive power when the Holy Spirit has come upon you" (Acts 1:8). Pentecost—literally the fiftieth day (from the Greek)—referred to the harvest festival seven weeks after the celebration of the Passover feast. In the New Testament, we read that it was on this day that the Holy Spirit was poured out on the Church by the risen Lord Jesus. Pentecost has thus come to symbolize not only the dramatic tongues of fire and inspired speech of the early disciples but also the recovery of unity and communion between people of many languages. There seems to be evidence that

Genesis 11 (which recounts the dispersion of languages at the tower of Babel) was among the assigned parts of the Torah (meaning "instruction," referring to the first five books of the Hebrew Scriptures) read in the Jewish temple liturgy on that very day. The term "Pentecostal" came to express power to witness and the recovery of the miraculous gift of glossolalia, as well as a new unity across barriers of heritage, nationality, and languages, as represented by the diversity of people in Jerusalem on that day who heard the mighty deeds of God proclaimed "as if in their own languages" (Acts 2:6, 11).

A Fully Trinitarian Faith

The Pentecostal movement is profoundly associated with the work of the Third Person of the Holy Trinity. The term "Pentecost" also speaks to the fact that the Spirit was "poured out" like life-giving water on a parched land at this milestone event in the history of salvation. It has been characteristic of Pentecostalism that pneumatological terminology (referring to the Holy Spirit—from the Greek *pneuma* for spirit, wind, or breath) has occupied a prominent place. Christian leaders have long realized that the Holy Spirit, the Third Person of the divine Trinity, has been neglected to varying degrees in the different confessional traditions. As far back as the earliest creeds of Christianity—the so-called Nicene and Apostles' Creeds—we find a predominant section on the doctrine of Christ followed by a much briefer treatment of the Spirit. In evangelical circles in Christianity today there is often a "functional binitarianism," that is, a focus on the roles of two Persons (specifically Father and Son), rather than a fully Trinitarian faith, expressing the tri-une nature of the orthodox teaching on the doctrine of God as Father, Son, and Holy Spirit. This situation is largely "functional" in the sense that theoretical lip-service is always given to the classic understanding of God as tri-une (Three in One), while references to the person and work of the Spirit are largely perfunctory or conspicuous by their absence in most expressions of Christian life and ministry.

A significant part of the work of the Spirit as seen in Scripture is that of unifying, linking God to human beings and believers to one another. In fact, the Holy Spirit is the Spirit of unity and love, the Spirit being rich in creating communion and relationships in the Church. There can be no true unity without God's Spirit, and wherever and whenever the Spirit is at work, *koinonia*, or fellowship, is created between people, often across traditional barriers of class, age, gender, and ethnic origin.

Two Twentieth-Century Spirit Movements

Interestingly, at the start of the twentieth century, *two* very different major religious movements emerged within Christianity virtually simultaneously and largely in isolation from each other. Both have influenced the global religious scene significantly. The first is the rise of the Pentecostal movement, while the second is the rise of the Ecumenical movement. However strange it may seem, both are, in a sense, "Spirit movements," each focusing on a different but deeply connected aspect of the Spirit's work. It is necessary to pursue the historical roots of these two movements briefly.

Ecumenism

Both movements originate ultimately in the New Testament era. Ecumenism sees itself as a witness to the Christian unity of the early Church, before historical, doctrinal, and ethical controversies fragmented the body of Christ into the wide-ranging denominationalism of contemporary Christianity. New Testament scholarship has recently made us more aware of the fact that even the unity of the first two centuries was never a uniformity in which the Church was made up of homogeneous congregations. Nevertheless, the differences that existed, even with regard to doctrinal emphases, did not lead to the widespread separation and schisms that have characterized Christianity since the sixteenth century. The goal of much ecumenical fervor in the twentieth century was to restore the original unity-in-diversity of the fledgling churches of the apostolic era and even to attempt to revive the "apostolic faith" of primitive Christianity. It is fascinating, if not ironic, that the World Council of Churches (with its headquarters in Geneva, Switzerland) launched a project at the end of the twentieth century seeking to recover what they also call the Apostolic Faith—the very term employed by William Seymour to name the new revival movement of Pentecostalism!

The more direct and immediate roots of the modern ecumenical movement can be found in the evangelical awakenings and the great missionary movements of the nineteenth century. International student ministry and youth movements such as the YMCA and YWCA also brought a new awareness of the divided nature of Western Protestantism. It was especially the confrontation with different cultures and other world religions in Asia and Africa that brought many Christian missionaries and evangelists to reflect on the biblical call to the unity of the Church. Ephesians chapters 2 and 4, as well as the prayer of Jesus in John 17, featured prominently in these deliberations. These ecumenists recognized the pivotal role of Christian unity in world evangelization. Jesus had prayed "that they may all be one so that the world may believe" (vv. 21, 23).

Yet the fragmented nature of Christians missions has discredited the gospel in many ways. Not only did fragmentation diminish resources, but missionaries found it difficult to explain to new believers why different denominational missionaries competed among themselves (even those within the same doctrinal family, such as Baptist or Lutheran) for converts in colonial settings. The first World Mission Conference in Edinburgh in 1910 gave new intentionality to the issue. Soon calls for a new Council to seek deeper unity among Christians emanated from sources as different from one another as the Ecumenical Patriarch of Eastern Orthodoxy in Istanbul, Turkey, the Protestant Episcopal Church (Bishop Brant), and the Disciples of Christ/Christian Church (Peter Ainslie) in the United States. Early on, the modern ecumenical movement sought visible unity chiefly by bringing many confessional groupings together in dialogue, in what is called "multilateral" ecumenism. This ecumenical approach led to the formation in Amsterdam in 1948 of the World Council of Churches (WCC). The major players in the WCC have been the mainline Protestant denominations, often theologically liberal, and the Eastern and Oriental Orthodox Churches of Eastern Europe and the Middle East. Since the Second Vatican Council (1962–1965), the Roman Catholic Church—by far the largest branch of Christianity, numbering over one billion adherents—has engaged actively in ecumenical discussions. Catholic discussion has taken place largely in the form of "bilateral" dialogue—dialogue with one other communion or confessional family at a time. In fact, the Roman Catholic Church has dialogued regularly with Pentecostal leaders for three decades.

Separations between the Two

More significant, nevertheless, than any similarities between these two movements that emerged at the beginning of the twentieth century has been the polarity and opposition separating them. The Pentecostal movement has tended to become associated or identified with theological conservatism and fundamentalism. The inaccuracy of this generalized classification will become apparent in the theological analysis pursued in the following chapters. In fact, Pentecostal and Charismatic perspectives differ from more evangelical or fundamentalist positions in many clear ways. Examples of such differences include attitudes toward the present-day occurrence of the gifts of the Spirit—the so-called charismata—and styles of worship, the role of reason, and the understanding of prophecy, among others.

Separations between "Spirit movements" and movements toward visible Christian unity have also been fueled by perceptions of ecumenism as necessarily liberal theologically and radical socio-politically. The limitations of this view will not be pursued here. Suffice it to say that given the New Testament imperative to Christian unity, a valid call to deeper fellowship, cooperation, and the visible expression of the oneness of Christ's body is an undeniable part of the gospel. The Christian Church in the twenty-first century must integrate these two aspects of the work of the Holy Spirit that emerged so strongly in the first decade of the twentieth century—both the reclaiming of the supernatural dimension of Christianity by Pentecostalism and the renewing of the call to the visible unity of the Church by ecumenism. Both movements may themselves need to be transformed in this process.

Pentecostalism

The more direct and immediate roots of the Pentecostal and Charismatic awakenings add a dimension to the picture of the Holy Spirit as the Spirit of unity and the Spirit of the miraculous. His miraculous activity beckons us beyond the confines of that which can be understood and defined by human logic and rationality.

Hebrews 13:8 was the rallying cry of early Pentecostal thinking: "Jesus Christ is the same yesterday, today, and forever." This affirmation implied that believers today could experience the power of the Holy Spirit just as it was manifested in the supernatural healings and exorcisms of the New Testament. The Church needed to rediscover openness, at least to the full range of charismatic manifestations described in Acts and the letters of Paul, including prophetic utterances with revelatory content, divine healing, the enigmatic sign of glossolalia, and the interpretation of these same tongues.

Pentecostals view their historical roots as stretching back to the first century, but it is undeniable that the foundations of the modern Pentecostal movement (like those of the ecumenical movement) are established in the eighteenth and nineteenth centuries. Before pursuing the development of Pentecostalism and the Charismatic movements at length in the following chapters, a brief outline of this history is in order.

The primary distinction that first needs to be drawn is between a *white-originated* (European-North American) heritage and a *black-originated* movement with roots in Africa, the Caribbean, and the African-American culture. The unearthing of the vital role played by slave revivals in the earliest origins of Pentecostalism has only come about in the last three decades. Swiss theologian Walter Hollenweger, an established researcher in the field of global Pentecostalism, gathered around him in Birmingham, England, a number of students from the Caribbean Islands. Gradually, a clearer understanding emerged of black-originated revivals that would later flow into mainstream Pentecostal spirituality through the Azusa Street revival.

Black-originated Pentecostalism

As far back as 1741 and 1783, slave populations experienced significant religious awakenings in the southern states of the USA and on islands such as Jamaica and Hispaniola in the West Indies or Caribbean. Further revivals took place in 1860 and in 1886 after the abolition of slavery. Racial prejudice seems to have adversely affected the writing and documentation of this history, and much research still needs to be done to write an adequate history. Although uprooted from their continent of origin, many black slaves brought with them a wellspring of African spirituality. This has been called "the invisible institution." Hidden from the public eye, spontaneous forms of worship were practiced on cotton plantations, often under large trees. The liturgy was oral, rather than written. The gatherings included the flamboyant, contemporaneous retelling of Bible stories, healing by prayer, sharing of dreams, visions, prophecy, hand-clapping, shouting, exorcism, testimonies, spirited dancing, glossolalia, simultaneous audible prayer, emotional singing, and full body worship, including swaying, jumping, raising of arms, and falling down. Many of these features would later feed into the empowered worship style of classical Pentecostals, and they also influenced the broader stream of most African-American Protestant churches. This explains why many black Baptist or Methodist churches seem more "Pentecostal" in their style of worship than their European-American counterparts. This

African heritage was very much part of the black Wesleyan-Holiness tradition as well, and it is from this background that William Seymour came.

White-originated Pentecostalism

The white-originated roots of classical Pentecostalism have been more extensively researched and documented. A focus on the Spirit can be found on the fringes of Christianity throughout the centuries, from the second-century Montanists through medieval sectarian movements to the radical Reformation of the sixteenth century and the revival meetings of the First Great Awakening. However, the first figure to stand out more clearly in the role of a proto-Pentecostal was the Scottish Presbyterian Edward Irving, who pastored a fashionable Presbyterian Church in Regent's Square, London in the 1820s. By the end of the decade, prophecy and tongues were heard in his services. In his Christology, Irving taught that Jesus assumed the same fallen humanity as we have and that the supernatural dimension of His life was due to empowerment by the Spirit rather than to His divinity. This perspective recognized that contemporary disciples of Jesus could then also move in the power and manifestations of the Spirit. Irving saw glossolalia as the "standing sign" of a person's baptism in the Spirit. Irving was ousted from Presbyterianism, more for his Christology than for his support of charisms. Out of his ministry developed the Catholic Apostolic Church, which reinstituted the practice of twelve original apostles and later an elaborate structure of ecclesiastical offices.

The historical link from Irving to Charles Fox Parham, who first formulated the concept of glossolalia as "initial physical evidence" of the baptism in the Holy Spirit, remains somewhat clouded in mystery. Perhaps it came via John Alexander Dowie of Zion City, in Evanston, Illinois, who grew up in a Scotland very much aware of the strange occurrences among the Irvingites. It could be that the missing link was Frank Sanford of Shiloh, Maine, where Parham witnessed Bible school students speaking in tongues several months prior to the dramatic breakthrough in Topeka, Kansas, in 1901.The details remain uncertain.

"Born in a holiness cradle"

Broadly speaking, it is clear that Pentecostalism arose out of the Wesleyan-Holiness movement. Both Parham and Seymour were steeped in this tradition. The Holiness movement of the last three decades of the nineteenth century had not only preserved but intensified John Wesley's focus on sanctification. The doctrine of Christian perfection came into new prominence, and sanctification was viewed in Holiness circles as a crisis experience, or step, subsequent to conversion, rather than an ongoing process. The Wesleyan teaching of a "Second Blessing" after conversion provided a theological framework in which the Christian life could be viewed as consisting of a series of distinct stages, marked by specific events. Under the influence of Wesley's designated successor, John Fletcher (originally from Switzerland), the initial Wesleyan focus on sanctification and holiness moved into more pneumatological categories (categories centered on the Holy Spirit). Fletcher replaced references to purity with references to enduement with the Holy Spirit's power. He was also the first to call the Second Blessing a "baptism in the Holy Ghost." Later the Keswick-Holiness and Higher Life movements' adherents were added to the mix and presented a different perspective on perfection. They saw the purpose of the second experience not as achieving purity of heart and intentions but as an "enduement with power for service."

By the time of Parham's teaching on Spirit baptism, there already was within Holiness circles in the United States an established view that saw the normal pattern of Christian discipleship as consisting of three stages: conversion, sanctification, and the baptism of the Holy Spirit. This innovative grid, which separated the purifying work of the Spirit in sanctification from the empowering work to enable witnessing, was disparagingly known as the "Three Blessing Heresy" by traditional Wesleyans. It was this three-staged pattern of B. H.

Irwin, however, that provided the "tinder box"—to use the apt analogy of Donald Dayton—from which the spark of glossolalia sprang to ignite the revival fires of Pentecostalism. Veteran church historian Vinson Synan, the undisputed expert in this field, concludes that it is safe to say that Pentecostalism in America was "born in a holiness cradle."

Speaking in Tongues

Isolated occurrences of speaking in tongues can be found throughout Christian history. Some claim that in the seclusion of Eastern Orthodox monasteries in Greece it never died out and has been continuously practiced for twenty centuries. Practically every major revival movement in the history of the Church testifies to the occurrence of strange tongues and utterances among the unusual phenomena often occurring on the margins of the movement. John Wesley recognized the role of the "French prophets"—French Huguenot refugees—in the manifestations taking place in his meetings.

The famous Cane Ridge camp meeting in Kentucky in 1801 included phenomena termed "godly hysteria," including jerking, dancing, and "holy laughter." The Church of God family of churches claims that the start of their Pentecostal outpouring took place in 1896, predating Topeka's Bethel Bible School and the work of Parham by five years. This date refers to an Appalachian revival in which glossolalia was very prominent.

The role of Charles Fox Parham has already been referred to above. He was a Wesleyan-Holiness preacher and healing evangelist who played a pivotal role in precipitating the whole Pentecostal movement, second in influence only to Seymour. The dramatic events at the start of the new century—January 1, 1901—at the Topeka Bethel Bible School belong to the collective consciousness of all Pentecostals. Parham, who was away conducting services in Kansas City, gave his forty or so students the task of studying the book of Acts, looking for the "evidence" of baptism in the Holy Spirit. They found the so-called "Five Cases" in which glossolalia either occurs or may be presumed (in chapters 2, 8, 9, 10, and 19). The missing link had at last been found—evidence for Spirit baptism. Following a watch-night service on that Old Year's evening, a student, Agnes Ozman, asked that hands be laid on her for receiving this gift; and in the first hours of the new century, she burst forth in an unknown language that she would speak for three days. Parham and the other students later followed suit. The phenomenon of tongues was seen as xenolalia—the speaking of unknown but existing languages with a missionary purpose. This was seen as parallel to the biblical events described in Acts 2. Although most Pentecostals soon abandoned this particular interpretation of the purpose of tongues, Parham maintained until his death that tongues were existing (but unlearned) languages given for evangelistic purposes.

It was directly from Parham, who swiftly spread the new doctrine of "initial physical evidence" further afield, that Seymour himself enthusiastically received it. At a Bible school set up in Houston, Texas, Seymour, being black, was initially only allowed to listen in on Parham's classes through an open door while sitting outside in the hallway. Seymour became convinced of this doctrine and would take it to Azusa Street when given the opportunity to preach in Los Angeles.

The founder of the movement, Seymour was himself later to abandon this theory of "initial evidence," choosing rather to see Christian love as the evidence of Spirit baptism—especially after he experienced rejection and racial prejudice from his erstwhile mentor, Charles Parham. The quest for evidence in itself is a rather remarkable sign of the times. At least two forces contributed to phrasing the question in this manner: namely, What is the initial physical evidence of the baptism or infilling of the Spirit? The first is cultural and secular in origin. In the broader culture, a significant interest in physical evidence stemmed from the tradition of British empiricism and scientific investigation focused, especially since Charles Darwin's *Origin of the Species* (1859), on fossil evidences and the search for the missing link of his theory of evolution. The second was of a more psychological and religious nature. In the Wesleyan-Holiness tradition, the theory that sinless (but not absolute) perfection could be attained often led to a restless seeking for assurance that the blessing had, in fact, been received. The frequent reoccurrence of sins after a crisis act of consecration led either to unhealthy denials or else to the conclusion that the experience had in fact not been the authentic article; and so a new quest was embarked on for the true and authentic "entire sanctification" experience. *Physical* evidence of the enigmatic, inner work of the Spirit would indicate that the much-desired-and-sought-after experience had indeed occurred.

Black and White Origins Converge

The black-originated movement—with its vibrant, ex-pressive style of worship and openness to things spiritual, uncluttered by a heritage of restricting rationalism and Gnostic inhibitions about the human body so prevalent in Western modernism—converged with the white-originated movement in the dynamic outpouring of God's Spirit that characterized Azusa Street. The white-originated movement brought with it a new "evidence" theory regarding the role of tongues, an eschatological fervor which expected an imminent return of Christ, and a doctrinal conviction regarding the encompassing nature of the Full Gospel. Above all, it represented an understanding of the supernatural and the miraculous that had been suppressed or denied in Western Christianity to varying degrees for at least three hundred years. That the white-originated movement had not entirely extricated itself from the rationalist heritage of modernism would become evident from the way in which parts of Pentecostalism soon aligned themselves with predominantly white American evangelicalism and fundamentalism known for their rationalistic view of truth that defined biblical teaching as made up of logical propositions. It is also part of the ensuing history that within two decades, black and white Pentecostals went their separate denominational ways, negating the costly unity forged in the revival fires of Azusa Street. It would take until 1994 before even the umbrella organizations linking black and white Pentecostal (and Charismatic) denominations would form a unified body. This "Memphis Miracle" led to the formation of the PCCNA—the Pentecostal and Charismatic Churches of North America.

Conclusions

This introductory chapter has thus set the scene for developing the focus of this book and leads to these conclusions:

1. Pentecostalism is seen as an empowering move of God's Spirit, bringing revival and a fresh impetus of global evangelistic and missional outreach.

2. This "First Wave" of the Spirit in the twentieth century led to a seismic re-evaluation of the role of the miraculous and the supernatural. Participants claimed that spiritual experiences and dramatic charismata and other manifestations of God's power were reappearing in unprecedented ways and measure—occurrences not widely experienced in the Church since the first centuries.

3. Pentecostalism erupted with an unusual unity, love, and fellowship across barriers of race, ethnicity, nationality, gender, and class.

4. This new movement brought the role of the Third Person of the Trinity to the forefront, redressing centuries of neglect of the Spirit.

2

Worldviews

T he Pentecostal and Charismatic movements did not
develop or emerge out of a vacuum. Although somewhat
isolationist and anti-cultural in nature, they were still
deeply influenced, either positively or negatively, by the cultural
and societal trends of their times. Pervasive ways of thinking and
patterns of perceiving often operate unconsciously or in a
subconscious manner. Yet the rise of Pentecostalism challenged
the dominant worldview held in the West at the beginning of the
twentieth century. Only within this context may we grasp the
intensity of societal reaction against the Azusa Street revival and
its full-scale rejection. We turn thus to a discussion of the worldview of *modernity*.

For a brief overview of the foundational presuppositions of
the modern mindset—what is called modernism—we will use the
analysis of world-renowned missiologist David J. Bosch. In
chapters 9 and 10 of his imposing tome, *Transforming Mission*,
Bosch analyzes the differing theoretical paradigms or conceptual
frameworks within which missionaries have operated in the history of Christianity, specifically modernity and post-modernity.

In this context, it is helpful to look first at the way he describes the modern mindset and then, contrastingly, what has come to be known as post-modernity.

Modernity

Historians generally see the modern era as starting in seventeenth- and eighteenth-century Europe. Thomas Oden sees it as stretching from 1789 (French Revolution) to the fall of the Berlin Wall in 1989. This period is sometimes called the Age of Enlightenment. This analogy of light suggests that the preceding medieval period was contrastingly dark—clouded by the superstitions of uneducated serfs who were gullible and unsophisticated and dominated by the institutional power of the Roman Catholic Church and its dogmas and inquisitions. The poet Alexander Pope expressed the mood of the Enlightenment well:

> The world lay bathed in darkest night,
> God said: Let Newton be, and all was light!

As the father of modern physics, Isaac Newton represented the scientific mindset of empirical inquiry, meticulous research, and accurate verification. The mysteries of the "enchanted universe," inhabited by fairies, goblins and demons that were thought to cause disease and bring curses, were dispelled by the bright clarity of logic and rational analysis. Scientists discovered that illnesses were caused by germs, not by witches. All the natural laws of the universe were fixed and clear, operating consistently and universally, like the law of gravity.

Seven Characteristics

Bosch outlines seven characteristics of the modern paradigm. First and foremost is *rationality*. Natural human reason is the point of departure for all knowing, and that which is logical and rational is of the highest value and importance in life. The French philosopher René Descartes succinctly expresses this approach in his maxim: *Cogito, ergo sum* ("I think, therefore I am"). He argued that he could doubt or skeptically challenge everything except the fact that he doubted. As a result, this process of thought authenticates his very existence. Rational thinking is accorded primacy and priority over being. A more recent popular slogan that embodies the same sentiment is, "You are what you know."

Second, the Enlightenment divides reality into *dualisms,* especially the tension between the so-called objective and subjective. Nature was seen as the object of the subjective, inquiring mind. Scientific analysis could produce reliable data that were objectively verifiable. The realm of the subjective human mind was very different, influenced by personal opinions or fleeting notions and values.

Third, Bosch recognizes in the modern worldview a simple, *linear causality.* There is a direct and mechanical correlation between cause and effect. All of reality was seen as operating according to the laws of mathematics and physics, including the complex structures of physiology and human behavior. Knowing the causes and outcomes gives comprehension and control. The scientific mindset banishes the dimension of the mysterious.

Fourth, the modern worldview is irrepressibly *optimistic.* There is a dogmatic belief in progress. Civilization is advancing and, through education and technology, we can confidently look towards the dawning of a better day and a brave, new world.

Fifth, in modernity, a pivotal role is played by the Enlightenment's concept of knowledge. True *scientific knowledge* is neutral, based on hard fact, and value-free. Knowledge is abstract and objective—totally independent of the personal views of the observer or researcher. A typical expression of this position would be a statement such as, "Two plus two is four whether you are Buddhist, Baptist, or an unbeliever." Facts have a life of their own and can be verified rationally or empirically. Mathematical and physical sciences yield the ideal forms of such knowing.

Sixth, Bosch states that in the modernist paradigm, all problems are in principle *solvable.* In time and with human effort, all the gaps in comprehension eventually will be filled.

Through intellectual discovery and invention and the accurate application of the scientific method, solutions can be found for all of life's problems. This expresses the "can-do" mindset of modern technology and engineering, and it is closely connected to the optimism referred to above. In fact, it should be clear that all of these characteristics are intimately related and interconnected.

Seventh, in a modern mindset, people are seen primarily as free *individuals*—masters of their own destiny, captains of their souls. Human beings have limitless potential. They are perfectible and autonomous, evolving according to their own free will and independent choices. The individual is self-sufficient and should not be limited or inhibited by group values or collective controls. This aspect is well represented by the "rugged individualism" of the West with its insatiable appetite for unrestricted freedom.

Evaluation

It is easy to recognize that modernity has placed an indelible stamp on much of our cultural heritage. In many areas, life is still driven and controlled by this paradigm. It is also true that there are countless aspects and insights of modernity that are helpful and valid. It is just as true that the modern mindset has produced a strong and one-sided slant to our understanding and perception of reality. I believe the major flaw of modernity can be expressed in the phrase "absolutizing the relative." The modern paradigm has given absolute value to rationality. The human mind, with its intellectual categories and concepts expressed in logical and scientific propositions, has become an idol—if you will, the goddess of sweet reason. As a result, moderns overinflate something with relative value to the detriment of all other considerations. Rational analysis does indeed occupy a legitimate place next to other modal dimensions of reality, such as economic value, moral guidance, justice, social sensitivity, aesthetic beauty, faith convictions, etc. However, where *one* relative aspect is made absolute, it seems to impoverish the rich variety of God's created reality and often calls forth, of inner necessity, its opposite pole or correlate. This phenomenon is commonly known as the pendulum swing from one extreme to another (as we shall presently see in post-modernism).

By overemphasizing rationality, the non-rational dimensions of life suffer neglect. Rationalist modernity sought to understand and control by dividing things into ever smaller segments. Academic life in modern universities, for example, is characterized by the repeated subdivision of disciplines, leading to advanced specialization in which the connectedness and integral nature of knowledge can easily be lost. It is even possible for a doctoral student to get a Ph.D. in theology by writing a dissertation on one Greek word that occurs only twice in Scripture! The whole is seen as no more than the sum of all its parts. This tendency of modernity is called an "atomistic" approach—the ongoing attempt to break things down into their smallest particles. (Ironically, the word "atom" in Greek actually means that which cannot be split or divided any further.)

A rationalist approach downplays the role of human emotion and will. It neglects the experiential dimension of life, rather focusing attention on the abstract and conceptual. Relating this evaluation to the faith of the Christian church, it is apparent that modernity does not agree with many of the basic tenets of Christianity. While we may appreciate rationalistic clarity in analyzing Scripture and developing doctrine, it is also true that we cannot express biblical truth exhaustively in logical or analytical terms. The basic foundation of Christian theism—a belief and trust in an infinite, loving, holy, and relational tri-une God—cannot be grasped or explained rationally.

Above all, this worldview of Descartes and Newton questioned *the supernatural dimension* of the Christian faith. As modernity gained influence in Europe, thinkers saw the miracles of Scripture increasingly as problematic. Initially, belief in God did not seem to present an insurmountable problem. Most modernists of the seventeenth and eighteenth centuries viewed the hypothesis of a creator favorably. Faith in God seemed tenacious, but modernism did question the orthodox understanding of the deity as being *both* transcendent and immanent. Modernists readily embraced transcendency: God was seen as the distant and infinitely wise Creator or Architect of the universe. In time, however, the relation between Creator and creation was undermined. God was seen as no longer actively involved in the world and the lives of human beings. Where God was still seen as having the ability to intervene, such occurrences were viewed as limited, exceptional, and increasingly rare. In full-fledged deism, God is portrayed more as a divine Watchmaker who created the world, then wound it up, and now allows it to wind down on its own. The Creator remains uninvolved, even oblivious, to his creation, just as the actual makers of the wristwatches on our arms have, in all likelihood, no idea what eventually happened to the watches they have made.

The deistic god of modernism is viewed as supposedly still being *transcendent*, but deism has abandoned the biblical corollary of God's being simultaneously *immanent*—involved and related to the work of His hands. It is especially in the realm of the so-called supernatural—the signs and wonders of Scripture—that modern sensitivities presented a problem to the Church. Some, like Thomas Jefferson, expressed their disapproval of the miraculous by literally cutting out those sections from the pages of the New Testament. Such an attitude opened the way for a watered-down Christianity that focused on a Jesus who was merely a great moral and rational Teacher, who lived out in practice the deeply profound Golden Rule, and who shared aphorisms of wisdom in His parables.

In this modern climate of what is called the era of the "liberal Jesus" of the late nineteenth and early twentieth centuries, Jesus became an ethical example, rather than the Son of God who atoned for our sin or the Risen Savior who conquered death. The English writer C.S. Lewis pointed out the inconsistency of the liberal scholars who portray Jesus merely as a wise Teacher while ignoring the many claims He makes for Himself—especially in the Fourth Gospel—which would be conceived as the ravings of a megalomaniac (that is, if they were not true!). Jesus saw Himself as the Light of the World, the Way, the Truth and the Life, the Bread of Life, the True Vine, the Resurrection and the Life, etc. Because it is impossible to view these universal claims of Lordship and redemption as the statements of a wise and benign, itinerant sage, many scholars operating with a modernist mindset simply reject the authenticity of large parts of the New Testament.

The rational, scientific worldview led to the large-scale reinterpretation and elimination of the supernatural dimension from the Christian gospel. Miracles of healing were explained away as spontaneous remissions or having been based on incorrect diagnoses. Those raised from the dead had only been temporarily comatose. The story of the walking on the water by Jesus and Peter led to a conjecture, devoid of geographical support, that they found a sandbar or a sandbank on which to walk. A choice example of this ingenuity of faithless human reason is the explanation given to the multiplication of the loaves and fish. Scottish New Testament theologian William Barclay asks if it could not have been, rather, a miracle of generosity, the conjecture being that most people would naturally have packed their own private picnic lunches but were reticent to share with others. The example of the little boy selflessly presenting his two loaves and five fish to Jesus shamed everyone else into sharing, and twelve basketsful of remains could be gathered.

Modern reconstructions of the Scriptures invariably tried to downplay, eliminate, or ignore the supernatural aspects in salvation history. The existence of supernatural beings besides God, such as angels and demons, also were "swept under the theological carpet." Rudolph Bultmann's demythologizing program was an example of late modernity's resistance to miracles. He found it incredible to believe in devils and spirits in an era that has harnessed electricity and can produce the wonder of electric light bulbs! Episcopal theologian Morton Kelsey calculated that a surprising 49 percent of the verses of the New Testament contain elements of the supernatural, such as healings, exorcisms, revelatory dreams, glossolalia, prophecy, and references to angels, spirits, etc.

Ultimately, the modernist view of the world reduces reality to materialism and naturalism, consisting only of different forms of matter. In this view, we are locked up within the space-time continuum and the natural laws of the universe. The universe is closed.

Post-modernity

After a good three centuries, the hegemony, or rule, of modernity in the Western world is currently being seriously challenged. The emerging worldview does not yet have a satisfactory name. It is simply entitled "post-modernity" to indicate that it comes after modernism. As with all major cultural shifts, there can be no precision regarding the date of the start of post-modernism. Some philosophers see it as emerging in 1907 with Einstein's breakthrough known as the theory of relativity, leading to the New Physics, in which such terminology as "uncertainty," "contingency," and "relationality" is introduced into what had been called supremely an exact science. Others place the rise of post-modernity much later in the era of the turbulent sixties, when authority figures and the established order were being challenged on an almost global scale. Some theologians see the work of Karl Barth as ushering in a new paradigm, whereas still others see post-modern theology emerging later in the "genitive" theologies of the seventies. By "genitive" is meant the theologies using the possessive case—theology *of* liberation, theology *of* revolution, etc. The explosion of these pluralist voices includes differing types of feminist theology, Holocaust, Black, Asian, and "Third World" theologies, to name a few.

To express something of the profound change of mood in post-modernism before considering the seven characteristics given by Bosch, the following anecdote may help. The tale is told of how modern and post-modern thinkers responded to a very simple question: What is a cat? Modernists immediately started gathering data. The help of various sciences was sought.

Information collected included the specific gravity of the cat's blood and other detailed facts, such as a statistically reliable estimate of the number of hairs per square inch on the cat's fur. The cat was dissected, the organs measured, weighed, counted, and classified. With all this information summarized in a data report, the modernist announced: "There you have it—that is what a cat is."

In contrast, the post-modernist required only one thing to illustrate the answer. "Bring me a mouse," was the request. "In the experience of a cat encountering a mouse, the true 'catness' of the cat will be revealed. The whole cat becomes alive and aquiver from whisker to claw." This little story is most instructive. Modernism focuses on detailed observation and analysis yielding generalized abstractions. It dissects the cat into its component parts. Apart from the cat's losing its life in the process (!), the knowledge of the cat also dies the death of a thousand qualifications. Post-modernism, however, seeks experience that is integrated and holistic, experience that incorporates every dimension of the cat. Post-modernism discovers the true nature of the cat in a particular, concrete *experience*. It would contend that the whole is infinitely more than the sum of its parts.

Seven Characteristics

In describing post-modernity, Bosch revisits the same seven characteristics outlined previously, now expressing the shift in worldview. First, post-modernity recognizes and acknowledges the realm of the *non-rational*. Human experience includes more than the analytical and conceptually reasonable. It includes the intuitive, along with mystery, metaphor, spirit, and the symbolic. The materialist expectation of Marxists that religion would become superfluous and die out has not been realized. In fact, in the post-modern world, religious faith—and especially what many vaguely term "spiritulity"—exerts increasing influence. The spiritual dimension is not necessarily irrational or anti-rational, but it does refer to another dimension different from pure rationality and abstract logic. Contemporary theologies have *turned to experience,* including theologies as diverse as Latin American liberation theology, feminist and womanist thinking (based on white and black women's experiences, respectively), process theology, and the experiential approaches found in Pentecostal and Charismatic ministries.

Second, in the post-modern paradigm, *holistic* thinking overcomes the separation and divorce between subject and object. Human beings are seen as part of nature and not as polarized over against it. Modernism fueled a destructive tension and dualism between human beings and their physical environment, viewed them as at loggerheads with one another, and led to environmental problems that disturb the global ecological balance. Post-modernism seeks to recover the place of humans within nature. It also seeks integration of the mind and body of the individual person. As a pervasive, global philosophy, holism was actually developed by the South African prime minister and politician J.C. Smuts in the 1920s.

Third, Bosch maintains that post-modernity has replaced rigid cause-and-effect thinking with a rediscovered *teleology* (the quest for purpose). Rather than seeking explanations by determining causes, post-modern approaches try to probe evolving goals and aims. There is a new contingency and unpredictability afoot, as well as an openness to the future. In theology, this is evident in a shift to eschatological thinking (reflecting how the future impinges upon and breaks into the present as God's reign in the world).

Fourth, the mood of post-modernism is no longer that of widespread optimism. It recognizes, for example, that the exporting of modern technology, Western developmental aid, and educational programs has in many cases exacerbated the problem in the "Two-Thirds" or Majority World. Thus, post-modernity bears a new sense of *pessimism* and caution. Societal and political problems have proven to be more complex and democracy not so easy to establish.

Fifth, major shifts have taken place in the realm of epistemology, or the science of knowledge. The neutrality and objectivism of modern ways of understanding have divorced knowledge from morality. Hungarian philosopher Michael Polanyi speaks rather of a personal, *fiduciary knowledge*—an act of knowing that is embedded in trust and commitment. It has become apparent that there are no "brute facts," but only interpreted facts that are culturally conditioned. Notions of neutrality undermine the responsibility and sense of accountability that people should have for their thoughts. A glaring example is the devising and deploying of weapons of mass destruction. The Nazi holocaust was perpetrated by highly educated people. Knowledge is not value-free. No one really comes to the act of knowing with a clean slate (*tabula rasa*).

Augustine warned: "Unless you believe, you shall not understand." This old adage expresses the tacit, probing nature of understanding. Knowledge seems to unlock itself more readily and more fully to those who come as participant observers within a fiduciary framework. The word "fiduciary" refers to the idea of trust or faith (from the Latin *fides*). This approach to knowledge provides room for uncertainty and for mystery. Catholic scholar Karl Rahner states that the lamp of knowledge is love. Post-modern wisdom recognizes the unfathomable nature of the universe and the humility of the seeker for knowledge to remain open for revision and open towards the future.

Sixth, in the post-Enlightenment era, Bosch sees a *chastened expectation* of success. Many problems are not being solved; they are becoming more complex and frustrating. Linking this to the fourth characteristic, he underscores that in the Majority World (as the Third World has been renamed, recognizing that it constitutes the majority of the world in both area and population), as well as in the affluent North, serious societal problems of differing kinds abound—poverty, injustice, environmental pollution, debt, economic exploitation, racism, sexual abuse. Many increasingly recognize the demonic nature of cycles of violence and addiction, and their confidence in over-coming them has eroded. Although not yielding to pessimism or despair, the post-modern approach is more aware of human limitations and the reality of evil.

Seventh, post-modernity replaces the unbridled individualism of modernity with a sense of connectedness and *interdependence*. It no longer views the individual as autonomous and independent of larger societal groupings. A new relationship to nature and to the planet has become popular. Also, ethnic and regional ties of clan, tribe, and local dialect are now more fondly cultivated. Survival requires a togetherness, rather than the splendid isolationism of "I am an island" and unlimited individual liberties or rights. In the Church, some of these tendencies can already be discerned in the call for *team* ministry rather than the "one flock, one shepherd" concept of a multi-talented individual who is expected to be good at preaching, teaching, evangelism, counseling, fund-raising, recruitment, missions, music, and youth work. Many dialogues between different doctrinal traditions in Christianity now focus on the biblical call to be the body of Christ with a profound shared life of communion, or *koinonia*, among the members.

These characteristics help us understand the transitional era in which we find ourselves. In the United States, it seems as if, generally speaking, a post-modern climate is already firmly established on the West Coast and in the Northeast. In the South and Mid-west heartland, the modern mindset still has substantial influence. These are, nevertheless, broad generalizations, and one is sometimes struck by the diversity of perspective found even among those sitting in the same pew at a Sunday service. Next to a couple who live (and dress) much as they did in the fifties may sit a young lady culturally aligned to the twenty-first century. This phenomenon is called "non-simultaneity." As a result, patterns of ministry need to be increasingly flexible and adapt to face the challenges of addressing people who are modernists, people who are post-modernists, and many who seem to be a bit of both—all at the same time.

Further Contrasts

Modernity was described as "the absolutizing of the relative"—the universal application of the *rational*. Post-modernity has challenged this primacy of reason and brought non-rational experience into play as well as the rational. As its primary attribute, post-Enlightenment thinking is characterized by *experience* itself (in a holistic sense). All experience is seen as part of the picture, and since each person's experience is different and has decisive impact on the way one sees and interprets life, post-modernism is thoroughly relativistic. Inclusivity and tolerance have become the watchwords and indifference the mantra. "There is no right or wrong"—things are just different. Whereas this has always been valid in some arenas, such as the realm of matters of taste—colors of toothpaste or flavors of ice cream—post-modern sentiments deny the validity of any universal rule or moral guidelines. The word "absolutes" has become suspect. The only absolute is that there are no absolutes, one could say. This view applies to ethical conviction, legal norm, moral value, sexual mores, and even religious doctrine. In effect, post-modernity has turned modernism on its head. Instead of "absolutizing the relative," it *relativizes the absolute*, or denies universal validity to any idea.

Within Christianity, for example, God is believed to be the Absolute Truth, the source and goal of all reality. A post-modern mindset finds such claims to universal validity to be arrogant. The truth-claims of Scripture are rejected. Jesus Christ is not seen as "the Way, the Truth, and the Life" (John 14:6), nor is it accepted "that there is no other name under heaven given among men whereby we may be saved" (Acts 4:12). Post-modern philosophers such as Michel Foucault and Jacques Derrida deny the existence of the meta-narrative, what is popularly called "the big picture." For them, there is no big picture—no all-encompassing vision that gives ultimate meaning or purpose to existence. Post-modernists universally see such a claim as thinly disguised power plays for control and ideological manipulation.

Modernity found the mere existence of God as a supernatural, transcendent being problematic. It found the involvement or intervention of such a being in human life and the terrestrial world unconvincing. The Church was hard pressed to "prove" logically that there is a God. Post-modernity, on the other hand, is surprisingly open to the spiritual realm. Today claims to supernatural phenomena and even extraterrestrial visitations are no longer rationally scrutinized or skeptically rejected out of hand. The spiritual and the divine are taken seriously—so much so that the task of the Christian Church is no longer to testify to the existence of God but, rather, to protest that there are not many gods but only One! Post-modernity acknowledges the realm of the supernatural, but it does not necessarily acknowledge the need to discern between positive and negative expressions of the supernatural, between the spirituality of Light and the deceptions of darkness, and ultimately between God and his angels and the realm of the demonic. This seismic shift toward postmodernism in global consciousness has affected the rise and growth of the "Spirit movements" of the twentieth and twenty-first centuries profoundly.

This brief interlude of a more philosophical nature has provided a cultural and societal background for understanding the Pentecostal and Charismatic world and its critics. Even the term "supernatural" can really only be grasped within the context of modernism, as shall become clear in the next chapter.

3

An Array of Churches

Against this rather sketchy backdrop of modern and postmodern views of reality, we now turn to survey the *major communions of Christianity* in order to locate the Pentecostal and Charismatic awakenings of the twentieth century more precisely and in their historical context.

Classically, Christianity divides into three branches: Orthodoxy, Catholicism, and then the multiple forms of Protestantism. The basic contention of this present study focuses on the twin concepts that underlie the Pentecostal and Charismatic movements of the twentieth century: *the quest for fully Trinitarian thinking and divine power imparted by the Spirit, including the recovery of the so-called supernatural dimension and the full biblical range of the charisms.* How do these foundational issues inform our understanding of the wide panorama of Christian communions?

Eight Christian Communions

The term "communion" needs to be defined in this context. It refers to the broad doctrinal groupings of churches. A global communion consists of individual, national denominations. The

Baptist communion encompasses Southern Baptists, National Baptists, American Baptists, and Free Will Baptists. (to mention only a few denominational traditions within the USA). Similarly, the Methodist communion includes Nazarene, Wesleyan, and United Methodist denominations, as well as African Methodist Episcopal Churches and Free Methodists. For the purposes of this overview, we will now survey the eight major communions that originated up to the year 1900.

Orthodoxy

First, we encounter the Orthodox tradition, which numbers about 200 million believers. This grouping stretches back to the first century A.D. and sees itself as maintaining the orthodox doctrinal heritage of the early Church Councils and undivided Christianity. There is a basic cleavage in the Orthodox fold between the *Eastern* Orthodox Churches of Greece, Russia, and the Balkan states, such as Romania, Bulgaria, and Serbia, and the *Oriental* Orthodox Churches in Asia and Africa, such as the Coptic (Egyptian), Ethiopian, Jacobite (West-Syrian), Armenian, and Mar-Thoma (Indian) Churches. The doctrinal distinction between these two parts of Orthodoxy has to do with our understanding of the humanity and divinity of Christ. The Eastern Orthodox Churches accept the authority of first seven Ecumenical Councils of Christianity, including the pivotal decisions at Chalcedon in 451. The Chalcedonian formula, accepted by Roman Catholics and Protestant Reformers as well, was that Jesus Christ is one Person with two natures, which may be distinguished, but never separated or fused. The Oriental Orthodox are either *pre*-Chalcedonian—the so-called Nestorians who lean towards seeing Christ as "two Persons" and who broke away in 431—or *non*- Chalcedonians. The latter seceded after the decision of 451 because they saw Christ as having "one [mingled] nature" and thus are called monophysites (Greek for "one nature"), instead of espousing the two natures of the classic Christian tradition. Recent ecumenical dialogues are attempting to restore a Pan-Orthodox unity.

Roman Catholicism

The second major division in Christianity is between the Orthodox and the Roman Catholic Church. Catholics number more than one billion members, with large concentrations in Latin America, especially Brazil and Mexico, and Southern Europe (Italy, France, and Spain). Significant numbers live also in the USA, the Philippines, Poland, and the Congo. The separation between the Western and Eastern (the Latin- and Greek-speaking) parts of early European Christianity is usually dated as occurring in 1054 and linked to a somewhat minor doctrinal point concerning the eternal origin of the Holy Spirit. The oldest and most ecumenical of the creeds of Christianity, the Nicene Creed, states that the Holy Spirit "proceeds from the Father." In Western Europe, it became customary, in about the seventh century, to add the word *filioque* to the creed at this point, signifying that the Spirit proceeds from the Father *and from the Son*. This phrase was initially added, so it seems, to underscore the equality of God the Father and God the Son over against the Arian heresy, which denied the full divinity and co-equal nature of Jesus Christ with the Father. This Arian influence was strong in France and Spain. The Eastern Church dissented strongly to this innovation, which no council of the whole of Christianity had ever approved. When pressed, Eastern theologians stated that the Spirit proceeded from the Father *through* the Son (Latin, *per Filium*).

Contrasts: Eastern & Western Developments

Although seemingly trivial, this distinction symbolizes or represents a significant difference in the subsequent doctrinal development of the Eastern and Western traditions. The West awarded Christology substantially more attention than Pneumatology (the doctrine of the Spirit). Some argue that this would have happened regardless of the *Filioque* doctrine because the New Testament itself is clearly Christocentric in its focus, with Spirit's primary task being to point towards and testify concerning the redemption of God in Christ. Nevertheless, the East

33

developed a more mystical spirituality with less focus on structure and on the Church as an institution. It is also claimed, as has been mentioned above, that the *charismata*, or manifestations of the Holy Spirit, were practiced in Eastern Orthodox monasteries throughout twenty centuries, while the more dramatic *charisms* of the Spirit gradually ceased in the West, except for marginal occurrences, until the prominent "Holy Spirit awakenings" of the twentieth century. In *Christian Initiation and Baptism in the Holy Spirit,* two renowned Roman Catholic scholars, Kilian McDonnell and George Montague, have documented the experiential dimension (with the occurrence of *charisms*) of Christian initiation for the first eight centuries. Christian initiation includes the whole process of becoming a Christian, incorporating instruction in the faith, baptism, as well as the celebration of the Lord's Supper.

Contrasts: Material and Formal Principles

For Protestants to understand the distinctives of the Orthodox and Catholic traditions, it is helpful to consider the attempts of the well-known nineteenth-century theologian Friedrich Schleiermacher in expressing this basic difference. He stated that Catholics subordinate the personal relationship between individual believers and Christ to their relationship with the Church as a body, whereas Protestants do the converse—they subordinate the corporate relationship between individuals and the Church to their personal relationship to Christ. The Catholic approach would apply also to the Orthodox. Although this formula is rather simplistic, it is interesting to note that in the Restorationist and Discipleship/Shepherding groupings of Independent Charismatics, many come down on the Catholic, rather than the Protestant, side of the issue as stated above. Schleiermacher's successor in Berlin, Twesten, devised a more complex conceptual tool to help us group the differences between the major branches of Christianity. He distinguished between *the material principle* and *the formal principle.* The material principle refers to our understanding of what the basic nature of salvation is—what believers would refer to as *the essential element* of redemption in Christ. The formal principle has to do with the most important way in which the Gospel is transmitted—what is the primary *means of communicating* this message of redemption.

Orthodoxy

In Orthodoxy, the formal principle is to be found in the *liturgy* of divine worship. Worshipers are seen as entering into the presence of God's glory through the beauty of prayers, gold-painted icons, ornate oil lamps, music, and incense, enabling doxology and adoration. The material principle of Orthodox teaching is *theosis*—becoming godly. This term was widely used in the time of such Church fathers as Irenaeus and Athanasius. The idea is that God became human so that humans could become "divine." This was not meant as a blurring of the distinction between Creator and creature but, in the language of Second Peter 1:4, it is rather a "partaking of the divine nature" by escaping from the corruption of this mortal world through the impartation of life eternal. The celebration of the triumph of the resurrection of Christ at Easter expresses this focal point. Although we may also view becoming godly in moral terms— being sanctified—the Orthodox perspective sees salvation as the bestowal of the life of God and His immortal, incorruptible nature.

Catholicism

In Catholicism, the formal principle is the *Church* itself. The Roman Catholic Church, as an institution of God's grace, is the vehicle for transmitting the fullness of truth and redemption, expressed through the seven sacraments administered under the authority of priest and bishop. The global unity of Catholicism is expressed through what is known as the Petrine office (the pope in Rome viewed as the direct successor to Peter, through the ongoing link of ordinations known as "apostolic succession"). The material principle of Catholic theology is the *incarnation* of

Christ. God's redemption comes to us through "the Word made flesh" (John 1:14) and coming to dwell among us. This concrete, material aspect is expressed tangibly in sacramental worship.

A Shared Heritage

The heritage of Orthodoxy and Catholicism dates back to the classical, medieval, and pre-modern eras. This shared heritage readily acknowledges *supernatural empowerment and the miraculous as part of their concept of reality*. Because of the perceived excesses of the Montanist movement in the second century and various other factors, mainstream churches became somewhat cautious and reserved concerning the practice of the *charisms* of the Spirit. To differing degrees, these churches then limited these manifestations to the clergy and the monastic orders or to the more holy individuals known as "saints." Similarly, these churches saw signs and wonders of the kingdom (or rule) of God as operating through physical relics and at the tombs of deceased apostles, martyrs, holy men and women, or apparitions of the Virgin Mary. Roman Catholics have recognized miracles of divine healing throughout the centuries, although not all attested healings are considered authentic—by Catholic and non-Catholic alike. In modern times, Catholicism and Orthodoxy have tended to deemphasize or limit the supernatural dimension somewhat, but neither has ever formally denied this dimension or relegated it to the past, as has been the case in much of Protestantism.

The separation between Eastern and Western Christianity and the doctrine of the Filioque seem to have had the unintended effect that the Western tradition (both Catholic and Protestant) has focused in theology more on the Second Person of the Trinity than on the Third Person. Much has been made of the so-called "neglect of the Spirit" and the doctrine of pneumatology as an "appendix," "after thought," or "Cinderella" of Christian doctrine. In the East, the more subjective or mystical approach in worship has been credited with preserving a stronger understanding of the role of the Holy Spirit. Eastern Orthodox theology, however, has not developed an extensive, academic pneumatology, in contrast to the work of some Western scholars. This situation underscores the basic contention of this study that the most urgent theological task of the twenty-first century is the development of a full-fledged Trinitarian doctrine!

Protestantism

As we move on to consider the endless variety of *Protestantism*, we should first briefly attempt to apply the concept of the material and formal principles to Protestantism as a whole. The *formal* principle seems relatively simple—Protestants see the gospel as coming primarily, not through divine liturgy or the church as an institution, but through *the Bible*, as God's Word of revelation to humanity. What, however, is the *material* principle of Protestant theology? Personally, I prefer the description "union with Christ through the Holy Spirit." Salvation is to be found through regeneration and new life in the Spirit through the atoning and substitutionary death of Christ on the cross of Calvary. Some, especially Lutherans, would prefer the more legal Pauline term "justification by faith." Evangelicals would speak of being "born again" through a conversion experience or accepting Jesus as Lord and Savior into one's heart. These different analogies all express the same basic truth—forming a relationship with God in Christ through the indwelling of the Spirit.

Reformation

The Protestant Reformation of the sixteenth century permanently shattered the unity of Christendom in Europe. That unity had existed since the Emperor Constantine the Great legitimated the Christian faith in the Roman Empire in the fourth century and the medieval understanding of Catholicism under papal authority subsequently established the Church in society. At issue was the means of salvation. Martin Luther protested against an understanding of meritorious works-righteousness in the late Middle Ages, seeking rather redemption "by faith alone." This protest also challenged a perceived "domestication" of the work of the Holy Spirit within the institutional structure of the Church. John Calvin later developed the doctrine of the *Testimonium Spiritus sancti internum* (the internal witness of the Holy Spirit) as a testimony to the truth of Scripture (over against rationalistic argumentation), and both Luther and Calvin emphasized the correlation of *Word and Spirit (Spiritus cum verbo)* over against so-called "enthusiasts" or fanatics who attempted to loosen the operation of the Spirit from the touch-stone of the Scriptures.

Four Sixteenth-century Communions

The sixteenth century gave Christianity *four* new major communions or doctrinal families of churches. The *Anglican,* or *Episcopal,* tradition, emanating from the Reformation in England, formed something of a bridge between Roman Catholicism and the continental Reformation. Attachment to the *Book of Common Prayer* expresses the Episcopal focus on liturgical worship and beauty of form. Episcopalians also are known for their tolerance of a wide variety of theological emphases, ranging from Anglo-Catholic "High Church" to evangelical "Low Church," under the same Episcopal authority. Secondly, the *Lutheran* Reformation has a strong confessional tradition, and the doctrine of justification by grace is central, as well as the dialectical tension between Law and Gospel. Thirdly, the *Reformed* communion, also known as Calvinist or Presbyterian, emphasizes the cosmic Lordship of Christ and the sovereign majesty of God, in contrast to human finitude and sinfulness. It also values orderly process in its governing structures. Finally, the *Baptists* were derisively termed "Anabaptists" (rebaptized ones) in the Reformation era because their idea of a believers' church excluded the baptism of infants. They focused on individual freedom (including freedom from the influence of the state) and on voluntary, moral decision-making. The American revivalist tradition expressed this notion of freedom by ever-present "invitations" to conversion or "altar calls."

Methodism

In the eighteenth century, a fifth major communion appeared on the Protestant landscape: *Methodism*. Its founder John Wesley underscored the role of human responsibility, coupled with God's universal initiating grace, and emphasized holy living in the doctrine of sanctification and in the quest for sinless perfection.

The "Two-Party System"

These so-called "mainline" Protestant communions number about 400 million globally, but they have become sidelined numerically by a few important trends: by the rise of more conservative evangelical churches; by losses to secularism since the late 1960s, especially in North America and Europe; and by a cultural or civil religion form of Christianity that accepts nominal membership and limited attendance (such as on Christmas, Easter and Mother's Day). These churches once greatly influenced American society (forming the so-called White Anglo-Saxon Protestant, or WASP, establishment of the fifties and sixties of the twentieth century) and, of special significance in this study, these had most strongly imbibed the predominant worldview of modernity. As a result, they clashed with classic Christian doctrine on the issue of the miraculous.

By the middle of the nineteenth century, a division was forming between those Protestants who were challenging the supernatural dimension of the Scriptures outright and those who accepted the miracle testimonies of the Gospels and Acts yet believed that the "age of miracles" was over. These two groups became known by polarizing terminology, such as liberal and conservative or ecumenical and evangelical. This bifurcation has been overstated. Many Christians just did not fit into this two-party analogy that resulted largely from the Modernist-Fundamentalist struggle over the Darwinian theory of evolution. African-American Christians, Lutheran and Reformed con-fessional Protestants, as well as Pentecostals and Charismatics, simply have not and do not fit easily into either of these two labels, or categories.

Adventism

The nineteenth century also presented us with a sixth, and smaller, Protestant communion—the *Adventists*. The initial-ly rather marginalized Seventh-day Adventist Church focused on the imminent return of Christ and the life of preparedness for this advent by, among other things, religiously keeping the Sabbath and dietary regulations. The Adventist movement influenced Protestantism much more broadly than merely as a particular denomination. It ushered in renewed interest in the prophecies of Daniel and Revelation and, from that, in the pre-millennial understanding of eschatology and of the division of Church history into several (usually seven) eras or dispensations during which God employs different strategies.

Cessationism

Many conservative Protestants who wished to maintain belief in the literal truth of biblical doctrines (disputed by more liberal theologians), such as Christ's divinity, virgin birth, literal resurrection, atoning death, and physical return, were drawn into what became known as the cessationist camp. These accepted the supernatural signs and wonders of the biblical era but limited them to bygone eras. The miracles had ceased, and God now worked "through the propositional truths of inerrant Scripture." Although avoiding the lure of modernism in its overtly anti-supernatural form, this knee-jerk response to modern skepticism was itself unwittingly a victim of the same modernist presuppositions. The present-day or contemporary occurrence of signs of the kingdom (or reign) of God, signs such as prophecy, miracles, and healing, were denied or rejected as spurious. Scripture also was understood and interpreted in a somewhat rationalistic manner, without due recognition of historical and literary context or narrative structure.

At the close of the nineteenth century and the beginning of the twentieth century, the modernist paradigm still reigned supreme. In secular culture, deism, with its Creator distant from our modern "space-time box," and worldviews such as naturalism and materialism had widespread influence. In the Christian Church, liberal Protestants consequently focused on the ethical and rational dimensions of the teachings of Jesus. With his "demythologizing" program, the Lutheran New Testament scholar Rudolf Bultmann proposed, in the 1950s, to extract the kernel of existential meaning of the text from the outer husk—the vestiges of outdated cosmology and primitive supernaturalism. On the other hand, consistent dispensationalists of a more conservative, "Bible-believing" background argued forcefully for the cessation of all miracles after the death of the last original apostle (calculated as no later than A.D. 150 by B. B. Warfield of Princeton) or perhaps after the closing of the canon or list of accepted books of Scripture in the fourth century.

Exceptions

It is important to realize that this dominance of a *modern* worldview was limited to the culture of the West found in Europe, in North America, and in segments of the population in other places where colonization had imported similar sentiments. Even in the West, however, it did not permeate everyone. African-American and Native-American churches of the United States, for example, remained open toward the supernatural and acknowledged and expressed the non-rational dimensions of the human psyche. The worship style and spirituality of many such communities resisted the limitations of the modern mindset and its arid intellectualism. Through them, the broader range of human existence, including the affective and the intuitive, sought expression. Christianity was being prepared for showers of blessing on the parched aridity of modernist conceptualism. Many believed it was "for a time such as this" (see Esther 4:14) that the Pentecostal and Charismatic revival movements of the twentieth century came.

The Modernist Roots of Rejection

The extreme reaction against and total rejection of the Azusa Street awakening by some committed evangelical believers cannot be adequately understood as a response to the theological innovations of the movement (which were relatively minor). The new teachings of the Pentecostal movement were not wholly foreign to Christian tradition and could be illustrated and supported from the book of Acts, letters from Paul, and the experience of the early Church. There were, admittedly, grave questions about the exegesis of several key passages by early Pentecostal leaders, but their views did not seem to place them beyond the acceptable boundaries of doctrinal diversity within the Christian tradition. Practically every Christian communion has had some teaching that many other Christians have found strange: the Roman Catholic view on papal infallibility for official pronouncements and the assumption of Mary to heaven; the Calvinist teaching on limited atonement and *double* pre-destination (an ordaining by God of people both to heaven and hell before the foundation of the earth); the Wesleyan position on sanctification as instantaneous eradication of the root of sin from the human heart—to mention just a few examples—have all been questioned by other Christians without rejecting these confessional groupings outright.

Pentecostalism, however, was met in many quarters by vindictive criticism and a strident and total censure. The pinnacle of this reaction, perhaps, was the Berlin Declaration of 1909 in which the Evangelical and Pietist associations of Germany publicly declared that "the tongues movement" of California emanated "from below," referring, of course, to the demonic realm. Charismatic manifestations were considered as signs of mental imbalance, or even insanity. A prominent American preacher called the Pentecostal movement "the last vomit of Satan," and newspaper reports in Los Angeles used such inflammatory phrases as "an amalgam of African voodooism and Caucasian insanity."

This fanatical rejection of early Pentecostalism did much harm. It isolated Pentecostals and turned them against culture, as seen especially in the strong anti-intellectual and anti-medical stances they expressed in the first few decades of the twentieth century. The ridicule and persecution of the "Holy Rollers," "hysterical babblers," and so forth called forth or strengthened a persecution mentality and a "Christ-against-culture" mindset among early Pentecostals. In many mainline churches they were treated as outcasts and classified as sectarian or cultish.

The foundational cause of this misguided censure is to be found, not in theology, but, rather, in the fact that Pentecostals were questioning the most basic *philosophical* presuppositions of modernist culture. Protestant Christianity, after a century or two of interaction with deist and naturalist forms of scientific modernism, eventually came face-to-face with its heritage of supernaturalism and decided it was too costly and embarrassing to be maintained. The skeleton of belief in miraculous signs and wonders was stored securely in the back closet in order to gain intellectual respectability in modern society. Some doubted whether the miracles of the Gospels had ever taken place, while others—more evangelical and conservative in their doctrine of Scripture—staunchly maintained a belief in supernaturalism in biblical times but avoided contemporary embarrassment by relegating all such phenomena to the dim and distant past. Modern Christianity caricatured Pentecostalism abusively because Pentecostalism shook the very foundations of modernism—the pervasive paradigm and framework that Christian modernism had struggled to develop over several centuries as it accommodated itself to the secular scientific rationalism of the day.

The attraction and threat of Pentecostalism was precisely this: here was a new and vibrant strain of Christianity that was claiming to represent an apostolic faith, manifesting the same miraculous power of the Holy Spirit of the first Pentecost of Acts 2. It was this testimony that brought hundreds of thousands of visitors to Azusa Street. This Pentecostal message touched a raw nerve and troubled the uneasy conscience of modernist Christians. Many troubled Christians recognized that the Church had compromised the truth of the gospel by surrendering its belief in the supernatural gifts of the Spirit in its eagerness to fit in its cultural context and to be accepted in the halls of secular academia. Faced with growing interest among the populace in the Pentecostal revival and its disarming claim that Jesus Christ is the same yesterday, today, and forever (Heb 13:8), modernist Christians tended to respond emotionally and to ridicule and isolate Pentecostal Christians, viewing them as heretical and satanically influenced or, at best, as sectarian. This rejection spawned yet another harmful reaction: the emergence in Pentecostalism of extreme or unbalanced views. As a result, it would take thirty to forty years before non-Pentecostals would take the teachings of this new revival movement seriously. This favorable attitude toward Pentecostalism occurred in what has become known as the Second Wave or the denominational Charismatic Renewal movement of the 1960s and 1970s. At the same time, the first Pentecostal churches were maturing in their theological thinking.

The term "Classical Pentecostalism" was coined by the Catholic ecumenist Kilian McDonnell in order to distinguish the original Pentecostal movement from the later movements. The vehemence of reaction against Classical Pentecostalism is a casebook illustration of how non-theological—in this case philo-sophical—factors often become paramount in the struggles between Christian Churches. As an historical parallel, consider the inordinate attention given to the rather small Socinian movement in the theological treatises of the seventeenth century. Ultimately, the struggle was not so much about the theological arguments or the social influence of the followers of the Italian reformer, Faustus Sozzini, working in Poland but, rather, about the philosophical and epistemological presuppositions they represented. The Socinians were the first to critique biblical supernaturalism from a modernist perspective, and, as a result, all orthodox apologetes of the era gave the Socinian heresies disproportionate attention. The outburst of Pentecostalism at the beginning of the twentieth century represents the converse of this movement. The Socinians, with their denial of all supernatural aspects of Christianity, may have signaled the start of unbridled modernism in the Church, and the Azusa Street awakening, with its equally unbridled supernaturalism, may in fact have signaled the impending demise of the modern era and the start of post-modernity!

Reconsidering the "Supernatural"

The term "supernaturalism" has been used repeatedly in our discussion up to this point. A clarifying word is probably overdue. "Supernaturalism" is an awkward term that unfortunately comes with its own "baggage." It was formed in contrast to the idea of "naturalism," which is a view of reality without any non-material influence. Naturalism would seek to understand and explain all things by means of the senses and the analytical study of the natural, empirical world. The Greek philosophical views of Plato acknowledged the existence of "ideas" or patterns from a superior, heavenly realm that could be remembered and reconstructed here on earth. They may even be innate (inborn) in human beings. These spiritual (non-material) dimensions of knowing included wonderment, intuition, beauty, prophecy, healing and ecstasy. Plato's successor, Aristotle, however, reduced this concept of knowledge to the rational and empirical. He declared that all knowledge starts with the five senses. Rational analysis could be added to that for classifying and comprehending the empirical data. Aristotelian logic and philosophy were reintroduced to the Latin-speaking world in the thirteenth century through the writings and translations of Jewish and Muslim scholars in Spain.

Thomistic Dualism

Up to this time, the thinking of Plato and Augustine had been paramount in Christian circles. The great Catholic theologian

Thomas Aquinas, who favored Aristotle, was responsible for dividing reality into the independent realms of *nature* and *grace*. In the realm of nature, which was seen as preparatory for the realm of grace (also termed super-nature), knowledge came through rational analysis. Here Aquinas found common ground with those of other religions. He believed even the existence of God could be logically demonstrated. Building on Aristotle, Thomas worked out five theoretical ways, or "proofs," of God's existence. God was seen as the "unmoved Mover" or the "uncaused First Cause." In the superior realm of the supernatural that Thomas called Grace, however, knowledge came by special revelation in the Holy Scriptures. It was the relative independence of the Thomistic concept of Nature that would later be developed into an all-encompassing naturalism. The relation of Nature and Grace was analogous to that of body and soul, reason and revelation, as well as State and Church.

The disastrous implications of this dualistic scheme were demonstrated by the papal bull of Pope Boniface VIII, *Unam Sanctam* (1302), in which he applied Aquinas' theory to claim the supremacy of the church over the state. This led to military crises as the pope, using his territorial authority and papal lands, pitted the church's temporal power against the kings of France and England and precipitated the most serious confrontation between church and state in the Middle Ages. This dualistic theory of Nature and Grace became more than mere concept. It led inevitably to the dissolution of the holistic vision of medieval Christendom *and* of the authority of Christian faith.

Rise of Modernism & Supernaturalism

Eventually, Renaissance culture and emerging modernist thinking struggled to become free not only from the tutelage and domination of the medieval Church as an institution but also from God and any constricting religious or ethical norms based on Scripture. This naturalism ultimately denied the existence of a supernatural Creator but, even in its less radical forms, the involvement or *intervention* of the deity was questioned. Deism abounded among the intellectual elites. They saw life as a closed circuit of cause and effect. Miracles violated the laws of nature.

In this context, the counter-claim of supernaturalism emerged. Those espousing the truthfulness of divine revelation advocated, in response to naturalism, what they called supernaturalism. God was not limited by his creation. He could supersede the laws of nature. It certainly is unfortunate that defenders of the truth of signs and wonders employed the category "supernatural," because the term bears in itself the "baggage" of an understanding of reality divided into two separate parts.

A more responsible way of expressing the truth of miracles would be to acknowledge that—in the words of Psalm 24—"the earth is the Lord's and the fullness thereof." God does not have to intervene from above like a lightning bolt from heaven. Rather—to use another poetic flourish, this time by Jesuit poet Gerard Manley Hopkins—this world is charged with the grandeur of God. God is both transcendent and immanent. He created heaven and earth. He may govern the universe according to regular patterns of secondary causes, but at any moment, He may choose to unlock special, hitherto unknown, potentialities embedded in the very fabric of creation to result in different patterns of operation. In this way, a miracle, for example, of walking on water, may take place by changes in molecular structure not yet grasped by physicists. This concept of a universe open to God can readily integrate the miraculous. This reality is rather clumsily expressed by the phrase "the super-natural dimension of reality."

The Pentecostal awakening of the twentieth century reclaimed and rediscovered a universe open to God and the miraculous; and this discovery would lead to a new understanding of the Holy Spirit's involvement in the life of the church. This awakening challenged Protestantism especially, which had embraced the worldview of modernism the most and was now being challenged to develop a more truly Trinitarian theology.

4

The First Wave: Classical Pentecostalism

*W*e turn now to an overview of the doctrinal teachings of Classical Pentecostalism. Vinson Synan has ably told the development of the whole story in *The Holiness-Pentecostal Tradition* (1977) and his more recent book *The Century of the Spirit* (2001), as has William Faupel in his *The Everlasting Gospel* (1996). In the present study, I am therefore not focusing on the historical narrative and development but, rather, on the theological history, or the history of doctrinal teachings unique to this movement. In his classic *The Theological Roots of Pentecostalism*, Donald Dayton uses the so-called Foursquare Gospel as a paradigm to capture the unique approach of Pentecostalism. The term "Foursquare Gospel" identifies four saving activities of Jesus Christ: Jesus as Savior, Spirit-baptizer, Healer of the Body, and the Soon Coming King. I have, however, chosen a different approach here and want to develop the doctrinal history of Classical Pentecostalism by probing six strands or themes that are found holding together the conceptual patchwork of the Pentecostal awakening: sanctification, or purity; empowerment; healing; premillennial eschatology; Spirit baptism and glossolalia; and unity across societal barriers.

1. Sanctification

Scholars have demonstrated convincingly that Pentecostalism has deep Wesleyan roots. Most of the earliest Pentecostal leaders came out of the Wesleyan-Holiness movement. Against the background of the established Church of England in the eighteenth century—with corruption and moral decay much in evidence, even among the clergy, John Wesley preached an impassioned vision of biblical purity. He called converts to "grow in grace," advance in holiness, press on toward the goal (Phil. 3:14), and strive toward perfection. With the strong focus on sanctification, an innovative teaching was developed, called the "second blessing." (The term itself probably comes from a reference to Second Corinthians 1:15 where mention is made of Paul's visit bringing a second blessing to the congregation—not really relevant to the later usage that developed.)

   Wesley thought that subsequent to conversion (or justification) there is a distinct second work of grace, that he also called entire sanctification. This occurred as a step or a crisis experience. Wesley developed this teaching in his classic exposition, "A Plain Account of Christian Perfection, as believed and taught by the Reverend Mr. John Wesley from the year 1725 to the year 1777," which has been the subject of much debate. According to the subtitle of the book, he is said to have believed and taught this view between 1725 and 1777 (and probably until the day of his death). The Wesleyan-Holiness tradition underscores that believers experience sanctification instantaneously and that it fully restores the image of God in the believer. It is also called entire sanctification, perfect love or heart purity. One's intention and love toward God are seen as becoming perfect. The root of sin is eradicated and plucked out of the heart—hence the designation of this view as "eradicationist." The mainstream Methodist tradition today focuses more on the progressive nature of sanctification and points out that Wesley states that this purity of intention and perfection in love need to be maintained by an ongoing work, both preceding and following the instantaneous replacement of evil motives from the heart.

It is important to keep two things in mind here. First, Wesley's teaching maintained (over against Calvinism and the teaching of the perseverance of the believer) that both sanctification and salvation can be lost and are not necessarily permanent in nature. Second, Wesley had a rather limited definition of sin, which he viewed as a "voluntary (or willful) transgression of a known law." Even with this narrow definition of what qualifies as sin, he does not teach an *absolute* sinlessness but, rather, a Christian perfection that, nevertheless, implies that all thoughts, words, and actions are governed by pure love. What continues to be imperfect in us are termed ignorance, mistakes, or infirmities, rather than (intentional) sins of the heart.

This innovative teaching was unique in the history of the Church. Sanctification had not previously been seen as something that may occur instantaneously. Never before had the attaining of perfection in this life been claimed and professed by a part of mainstream Christianity. Just as momentous was the fact that Christian believers could now readily be classified into two distinct groups on the basis of a specific experience. This has generally led to a measure of elitism and divisiveness within Christian churches. It is easy to interpret this view as implying that there are two classes of Christians: first-class believers who are saved and sanctified, and second-class believers who are "just" saved. In itself such a classifying of Christian is always unacceptable. Paul distinguishes between carnal and spiritual believers and between those who can digest solid food and those still needing only milk. The innovation lies in the fact that the demarcation line has become visible and accessible to others and is based on subjective religious experience.

This "second blessing" thinking is called a theology of subsequence, underscoring the fact that apart from conversion there is another event in the Christian life distinct from and subsequent to one's becoming a believer. Where a more encompassing view of the nature of sin is maintained, the idea of people attaining perfection in this life is consistently rejected. The Christian life is viewed as an ongoing process of sanctification, filled with ups and downs, and perfection always eludes us this side of the grave. The Orthodox and Catholics understand that some individuals reach higher levels of sanctity—usually through martyrdom, mystical encounters, or suffering for the sake of the gospel. They may then be beatified or canonized as "saints." In the churches of the Protestant Reformation, however, all believers are considered to be saints, their holiness lying objectively in Christ rather than in their personal, subjective holiness. In Reformed circles, the reigning sentiment is that all believers are sinners and that this is pointed out without much compunction. Lutherans hold fast to the classic statement of Luther that we are *simul iustus et peccator*—simultaneously justified and sinful. When taken as a summary statement of the Christian life, this maxim seems to award both components equal weight. Where grace is furthermore taken to imply the exclusion of human responsibility in our daily walk, a defeatist attitude can creep into one's view of salvation.

It is precisely at this doctrinal point that Wesley protested against the Reformational heritage, as it was presented to him by some Moravians. Over against an attitude that saw Christians as being sinners as much as they were saved, Wesley wished to emphasize Christian growth and advancement, stressing that a faith that does not bear fruit in holy living is dead. We need to grow in grace! Methodists have classically focused on sanctification.

Another complicating factor is that this climate of perfection or entire sanctification tends to give rise to a major psychological difficulty. If it is, in fact, *not* possible for Christians to reach perfection before death—a view that most believers have espoused throughout the history of the Church, then it is inevitable that sin will surface again in the life of an individual who claims to have had a sanctification experience in which sin has been eradicated. When someone in such a situation falls into sin again after the experience of the second blessing of sanctification, two options open up: either one denies and suppresses this sin from one's consciousness, or one acknowledges that it was a sin and, as a result, one seeks further to discover and experience the authentic step of entire sanctification. Such a believer seeks another experience of yielding and holiness. Perhaps another event may yield the true article—the elimination and eradication of sin. As a result, the Christian life can become event-centered, fixated on particular experiences.

This theological framework was passed on to Classical Pentecostalism by Wesleyan-Holiness evangelists. The fact that entire sanctification was seen as occurring instantaneously compounded the issue. The Christian life came to be seen as a series of progressions, punctuated by works of grace. To conversion and sanctification, the early Pentecostals now added a third stage—baptism in the Holy Spirit. All three stages were accompanied by a dateable experience or crisis-event, rather than something progressive or ongoing. Some of the early Wesleyan-Holiness Pentecostals originally divided these stages between the Second and Third Persons of the Trinity. The Son of God was seen as operative in our conversion and sanctification, with the Holy Spirit coming upon us only at stage three or Spirit baptism. This unorthodox separation of the work of the Trinity was explained by such popular slogans as "The Holy Spirit cannot come to an unsanctified heart," implying that both conversion and sanctification had to precede the working of the Spirit in "the baptism of the Holy Ghost."

Doctrinal objections to this way of speaking abound. Augustine had already outlined, in the fourth century, that the external works of the Trinity are indivisible. The external works are the works related to the world and our salvation. (The internal or inner workings of the Trinity refer to the intra-trinitarian relationships of the Father, Son, and Spirit.) Even though there may be an attributing of a particular divine work as being more specifically related to one Person of the Trinity—the

Father as Creator and the Son as the Mediator or the One who was incarnate—none of these works occurs in isolation *without* the other two Persons. In like manner, it is not possible to exclude the Holy Spirit from conversion. Are we not "born again" of the Spirit of God? The same is true of our sanctification. In time, this view would fade into the background and the idea that sought to limit the operation of the Holy Spirit to the third stage would no longer be taught. Unfortunately, this doctrinal shift away from seeing a "clean" heart as prerequisite for Spirit baptism may have resulted in less emphasis being placed on maintaining high moral standards in the Church.

Early on a very serious challenge to the Wesleyan-Holiness concept of sanctification was presented by William H. Durham of Chicago. This challenge led to a fundamental split within Classical Pentecostal ranks and precipitated the distinction between what has come to be known as the three-stage and the two-stage Pentecostals. Those within the Wesleyan-Holiness tradition—e.g., the Pentecostal-Holiness Church, the Church of God (Cleveland, TN), the Church of God of Prophecy, and the largest North American Pentecostal denomination (with over five million members in 2000), the Church of God in Christ— remained, with varying degrees of stringency, within the "three works of grace" camp. The three works of grace, or stages, of the Christian life were conversion, sanctification as an event, and baptism in the Spirit.

William Durham (1873–1912), however, was from a Baptist background. He traveled to Azusa Street where he received a powerful infilling of the Spirit at the hands of William Seymour in March, 1907. According to William Faupel's study *The Everlasting Gospel: The Significance of Eschatology the Development of Pentecostal Thought,* Seymour prophesied that the Spirit would fall upon the people wherever Durham would preach (p. 232). His church in Chicago soon became a prominent center for Pentecostalism, influencing thousands in the Midwest and Canada. After Zion City (built by John Alexander Dowie just north of Chicago) foundered after the loss of its leader and

Parham became discredited due to (unsubstantiated) charges of immorality, Durham took a larger leadership role, which added significance to the bombshell that he dropped at an annual Midwest Pentecostal Convention held at the Stone Church in Chicago in May, 1910. He spoke on "The Finished Work of Calvary." The indomitable researcher of Pentecostalism, Swiss theologian Walter Hollenweger, would later describe Durham as "the one original theologian of the Pentecostal Movement" (in Faupel, p. 261).

Durham's message presented the fledgling Pentecostal movement, still in its theological infancy, with its first schism and doctrinal controversy. Simply stated, Durham denied the so-called second work of grace. He rejected the idea of an eradication of sin through a "sanctification" experience. From experience, he noted that all believers were still subject to sin— even those who claimed perfection or entire sanctification. He argued that the atoning death of Christ included both our initial experience of conversion and also our sanctification, which would continue throughout our lives. He taught gradual progressive sanctification, which really is the view of all Christians except the Holiness movements. Many Pentecostal leaders deemed this view theologically sound, and it became a cornerstone of the doctrinal tenets of the Assemblies of God, founded in Hot Springs, Arkansas, in 1914.

Seymour prevented Durham from teaching this doctrine at Azusa. Parham too was quick in his vehement condemnation of this "new" teaching. He saw Durhamism as diabolical and Durham as guilty of "the sin unto death." Durham may have been influenced by the desire to gain ascendancy as the pre-eminent leader of Pentecostalism, but his doctrinal contribution should be evaluated on its own merits. He had come to question the Wesleyan understanding of the eradication of the root of sin and the idea of two stages of salvation or "subsequence" in the Christian life—hence, the "Finished Work" concept. He maintained that there were no pre-conditions of instantaneous sanctification and no higher degrees of holiness necessary for receiving the baptism in the Holy Spirit. Anyone who trusted in Christ as his or her Savior, standing on the Finished Work of Calvary, could be empowered by God's Spirit. The three distinct experiences were thereby reduced to two.

Many years later, some denominational and 'Third wave" Charismatics in the 1970s would take up the line of Durham and also apply his reasoning to Spirit baptism. "Does the Finished Work of Calvary not also include the baptism in the Spirit?" would be the logical question. Is a second definitive experience after conversion, namely of Spirit baptism, a prerequisite for the operation of the *charisms* of the Spirit, or may anyone who has become a Christian and walks with the Lord receive these manifestations and be a channel for God's grace, revelation, and miraculous power?

Within Classical Pentecostal churches of the Wesleyan-Holiness tradition, there has been a gradual softening of the insistence on sanctification as a definite second work of grace. Although it is still maintained among the fundamental truths by some denominations, it is rarely emphasized today. The Church of God in Christ is, perhaps, the least dogmatic about maintaining it. A focus on holiness and biblical moral standards of holy living, however, remained throughout Classical Pentecostalism and was certainly not limited to those teaching a Christian life of three stages or experiences. This valuable heritage should never be surrendered, and the prevalence of moral lapses in Church leadership in the twentieth century underscores its importance.

2. Empowerment

The second major theme of Pentecostalism is empowerment, or the enduement with power from above. Under this rubric, the Keswick-Holiness view will be discussed. The Higher Life and Keswick-Holiness movements were an adaptation of the Wesleyan-Holiness understanding of the Christian life. They maintained the two-stage grid and the need for a subsequent second work of grace after conversion. However, they redefined the nature of this second blessing. The word "Keswick" refers to a town in northwestern England—in the Lake District—home to annual spiritual conventions since 1875. The original title of the meetings expresses the mood well: "The Convention for the Deepening of the Spiritual Life." Keswick teaching has greatly influenced the genre of popular devotional literature. Customary metaphors and expressions that capture the essence of this spirituality include "the upward way," "the higher life," "the upper room," "the deeper walk," "consecration on the altar," "reckoning yourself dead to sin," "resting in the Lord," "letting go and letting God," "self-denial," and "cross-bearing." A typical example would be Oswald Chambers' well-known devotional *My Utmost for His Highest*. Many hymns written in the nineteenth century encourage those tarrying at the altars to receive pure hearts and the impartation of power.

The Keswick-Holiness movement did not follow the Wesleyan idea of sanctification as purity of intention and the eradicating of indwelling sin. It focused instead on achieving a life of victory, striving after a perfection of practical living by consecration, and passively surrendering to God. Romans 6:11–14 is a pivotal scriptural reference. One enters the upward way, not by conscious self-effort, but by reckoning one's self dead to sin and alive to God. Sin will have no dominion over those who are under grace rather than under the law. The idea of "resting in Jesus" with inner passivity has led some to describe the Keswick idea of holiness as "suppressionist": sin is not supposedly eradicated, but it is not allowed to come to the surface, as it were. The key to the higher life is an agonizing act of complete personal consecration and self-denial, which is the inescapable pre-condition for the ongoing process of sanctification. This step, which enables the believer to live in victory should, ideally, follow directly after conversion but frequently does not. In that sense, the Keswick-Holiness movement also bequeathed a two-stage framework to its successors. Believers could be divided into two groups: the "victorious," who were the normal empowered Christians, and the "defeated," whose lives were considered substandard or worldly.

In chapters 3 and 4 of his classic study *Theological Roots of Pentecostalism*, Donald Dayton carefully outlines the gradual shift within Holiness circles from the more Wesleyan focus on purity to a more Keswick underscoring of power and enablement. This change relates also to the use of Pentecostal and pneumatological language, originating with a contemporary and fellow-laborer of John Wesley, John Fletcher. Fletcher brought the book of Acts into greater prominence in the discussion. At that time sanctification was described as receiving the "Pentecostal baptism of the Holy Ghost." Soon, however, the Pauline emphasis on ethical behavior came to be eclipsed by a more Lucan perspective on the enduement with power to live the Christian life victoriously. At Oberlin College in Ohio, a new revivalist focus entered the Holiness movement. The Pentecostal language of enablement came to supersede the more ethical categories of the Pauline epistles and Wesley's emphasis on the fruit of the Spirit. Asa Mahan, president of Oberlin College, played a pivotal role, and the shift seen in the titles of his two books on sanctification illustrates the paradigm change that was taking place. In 1839, Mahan published *The Scripture Doctrine of Christian Perfection*. In 1870, his new book was titled *The Baptism of the Holy Ghost*.

Gradually, the Holiness movement became broader in its focus and developed in a more Reformed and less Wesleyan way. The great preacher of the Second Great Awakening, Charles Finney, did much to popularize a new revivalist understanding of Spirit baptism as an empowering for service. The change was not without tension. Phoebe Palmer, one of the most influential Keswick-Holiness speakers known for her "altar theology" and call to sanctification and consecration, attempted to synthesize the two motifs by declaring "holiness *is* power." Another solution equally unacceptable to Wesleyans was the so-called "three blessings" view alluded to already. It divided the "second blessing" into two parts—a sanctification experience for purity, followed by a third experience for spiritual power. It is easy to see that the pathway for early Pentecostalism and its use of a three-staged understanding of the Christian life and a theology of subsequence had been well paved and prepared by the Holiness preachers. There was a need somehow to incorporate the impartation of power for Christian service as something distinct from sanctification. B. H. Irwin of the Fire-Baptized Holiness Church took this development to the extreme when he added strange, additional baptisms of "dynamite," "luddite," and "oxidite " to the first three stages. These excesses were soon discarded, but the "pre-Pentecostal tinderbox" had been thoroughly prepared. With this apt analogy, Dayton expressed the idea that the Holiness movements had supplied the whole framework for Classical Pentecostal theology. All that was lacking was a spark to light the fire, and this spark would be the doctrine of glossolalia as "initial evidence" formulated by Charles Fox Parham.

From these Keswick and revivalist motifs would, in time, emerge a new understanding of the work of the Spirit. It rejected the Wesleyan doctrine of sanctification as perfection and as a step or crisis-event that may occur instantaneously and would consequently shift the believer into an entirely different level of sanctity. When William Durham preached his historic sermon on the Finished Work of Calvary in 1910, it would fall on ready ears and soon gain wide acceptance. Foremost among the forces that facilitated this fundamental change in early Pentecostalism was the Keswick understanding of Spirit baptism as an enduement with power. With sanctification understood as a life-long process in Finished Work circles, the empowering work of the Spirit—a work that revivalists such as Torrey and Moody would see as a definite spiritual experience of empowering—was now linked in Pentecostal circles to the gift of tongues.

For this reason, the second major grouping of Classical Pentecostals is widely known as the Keswick-Holiness Pentecostals. They hold to a two-stage pattern of Christian living and are represented by such denominations as the Assemblies of God, the International Church of the Foursquare Gospel, and the Open Bible Standard Church. Because the Assemblies of God (headquartered in Springfield, MO) is the largest Pentecostal denomination globally and greatly influences Pentecostal thinking, many observers believe that the two-stage approach is the definitive or typical Pentecostal position. This grouping of Classical Pentecostalism is sometimes also referred to as the Baptistic Pentecostals. This designation is not really helpful. It attempts to allude to the non-Wesleyan emphasis and the fact that many of these Pentecostals came out of Baptist or loosely Reformed backgrounds. However, the word "Baptistic" evokes associations of the mode of water baptism as immersion of believers, and this is equally true of the three-stage Wesleyan Pentecostals. (It is a lesser-known fact that some non-North American Pentecostals actually practice the sprinkling of infants, e.g., leading Pentecostal bodies in Germany and Chile.)

Empowerment by the Spirit is a dominant motif in all of Pentecostalism. The primary text is Acts 1:8, where the coming outpouring of the Spirit on the Day of Pentecost is described in these terms, "But you will receive power when the Holy Spirit has come upon you; and you will be my witnesses. . . ." The whole Pentecostal movement has come to be known for its evangelistic fervor and missionary outreach. Oral Roberts University scholar James Shelton captures the essence of the Lucan perspective as reflected among Pentecostals with his (dissertation and) book title *Mighty in Word and Deed*. How this enduement with power came to be linked to glossolalia will be developed in a following section.

3. Healing

The third major theme is that of healing. Some would ask if healing may not even be more characteristic of Pentecostalism than Spirit baptism. Although the modern healing movement actually predates the Azusa Street revival by several decades, the divine healing of the body and Pentecostalism became closely intertwined. Physical healing was the most frequent demonstration of God's power alluded to in the early Pentecostal motto that Jesus Christ is the same yesterday, today, and forever (Heb 13:8). The North American healing movement received its major impetus from Europe, especially from the testimonies and writings of Johann Christoph Blumhardt, Dorothea Trudel, and Otto Stockmayer in the 1840s and '50s. The remarkable awakening in Britain, centered on the ministry of Edward Irving in the 1830s, also included miraculous healings.

A number of Holiness evangelists and evangelical preachers became involved in the modern "faith cure" movement of the late nineteenth and early twentieth centuries. Prominent among them were Dr. Charles Cullis, W. E. Boardman, Carrie Judd Montgomery, A. B. Simpson, A. J. Gordon, and Captain R. Kelso Carter. Dayton connects significantly the specifically Wesleyan understanding of sanctification as instantaneous and "entire" (or perfect) with the popular expectation of healing at that time. Kelso Carter in his earlier book, *The Atonement for Sin and Sickness* (1884), argued that healing was included in the atonement of Christ and was thus automatically available to believers (Dayton, p. 129). He also rejected the use of doctors and medicine. Having claimed or experienced the instantaneous and entire sanctification of his soul, he consequently expected the total and instantaneous healing of the body as well. When he actually experienced such a healing, he was not reluctant "to universalize his own experience" (Dayton, p. 130). A later illness, however, was healed only after he took some medicine. Following a three-year struggle, Carter revised his theological views. In a later publication, *"Faith Healing" Reviewed after Twenty Years* (1897), Carter retracted his anti-medical stance and no longer saw continuing disease as a sign of lack of faith or continuing sin. He taught that the effects of the atonement were not necessarily or automatically applied in each individual's experience. Healing was based on a special answer to prayer rather than on the universal provisions of the atonement. It was, however, the earlier view of Carter that most significantly affected the early healing movement and became the general view in Pentecostal circles during the first few decades of the twentieth century. According to Paul Chappell, the well known phrase "Healing is in the Atonement" originally indicated an anti-medical stance. John

Alexander Dowie, who built Zion City north of Chicago, went even further in his rejection, as is apparent from the title of one of his popular sermons: "Doctors, Drugs and Devils; or the Foes of Christ the Healer."

By the last decades of the nineteenth century, divine healing had become part and parcel of the Holiness movement in the United States. Charles Parham experienced a personal healing and set up a healing home in Topeka, Kansas, in 1898, and he conducted healing revivals in neighboring states. William Seymour of Azusa Street reported that the Pentecostal awakening in Los Angeles included the healing of all manner of diseases. From Parham's followers in Zion City came a number of Pentecostal healing evangelists, such as John G. Lake and Gordon Lindsay, who spearheaded significant international ministries. The founder of the International Church of the Foursquare Gospel, Sister Aimee Semple McPherson, had a widespread healing ministry.

After World War II, a major healing revival era commenced with the tent crusades, radio, and television programs of the two post-war giants, William Branham and Oral Roberts. David Harrell's volume, *All Things Are Possible* (1975), documents the ministry of the major healing evangelists of the 1950s. Branham's ministry was characterized by spectacular healings and able supporters, such as Gordon Lindsay, Ern Baxter, and F. F. Bosworth. Unfortunately, it unraveled as he fell into doctrinal error and held inflated views of his own significance. The healing ministry of Roberts was, in many ways, unparalleled in scope and lasting significance. Emanating from a Pentecostal-Holiness background, which was both anti-intellectual and anti-medical, he transcended these limitations, founding both a prominent university and a large hospital in Tulsa, Oklahoma. Even though the hospital did not succeed financially, it integrated medicine and healing prayer in a holistic vision of ministry to the whole person—body, mind, and spirit—that still characterizes Oral Roberts University.

The healing impetus of Classical Pentecostalism would be carried further in the ensuing denominational and independent Charismatic movements by such prominent healing evangelists as Kathryn Kuhlman, Francis MacNutt, John Wimber, Kenneth Hagin, and Richard Roberts.

4. Premillennial Eschatology

The fourth major theme of Pentecostalism is premillennial eschatology. This also represents the final element in the traditional Foursquare Gospel: namely Jesus Christ is "the soon and coming King." In his benchmark study on Pentecostalism already mentioned, *The Everlasting Gospel: the Significance of Eschatology in the Development of Pentecostal Thought* (1996), William Faupel seeks to illustrate the importance of eschatology in the rise of Pentecostalism and overviews well the whole development of the movement from its conception to its doctrinal controversies over sanctification and the Trinity.

The Methodist and Holiness traditions generally tended toward a *post*millennial eschatology in which a transforming work in society by believers prepares for the return of Christ. The optimism inherent in the teaching of human perfection attained through sanctification made initially sustainable the idea that society would gradually transform as preparation for the coming of the millennium. Such a view has the effect of considering the Second Coming as less imminent, since the symbolic millennial kingdom which still has to precede Christ's advent develops only gradually over time.

In eighteenth-century Methodism, Fletcher again steered a course different from that of Wesley. He taught a doctrine of three dispensations correlated to the Persons of the Trinity. In the era of the Spirit, he expected the imminent return of Christ and even predicted the date of the Second Coming (before 1770!). The Oberlin perfectionism of Charles Finney radicalized the post-millennial vision of ethical transformation. Finney appealed to the Church to reform the world and thereby to usher in the king-dom. With his strong Arminian bent (even though his denominational background was Presbyterian and Congre-gational), he underscored human responsibility, claiming that if only the church would do her prophetic duty, the millennium would come in six months (Dayton, p. 155). Dayton shows how this most radical wing of postmillennialism eventually flipped over into its opposite—premillennialism—because society failed to transform as expected and the initial optimism faded into despair (p. 158). When human effort failed to transform society, adherents focused instead on divine intervention in an apocalyptical way.

This new premillennialism became attractive also to those from Reformed backgrounds because of their tradition of divine sovereignty. A new climate emerged in which believers expected the return of Christ in a sudden and apocalyptic fashion. The message of early Pentecostalism seemed to mesh well with this expectation. The Second Coming would be ushered in by the "latter rain"—the return of the supernatural manifestations of the Holy Spirit. In the last decade of the nineteenth century, many expected God soon to restore all His gifts to the Church. Charles Parham linked the gift of glossolalia to a final worldwide evangel-istic outreach bringing in the ripe harvest before the return of Christ. To the day of his death in 1929, Parham maintained that the gift of tongues, which was occurring widely in Pentecostal circles, was actually xenolalia (the occurrence of existing, but unlearned languages). He saw Acts 2 as parallel: there the apostles received supernatural divine enablement to speak known languages and to proclaim the mighty deeds of God in these languages, which they themselves had never studied. In like manner, early Pentecostal missionaries traveled abroad on one-way tickets to evangelize with the help of the gift of tongues. This heady expectation was soon shattered. Experience taught the missionaries the hard lesson that they had to learn languages through the regular demands of study and practice, and early Pentecostals began to view the gift of tongues in a different light—as glossolalia: this gift was for private, personal edification, or for communicating in a congregation, when coupled with the gift of interpretation.

This theological transition occurred with amazing speed. Within two decades, very few advocates of tongues as "an equipping for missions" remained. This is not to deny that, occasionally, the phenomenon of xenolalia was attested to in assemblies. Someone would be speaking in tongues in a gathering, only to be surprised later by discovering that another person recognized the tongue as an existing foreign language and understood it. Such testimonies abound but actual documentation usually eludes the researcher.

The early pioneers Edward Irving and John Alexander Dowie believed that the "nine-fold" gifts of 1 Corinthians 12 needed to be restored before the Second Coming of Christ. In like manner, Frank W. Sandford of Shiloh, Maine, expected manifestations of the Spirit in his deeply eschatological vision. After a visit to Palestine, his focus on the imminent return of Christ sharpened. He also embraced the elitist British-Israelite theory, which taught that Britain and the United States were actually the ten lost tribes of Israel. Sandford passed this view on to Parham, who visited him in the summer of 1900 prior to the pivotal outbreak of tongues at Topeka, Kansas, in January, 1901. In Maine, Parham witnessed glossolalia among the students at Sandford's Bible school, but Sandford himself did not assign any great significance to this manifestation. Parham however was convinced that the Second Coming of Jesus would occur right after a global revival, precipitated by the miraculous evangelizing efforts of recipients of "instant missionary tongues." James Goff, who wrote a biography of Parham, *Fields White Unto Harvest* (1988), points out that Parham may have been influenced by a report in a Holiness journal that a missionary, one Jennie Glassey, received an African dialect in the Spirit in 1895, by which she could subsequently read, write, translate, and sing while no longer in a "trance." The analogy of Acts 2 formed the natural foundation for these unsubstantiated claims. As just referred to, many disappointed missionaries, having initially left on one-way tickets with the expectation of finding a heathen tribe that could understand their utterances in tongues, nevertheless rose to the occasion and learned the languages in the usual fashion. They became powerful instruments of the gospel and spread Pentecostalism across the globe.

The shift to a premillennial imminent return of Christ fueled the missionizing fervor of Holiness and Pentecostal believers in the United States. On the other hand, it also exacerbated the split forming within Protestantism between what is sometimes called the "Mary" and the "Martha" approaches to Christian discipleship. The "Mary" approach, also known as evangelical, focused on conversion, holiness, prayer, personal devotion, witnessing, evangelizing, and mission, whereas the "Martha" approach, sometimes called mainline, ecumenical, or social gospel, focused on societal transformation, mercy ministry to the marginalized, and, as the decades of the twentieth century continued, on the visible unity of the Church. This simple but stereotypical bifurcation of Protestantism into two parties was, in fact, a gross over-simplification. Many constituencies would never fit neatly into either camp—not the least, Classical Pentecostalism, which initially labored largely among the marginalized and disinherited of society.

5. Spirit Baptism and Glossolalia

The fifth major theme of Pentecostalism is a miraculous baptism in the Holy Spirit evidenced by speaking in tongues. (This will already be clear since there is a significant degree of overlapping between these broad themes.) Accounts of the advent of the Pentecostal awakening of the twentieth century agree that Charles Parham linked a "baptism of the Holy Ghost" and speaking in tongues. Spirit baptism was first seen as designating an experience of entire sanctification for some in the Wesleyan-Holiness movement who had started using pneumatological language and developed a preference for the book of Acts in expressing it. This development formed a bridge to a Keswick-Holiness view of sanctification in which Spirit baptism was interpreted as an enduement with power rather than an instantaneous moral perfection in love and inward motivation. Parham embraced both of these positions and interpreted them as two successive events after the primary experience of conversion. These were dubbed the "three blessings." However, after the dramatic outburst of tongues at the Bethel Bible School in Topeka, Kansas in January 1901, Parham altered his view of the third stage. It was still seen as an enduement with power. It was still called the baptism of the Holy Ghost, with the prior second stage of sanctification being described in classically Wesleyan terms of eradication of the root of sin or of the Adamic nature from an individual believer. The third stage, however, was now decisively linked to the outpouring of the gift of tongues, reminiscent of the first chapters of Acts. That is why the term "Apostolic Faith" played such an important role in the early stages of the movement. Tongues signified a new outpouring of the apostolic languages. Parham called tongues the "Bible evidence." This pivotal linkage underscores the claim of many that Parham was the Father of Pentecostalism.

Precedents

Historians can point to a broad variety of occurrences of tongues. Not only have there been periodic outbreaks in many evangelical revival movements and sectarian fringe groups throughout Christian history, but tongues also occur in non-Christian religious and purely secular contexts. Among the oldest parallels may be the frenzied ecstasy of the pagan Oracle of Delphi in Greece. Also noteworthy is the phenomenon among the Shakers and the early Mormons in the nineteenth century. Eastern religions which believe in reincarnation explain tongues as recollections from a previous life, while Jungian psychology considers it an illustration of the theory of a universal human collective unconscious. As with all religious manifestations, a tripolarity principle of origin applies. Tongues may have a divine origin—the Holy Spirit, or else come from a demonic source for the purpose of diabolical deception, or arise simply from human nature (the flesh) itself. Examples of flesh-related religious manifestations may include hypnotism, hysteria, and phenomena arising from autosuggestion, societal stress, drug usage, willful fabrication, unconscious manipulation, personality disorders, or regression. Early psychological investigations of Pentecostals in the twentieth century tended to attribute glossolalia to such forms of pathology, but in time more scientific studies showed that tongue speakers do not deviate from the normal range of personality inventories.

Edward Irving's "Standing Sign"

There is one clear precedent for Parham's position on tongues—the case of the Scottish theologian Edward Irving, in the 1830s. In "Edward Irving and the 'Standing Sign' of Spirit Baptism," church historian David Dorries shows that Irving believed in a baptism with the Holy Ghost separate from and subsequent to regeneration and sanctification. Irving saw glossolalia as the sign of such a baptism (in McGee, ed., *Initial Evidence,* p. 47). Does this mean that Irving taught the same doctrine as Parham? Only to a degree! Dorries points out that he would have been uncomfortable with the term "initial evidence." He rejected the idea of an "empirical spirit," which focuses on evidence, in the realm of the supernatural. His preferred term was tongues as "the standing sign" of the baptism with the Holy Ghost (p. 48). As mentioned previously, we lack evidence that connects Parham and Irving directly. Certainly John Alexander Dowie, who built Zion City in Illinois at the start of the twentieth century, could have fulfilled this role. He was born in Edinburgh, Scotland, where he attended New College in a milieu in which the innovations of Irving would still have been widely discussed. Dowie called his church the Christian Catholic Apostolic Church. Irving's movement had used the term Catholic Apostolic Church. The similarity is telling. Dowie died before the establishment of the Pentecostal movement but did not seem to have been impressed by the gift of glossolalia. Frank Sandford of Shiloh, Maine, whose message paralleled and mirrored that of Dowie in many respects, later found Pentecostalism to be shallow and fanatical (Faupel, p. 157).

Charles Parham's "Initial, Physical Evidence"

Consideration of Irving as a precedent to Parham raises the question of why Parham chose the terms he did to express his understanding of Spirit baptism. He called glossolalia "the initial, physical evidence of the baptism of the Holy Ghost." Careful attention must be given to these words. The term "initial" has the connotation of the first of a series. The phenomenon of tongues was seen as the breakthrough event, ushering in the possibility of other manifestations of the Spirit—usually seen as the nine-fold gifts of 1 Corinthians 12. The original teaching of tongues as the *initial* evidence, with the *secondary* evidence then being the fruit of the Spirit or, more specifically, love, has now generally been forgotten. The phenomenon of tongues is still seen as initial, in the sense of providing the prerequisite entrance or gateway to life in the Spirit where the *charismata* are then to be experienced.

This view raises many questions. The pivotal gateway role cannot be supported by any biblical reference and is counter to the experience of many individuals. It is also interesting to note that the restoration of the gift of divine healing in the modern healing movement in North America from about 1850 onwards clearly predates the restoration of a widespread occurrence of glossolalia after the milestones of Topeka, Kansas (1901), and Azusa Street, Los Angeles (1906). Nevertheless, no one has advocated healing as the initial (corporate) sign of the twentieth century awakenings.

The term "physical" makes the nature of the manifestation specific. It was not merely internal or spiritual but could be externally verified by the senses. It was an audible sign, rather than a moral or mystical transformation that could be doubted or questioned more easily. This brings us to the next aspect, namely "evidence." Ever since Thomas Aquinas introduced Aristotelian categories into the mainstream of Western philosophical thought in the thirteenth century and Francis Bacon advocated empirical, rather than metaphysical, inquiry, science has emphasized verification by sensory observation. As noted above, this emphasis was heightened further in the nineteenth century by the theories and publications of Charles Darwin. Assemblies of God theologian Russell Spittler, previously of Fuller Seminary, speaks of the shift from the Wesleyan concept of assurance to the notion of empirical evidence. In "Glossolalia" he writes: "This exchange was doubtlessly facilitated by the rise of a popular scientism after the Civil War. Darwin published *Origin of the Species* in 1859 and *Descent of Man* in 1871" (in Burgess and McGee, eds., *The Dictionary of Pentecostal and Charismatic Movements,* p. 339). Although it is clear that conservative Protestants, among them participants in the Wesleyan and Keswick-Holiness movements, responded negatively to the theory of evolution and the popular quest for the missing fossil link, Spittler suggests that they may have succumbed to the empiricist mentality—"one gets at truth by 'citing evidence'" (p. 339).

Coupled with the ongoing frustration experienced within Holiness circles regarding certainty about whether one had, in fact, experienced entire sanctification and the eradication of the root of sin, the claim of physical evidence became deeply attractive. It did indeed function as the spark in (what Dayton calls) the pre-Pentecostal tinderbox!

As we have seen, Parham did not approach the issue of tongues as a *tabula rasa*, or a clean, unwritten slate. He had read of the remarkable account of a particular missionary who claimed to have acquired an African dialect supernaturally. Synan and Faupel state that this person, Jennie Glassey, was a student at Sandford's school. Parham expected the restoration of the gifts of the Spirit in a "latter rain" outpouring, precipitating a worldwide revival before the return of Christ. He had witnessed students speaking in tongues at Frank Sandford's "The Holy Ghost and Us" College in Shiloh, Maine. Consequently, Parham's seemingly innocent question to his students to study the experience of the first believers from the book of Acts to "see if there is not some evidence given of the baptism so there may be no doubt on the subject" was probably a loaded question (Faupel, p. 171). James Goff, R. M. Anderson, and W. Faupel all seem to agree on this point. Upon Parham's return from a three-day preaching tour in Kansas City, he was "surprised" to find an almost unanimous answer from the class: When the baptism of the Spirit came upon people, they all spoke in unknown tongues (Faupel, p. 175). Faupel states that there was not total unanimity on the point. Parham's sister-in-law had concluded in her own mind that "any of the nine gifts would prove the Baptism" (Faupel, p. 175).

New Testament scholars are becoming increasingly aware that when present-day researchers approach a text with their own contemporary questions, asking something that would not have been an issue in the author's time and context, they are easily deluded and often find the answers they had anticipated or sought. However, the historic die had been cast. The answer of the students, anticipated and perhaps engineered by Parham, provided the spark for the fire of Pentecostal revival. A movement had been born that would irrevocably change the religious landscape of the globe in the twentieth century.

The Classical Pentecostal Doctrine & Present Practice

The classic formulation of the case for initial evidence from Acts soon came to center on the "five episodes" in chapters 2, 8, 9, 10 and 19, respectively: the Day of Pentecost, the Samaritan Pentecost, the conversion of Paul, the house of Cornelius, and the disciples of John in Ephesus. The coming of the Spirit was accompanied by the mention of glossolalia in chapters 2, 10, and 19, and, so it was argued, could be assumed in chapters 8 and 9. It was claimed that the five cases all illustrate subsequence—the baptism in the Spirit coming subsequent to conversion. The same two-fold pattern was seen as being illustrated in the life of Jesus (the Holy Spirit overshadowing Mary at His conception and, subsequently, coming on Him at the baptism in the Jordan) and in the lives of the apostles (first stage was their supposed conversion—located by Old Testament scholar Howard Ervin at the point when Jesus blows upon the disciples in John 20:22, and the second stage on the Day of Pentecost). These arguments are hardly compelling when examined in the light of serious contemporary biblical scholarship. Consequently, the validity of these arguments will be probed further in the following chapter on the denominational Charismatic renewal.

Speaking in tongues as a sign of the baptism of the Holy Ghost (now usually called Spirit baptism) was a much-sought-after experience in Pentecostal churches. Sometimes it was required for service in congregational leadership. Special tarrying meetings were held in the early days at which seekers would tarry for hours and seek to prepare their hearts for this dramatic breakthrough. Confession of sin and personal holiness were part of the preparation which could sometimes lead to heightened emotions. These meetings played a role in fostering the process of sanctification but were later abandoned as too emotional or open to manipulation. They were usually successful in achieving the desired result. The practice of special times or services at which seekers are prayed for to receive the baptism still continues. Statistically, however, there has been a gradual decrease in the percentage of the members of Pentecostal churches who claim to speak in tongues, both personally and as a gift in the assembly. By the year 2000, it had dropped to about 30%, even in denominations where it is highly prized. Some put this down to an increase in worldliness in the church or the lack of proper teaching from the pulpit; others argue that tongues is only one of the charismata and that not everyone needs to receive this gift—going against the traditional Pentecostal teaching that it plays a pivotal role and is the initial, physical evidence of Spirit baptism.

6. Unity across Societal Barriers

The sixth major theme of early Pentecostalism was unity across societal barriers. It has been convincingly argued that the Day of Pentecost and the outpouring of the Spirit on the fledgling Church symbolized the reversal of the tower of Babel. Catholic biblical scholar George Montague notes that the prescribed cycle of Torah readings on this Jewish harvest festival, seven weeks after the celebration of the Passover, included a reading from Genesis 11—the tower of Babel episode, where language had become a divisive factor. The coming of the Spirit at Pentecost, the outpouring of the Spirit on the Church as described in Acts 2, was seen by Luke as an enduement with power to witness and evangelize. The *unitive* function of this experience, however, is equally significant. Luke rattles off an impressive list of countries represented among the crowd who had gathered, and theologians find similarities to other lists in ancient geographical texts. With a certain rhetorical flourish, Acts 2:5 proclaims that there were Jews in Jerusalem "from every nation under heaven." The disciples gathered in the Upper Room were united with one accord, and they were all filled with the one Spirit, enabling them to proclaim the powerful deeds of God in a way that all present heard them speaking in their own languages.

The Holy Spirit is unquestionably the Spirit of unity. Wherever the Spirit is truly at work among believers, our self-erected barriers and societal divisions, such as those based on class, race, gender, age, and national origin, break down. Conversely, wherever there is a coming together of people in truth and love, one may conclude that the Spirit of God is at work. There is however also another kind of seeking unity—for evil purposes or merely for the sake of unity itself. That reflects the spirit of arrogance seen at the Tower of Babel. The New Testament, however, places a very high premium on unity among believers. This call to unity is part of the prayer of Jesus for his disciples (and their followers who will come to believe through their words) in the Farewell Discourse of John 17. The credibility of the gospel is at stake: "That they may all be one . . . so that the world may believe." The same theme of unity is also prominent in Ephesians 2 and 4.

It is thus possible to argue that the collective baptizing of the Church in the Spirit at Pentecost was not only for the purpose of empowering for witness, but also for fostering unity. Or to say it in a different way, the empowering of the Spirit includes the enablement to cross barriers of estrangement and separation, to find love, communion, and true unity among people. In Ephesians 2:14, Christ is seen as our Peace—the One who breaks down the dividing wall of hostility between Jews and Gentiles, reconciling both groups into one body.

As pointed out in chapter one, the modern ecumenical movement that chronologically overlaps with the rise of Pentecostalism at the beginning of the twentieth century has sought to further the visible unity of the body of Christ. It is becoming clear to some representatives of both these movements—the ecumenical and Pentecostal movements—that they need to learn from one another. American Disciples of Christ theologian, Paul Crow, a one-time leading figure in the Faith and Order Commission of the World Council of Churches, decries the lack of spiritual fervor in the ecumenical movement, ascribing the present-day malaise and lethargy to the poverty of the Spirit that plagues many churches. Swiss New Testament theologian Oscar Cullmann states simply that, without the Holy Spirit, ecumenism is not possible.

Similarly, in the heritage of the pioneering ecumenical pastor, "Mr. Pentecost" (David du Plessis), Assemblies of God theologian Cecil M. Robeck of Fuller Seminary has become deeply involved in ecumenical dialogue with the Roman Catholic Church through the bilateral International Roman Catholic-Pentecostal dialogue. He has chaired for the Pentecostal side in this dialogue and with multilateral ecumenism in commissions of the World Council of Churches.

The issue of unity encompasses increasingly more than matters of doctrinal significance and differences in ecclesiastical polity. Today, the deepest cleavages within the body of Christ may relate to societal issues such as ethnicity, homosexuality, environmental policy, and the ordination of women.

In early Pentecostalism, there was a brief season of unity and harmony across racial barriers that did not escape the notice of the public eye. In September of 1906, the *Los Angeles Daily*

Times carried scathing articles on the Azusa Street revival that was just gathering momentum at that time. It was the mingling of black and white worshipers in a time of Jim Crow laws that drew the most attention. Cecil Robeck, who has authored a major study on this revival called *The Azusa Street Mission and Revival*, previously documented this point in his essay "William J. Seymour and 'the Bible Evidence.'" Robeck refers to a newspaper headline, "Whites and Blacks Mix in a Religious Frenzy," and then quotes a Baptist pastor who declared Azusa Street to be "a disgusting amalgamation of African voudoo [sic] superstition and Caucasian insanity" (in *Initial Evidence*, p. 79). The intensity of this criticism reveals that something truly remarkable was happening in the Pentecostal movement at a time that church historian Vinson Synan has described as "the very years of America's most racist period, between 1890 and 1920" (*Pentecostal-Holiness Tradition*, 2nd ed., p. 167). For the first two decades, Pentecostalism resisted these societal pressures and was an interracial movement.

Due to the early legal incorporation of the Church of God in Christ in 1897, this largely black denomination, led by Bishop C. H. Mason, gave ordination credentials to several hundred white ministers of independent Pentecostal churches. A major benefit of ordination at this time was reduced rates for clergy in rail travel. In time, however, societal pressure led to a separation of the ways. The Assemblies of God, founded in 1914 in Hot Springs, Arkansas, became a largely white Pentecostal denomination. Many Protestant denominations had also split along racial lines at the time of the Civil War over the issue of slavery. Vinson Synan reports that by 1929, 90 % of all black Christians belonged to churches restricted to their own race (Synan, p. 168).

Another racially charged issue in Pentecostalism was the debate about the "founder" or "father" of the movement. Supporters of Parham could claim that the occurrence of glossolalia in Topeka, Kansas, was the first of the twentieth century. Supporters of Seymour pointed out that the Azusa Street awakening had far greater impact and numbers. The issue of race featured prominently in this matter. Parham was perceived by many as being racially prejudiced, and the supporting evidence for that is impressive. He was a British Israelite, which gave prominence to the role of the "Anglo" race as supposed successors and descendants of the ten lost tribes of Israel. Parham had also condoned "Southern White sensibilities" by requiring Seymour (the son of freed slaves)—at least initially—to sit outside in the hallway at his Bible College in Houston. It is also widely claimed that Parham supported the Ku Klux Klan, and Synan documents that Parham gave a speech to the Klan in Michigan in 1927. This clearly shows his willingness to be associated with them but, to his credit, he did tell them that they could achieve their ideals only by first being "saved" (Synan, p. 182).

Together with inconclusive moral charges made against Parham, his racial views made him unacceptable to many—both black and white—for the role of the true Father of Pente-costalism. Seymour, who in my personal evaluation indisputably deserves to be acknowledged as having fulfilled this role, was automatically excluded from the honorable position of founder in the eyes of many white Pentecostals. Faced with this dilemma, the best option for many was the pious observation that Pentecostalism has no founder but the Holy Spirit Himself.

The subsequent developments should not, nevertheless, detract from the remarkable legacy of Azusa Street as a brief intermezzo of true unity in the Spirit. It was much more than an issue of black and white. Reports of that time include a remarkable list of ethnic and national origins among the early participants of the revival: Mexicans, Armenians, Italians, Chinese, Russians, Indians, and many more. It is perhaps significant to recall that what many of these people had in common was that they had not come through the rationalist tradition of the Western "Enlightenment," with its modern scientific mind-set. They did not disparage the non-rational dimensions of humanity, and many eagerly embraced the supernatural and the "full gospel" which touched them body, soul, and spirit. The undercurrent of expressive spirituality that was part of what was called the "Negro tradition" flowed freely into the new openness to all the manifestations of the Spirit. Dubois's statement that the religious goal of the Negro was "to be mad with supernatural joy" perhaps explains the readiness of many black people to accept Pentecostalism and also the fact that to this day a more "Pentecostal" style of worship is found in many non-Pentecostal black churches (Synan, p. 178).

The racial division of Pentecostal churches continues to this day, but a significant milestone was reached in 1994, when the separate umbrella organizations for white and black Pentecostal denominations were disbanded and a new interracial association formed. At this time, independent Charismatics were also included. This "Memphis Miracle" has been referred to above.

The theme of unity remained an integral part of the Pentecostal and Charismatic movements, even though it sometimes became more of an undercurrent. The German Systematic Theologian Eberhard Jüngel captures something of this deeply unitive work of the Holy Spirit when he expresses the distinctive role of the Spirit as His capacity to be rich in relating and the creating of new relationships within the divine life that we come to share as the body of Christ. As believers, we are drawn together by the indwelling of the one Spirit who has come to inhabit us and make us into a dwelling place of the triune God (Ephesians 2:22).

The role of two Classical Pentecostals will remain synonymous with ecumenical unity and bridge-building—David du Plessis, nicknamed Mr. Pentecost, and Vinson Synan, who spearheaded most of the large Charismatic conferences of the 1970s and 80s and facilitated dialogue across the denominational spectrum.

With these six pervasive and overlapping themes, the basic doctrinal development of Classical Pentecostalism has been outlined. However, the picture is not complete. Some major issues remain to be discussed. The first of them is the issue that, above all others, stretches the thinking of orthodox researchers to the limits. It has come to be known as the "New Issue." On the margins or periphery of mainstream Pentecostalism we find a non-Trinitarian group known as the Oneness, or Jesus Name, Pentecostals. In fact, they form the third major division of Pentecostalism apart from the Wesleyan and Keswick-Holiness Pentecostals. Their doctrine and practice set them apart.

The New Issue

The fledgling Pentecostal movement was still reeling from the divisions precipitated by the "Finished Work of Calvary" controversy when the "New Issue" broke. Faupel points out that although there were some previous indications, the debate actually surfaces at a camp meeting in Arroyo Seco canyon in the Los Angeles area in 1913. Maria Woodworth-Etter had held a spectacularly successful crusade in Dallas the year before, and she had been invited to bring her message, aimed at healing the division after the "Finished Work" controversy, to Los Angeles. Instead of the camp meeting bringing reconciliation, another doctrinal storm erupted there. A speaker preaching from Jeremiah 31:22 declared that God was about to perform "a new thing." Next, a Canadian, R. E. McAlister, pointed out at a baptismal service that according to Acts, the early church baptized people in the name of Jesus Christ, rather than in the Trinitarian formula of Matthew 28:19. This startled many people. That night, a minister named John G. Scheppe prayed and reflected deep into the night. He ran through the camp in the early hours of the morning shouting that the power of Jesus to save and heal was connected to being baptized in His Name. He announced that everyone should be rebaptized in the name of Jesus only (Faupel, p. 280).

Thus commenced the New Issue. It evolved steadily. At first, the focus was on the correct form of baptism. Acts 2:38 became the rallying cry—the words of Peter to the first converts on the Day of Pentecost: "Repent, and be baptized every one of you in the name of Jesus Christ so that your sins may be forgiven; and you will receive the gift of the Holy Spirit." This would eventually become the doctrinal slogan of Oneness Pentecostals. Instead of three or two stages, there is only one event by which people are saved, and it includes all three actions mentioned in this verse.

First, there is the need to repent, which is doctrinally unproblematic. Next, water baptism (after coming to faith and by immersion) must be administered only "in the Name of Jesus," which means that that phrase must be spoken during baptism, instead of "in the name of the Father and of the Son and of the Holy Spirit." Those baptized in the Triune Name had to be rebaptized, even though they widely recognized their baptism to be an act of obedient faith done in Jesus' name (in the sense expressed in Col 3:17). Third, one must receive the gift of the Spirit, which was interpreted as always including glossolalia. Therefore, if one does not speak in tongues, one is not saved!

The wider implications of the extreme exclusiveness of this view of salvation are not always grasped or acknowledged. A simple literalism ("that is what the text says") often leaves sincere people unaware of the fact that such a theology excludes as unsaved virtually all of Christianity throughout church history, because baptism administered voicing only the name of Jesus is a novel twentieth-century phenomenon. Similarly, reception of the gift of the Spirit requiring the sign, or evidence, of tongues also excludes the vast majority of Christians alive today as well as in the past. The soteriological stringency and exclusivity of this position is actually as great a doctrinal stumbling block as is the Oneness view of the Godhead, to which we now turn.

Use of the "in the Name of Jesus" baptismal formula in Acts influenced the evolution of a strange doctrinal position regarding the Name of God. The reference in the Great Commission of Matthew 28:19 to baptizing people "in the Name of the Father, and of the Son, and of the Holy Spirit" uses the singular form for *name*. Instead of interpreting this in a Trinitarian way, the single name was taken as referring to Jesus. Coupled with the worship patterns of Holiness and Pentecostal believers, which were strongly focused on Jesus, a view evolved that the Lord Jesus Christ is the Father, the Son, and the Spirit. It is not easy to understand this doctrinal aberration, and there are various interpretations of this view. It is probably not accurate simply to call it Unitarian. The Unitarian-Universalists of today developed out of New England deism and the denial of the divinity of Christ.

Oneness Pentecostals (some prefer to be called "Apostolic Pentecostals," but see below for other uses of this adjective) maintain the full humanity and full divinity of Jesus Christ. There seems—at least among the more sophisticated presenters of this view—to be an acknowledgement of some form of three-foldness in the revelation of God. It is perhaps more accurate to describe this view as a new form of modalism, in which Jesus, rather than God the Father, is manifested simultaneously in three different ways.

The deepest divergence of Oneness belief from orthodox doctrine is its rejection of the classic confession of the tri-unity of God as *eternal*. Faupel describes the Oneness Pentecostals' understanding of any three-fold manifestation in God as "temporal and transitory" (p. 286). What implications such a view could have for our understanding of Jesus Himself praying and speaking to His Father and for the significantly Trinitarian event of the baptism in the Jordan is unclear. It leaves one puzzled and bewildered. Faithful orthodoxy needs to maintain the tension that God is both three and one. This truth expresses both *identification* of the Three Persons with one another as well as *distinction* (but never separation) from one another. Exegetical debates with Oneness Pentecostals usually revolve around individual scriptural passages that express the identification. John's Gospel, for example, maintains that the Word (Christ) was God (1:1) and that "I and the Father are one" (10:30), expressing identification; but it also asserts that the Word was *with* God (also 1:1), expressing distinction.

Oneness Pentecostals, represented in such denominations as the United Pentecostal Church International and the Pentecostal Assemblies of the World (predominantly African-American), are usually counted in worldwide statistics of Pentecostalism but are not included in the associations of Pentecostal denominations. Throughout Christianity, the doctrine of the

Trinity has always been considered as a touchstone for doctrinal orthodoxy. The academic association The Society for Pentecostal Studies (SPS) forms an exception in this regard. Oneness Pentecostals have long been included as members, as well as in the Society's leadership. A Oneness-vs.-Trinitarian debate continues, part of which was hosted by the Society in a several-years' dialogue reported on in 2008 in the Society's journal, *Pneuma* (volume 30, issue 2, pp. 203–224).

In a significant contribution to this dialogue, Kenneth Gill's "The New Issue Reconsidered," delivered at the 1990 Annual Meeting of the SPS (and published in its papers), outlines five criteria for a viable formulation of the Trinity. First, there is the divinity of Christ. Second, God must be seen as having internal consistency, as being one. On these two points, there is unanimity between Trinitarian and Jesus' Name Pentecostals. Third, the three persons/modes of the Godhead must function simultaneously. Fourth, each person/mode must be God himself and not mere appearance. On these two points, there is still debate within the Oneness ranks, but Gill maintains that there are non-Trinitarian Pentecostals who would agree with orthodox Trinitarian doctrine on these points, provided that the term "person" is not used. The fifth criterion is the major stumbling block. God exists *eternally* as Father, Son, and Holy Spirit (p. 25). Whereas within Oneness ranks some acknowledge a threefold nature of God, it is always limited to God's temporal dealings with the world within salvation history (the economic Trinity) and does not extend to God's eternal nature, or being (the ontological Trinity).

But the eternal nature of the tri-unity of God is an essential pillar on which the credibility of the gospel rests. If God were to be unitarian in His eternal essence and triune only in His revelation to the world, the conclusion follows that God actually is not as He has revealed Himself. That would make His revelation inauthentic and the plan of salvation not credible.

In the practical interaction between Trinitarian and non-Trinitarian Pentecostals, it is remarkable that the doctrinal difference regarding the Godhead can easily be overlooked. Pentecostals are generally seen as focused on the Foursquare Gospel—Jesus as Savior, Spirit-baptizer, Healer, and Coming King—and both of these groups share this focus. One sometimes hears of Trinitarian Pentecostals visiting or even joining a Oneness church and not noticing any difference for several months. A remarkable unity in worship and in spiritual experience between the two should caution Trinitarians against pronouncing an overly hasty condemnation. (Anglican theologian David A. Reed, who was raised in Oneness Pentecostalism, has offered the most thorough study of the Oneness movement, with a generous evaluation from an orthodox Trinitarian view, in *"In Jesus' Name": The History and Beliefs of Oneness Pentecostals* [Deo Publishing, 2007].)

Often the legalistic practices of some Oneness groups affront other Pentecostals more immediately than the matter of the Trinity. Rules such as no cutting of hair for women and no television or movies for all are still common and occasionally lead to dissension and schism. By the strange quirk of history alluded to in chapter one, the original name of the Azusa Street Mission and of the periodicals of both Parham and Seymour—*Apostolic Faith*—has in North America come to be associated with the Oneness Pentecostals rather than with the Pentecostal movement as a whole. The largest Pentecostal body in South Africa is Trinitarian but is still called the Apostolic Faith Mission because that name was introduced very early and has been retained.

Critique

Pentecostalism has come in for a strong measure of criticism from other Christians—especially from conservative and evangelical groups. Cessationist and dispensationalist believers considered the claims of the reoccurrence of all the *charismata* as fraudulent. Some even associated the movement with demonic deception. Mainstream Christianity in the West that had been most thoroughly influenced by modernism and had accepted rationalist and materialist presuppositions was also profoundly critical of the resurgence of what was termed "primitive superstition" and "blatant supernaturalism." More than anything else, it was the element of the miraculous that led to the shaking of the foundations of the established Churches in a modernist culture.

However, there was also the critique on a micro rather than a macro level. In drawing this section on Classical Pentecostalism to a close, it may be helpful to look briefly at the assessment of a leading Reformed evangelical author, Frederick Dale Bruner, who published in 1980 his research done in Germany, under the title *A Theology of the Holy Spirit: the Pentecostal Experience and the New Testament Witness*. In this scholarly volume, he summarizes his major objections to Pentecostal doctrine under three rubrics: (1) the doctrine of subsequence, by which he means the fact that Spirit baptism is seen as an experience subsequent to conversion (a second or third blessing); (2) the doctrine of initial evidence, with glossolalia required for Spirit baptism; and (3) the doctrine of "conditions."

By "conditions," Bruner refers to the belief of some Pentecostals that seekers, especially at old-fashioned "tarrying meetings," must prepare for the coming of the Spirit in various ways (e.g., by worship, earnest expectation, prayer and fasting, obedience, restitution, repentance, etc.). Such preparation Bruner judged to be a form of "works-righteousness" that denied the Reformational concepts of living by faith and relying only on God's grace.

Personally, I do not find Bruner's evaluation to be valid. It is always important to note the genre of one's sources. The word "conditions" is, of course, technically suspect to a trained systematic theologian, and with good reason, but used in popular, revivalist, and inspirational writings, testimonies, or sermons, it probably reflects nothing more than fervency and a protest against "cheap grace." In Hebrews 12, believers are exhorted to resist sin to the point of shedding one's blood (v. 4), to lift drooping hands and strengthen weak knees (v. 12). It is a misunderstanding of the gospel to caution against effort, fervency, and passion in good works. The error lies not in the striving but in considering that any of this has meritorious value! Good works are an essential part of our Christian life, but they express among other things our gratitude for salvation and are not a precondition for salvation!

The critique of Bruner lines up with what Durham called the "Finished Work of Calvary." Bruner warns against the error that the gospel may be seen as sufficient for the beginning but not for the continuing and completing of the Christian life or as sufficient for bringing the Holy Spirit initially but not fully. What is needed, instead, is a deeper understanding of what was wrought on the Cross. The victorious Christian walk does not require anything "extra" in addition to the atoning sacrifice of Jesus Christ, but the Cross needs to be appropriated and the consequences and dimensions of it understood more fully. (The first two objections of Bruner—subsequence and initial evidence—have been referred to above and will be pursued further in the following chapter on the Second Wave of the Spirit, the Charismatic movement of the 1960s and 1970s.)

Broad sociological factors, as well as an overreaction to the paradigm shift in theology signaled by Pentecostal thinking, resulted in the isolation of Pentecostalism from the rest of Christianity for several decades. It is also true that between 1935 and 1947 there was an embarrassing scarcity of charismatic manifestations in many Classical Pentecostal churches. Their isolation from mainstream Christianity was overcome only at the time of the denominational Charismatic movement of the 1960s. By that time, several Pentecostal denominations had become large and influential. They had established denominational headquarters, undergraduate colleges, and theological seminaries. However, before looking at the Second Wave, we consider another development within Pentecostal ranks that occurred in the late 1940s, which also had significant doctrinal importance.

The "New Order of the Latter Rain"

The "New Order of the Latter Rain" was the name given to a revival movement that originated in North Battleford, Saskatchewan, Canada, in 1948. George Hawtin, who had been associated with the Pentecostal Assemblies of Canada, (a sister denomination to the Assemblies of God in the U.S.) was president of Sharon Orphanage and Schools in North Battleford and a central figure in the early part of the revival. In February 1948, a revival broke out with remarkable words of prophecy and healings. There was a remarkable hunger for God among the students. Instead of leaving for vacation, many stayed on campus to seek the Lord together. They received inspiration from Pastor Reg Layzell of Glad Tidings Assembly in Vancouver. He taught from Psalm 22:3 on how the Lord, the Holy One, is enthroned on the praise of Israel and inhabits the praises of His people. There was a birthing of understanding worship as a sacrifice of praise. There was a new focus on the impartation of the *charismata* through the laying on of hands (rather than at the old tarrying meetings of early Pentecostalism).

The movement itself was soon discredited in the eyes of the major Pentecostal denominations, but some of the doctrinal emphases and innovative teachings went underground, as it were, only to resurface later in parts of the Independent Charismatic movement. William Branham, known for his amazing healing crusades and, unfortunately, for his doctrinal aberrations towards the end of his ministry, was associated with the Latter Rain movement. Branham's crusade in Vancouver in 1947 had impressed the teachers of Sharon Bible School in North Battleford deeply. That led to his involvement in the movement.

This revival paralleled the Azusa Street awakening in many ways, according to Stanley Frodsham, a leader in the Assemblies of God and editor of the *Pentecostal Evangel*. However, he was soon pressured to resign as editor due to his association with the "Latter Rain" movement. The distinctive teaching of this movement includes the restoration of the fivefold ministry of Ephesians 4:11, especially the offices of apostle and prophet; the ministry of deliverance; the concept of the laying on of hands to impart spiritual gifts, which was seen as part of the foundational truths of Hebrews 6:1–2; and a new focus on exuberant worship with rhythmic dancing, singing in the Spirit, clapping, shouting, and swaying of limbs. This focus was associated with restoring the "Tabernacle of David" and a renewed interest in supporting Zionism and the State of Israel.

The theme of restoring the tabernacle of David (see Amos 9:11 and Acts 15:16–17) became a major concern. This historical interlude after David brought the Ark up to Jerusalem and before the building of the temple by King Solomon—a period of about 38 years—was viewed as a New Testament oasis in the Old Testament dispensation. It was an era of peace, with more freedom for the expression of prophecy and revelation. Exuberant worship—note the leaping, jumping, and praising God by King David that was frowned on by his wife Michal—took the place of the regular system of animal sacrifices. The worship led by the Levites and singers with their musical instruments was unceasing, as about 4,000 people worked together in shifts (1 Chron. 15–17). This is also the first time mention is made of choirs.

The seminal writer of this movement, George Warnock, stated that through God's presence we see the invisible, hear the inaudible, hold the intangible, declare the unspeakable, and do the impossible. Warnock's book *The Feast of Tabernacles* advocated anew the celebration of the third great Jewish feast— The Feast of Tabernacles, or Booths. He maintained that while the Passover was fulfilled at Calvary and the Feast of the Weeks (Pentecost) was fulfilled at the outpouring of the Spirit on the Day of Pentecost, the Feast of Tabernacles is yet to be fulfilled. It should be noted that the State of Israel was established in the same year that the New Order of the Latter Rain started. The establishment of the Christian Embassy in Jerusalem was also an outflow of this focus on Israel.

Revival historian Richard M. Riss points out in his article "Latter Rain Movement" that the popular magazine of the independent or non-denominational Charismatic movement,

Logos Journal, grew out of a Latter Rain publication (Burgess and McGee, *Dictionary*, p. 534).

Michael Moriarty, who wrote a very negative critique titled *The New Charismatics*, adds a few further characteristics of the Latter Rain movement. He highlights the anti-establishment tenor of the movement. They saw Protestant denominationalism as akin to "Roman Catholic perversion." Both emanated, according to Branham, from the seductions of "Nicolaitanism" and "Balaamism" (pp. 65–66). The practice of deliverance it seems was even used for sinful habits of the flesh (which many, myself included, would maintain require crucifying rather than exorcising) and became more prominent, as well as fasting. There was a new wave of prophecy which functioned not only as encouragement and exhortation (1 Cor 14:3) but also as detailed, directive revelation.

After a period of amazing success, Branham's ministry started to derail. He declared that he himself was the angel to the church of Laodicea and attacked Classical Pentecostals as representing a "Jezebel religion." The General Council of the Assemblies of God identified six errors of the Latter Rain movement in a resolution in 1949, and condemnations of this kind were the principal factor in the rapid decline of the movement thereafter. Classical Pentecostal leadership felt threatened by the revival and especially the new doctrine that the church is founded on the ministry of present-day apostles and prophets. This view later became prominent in the Restorationist stream of the Independent Charismatic movement. Pentecostals also questioned the imparting of the charismatic gifts such as tongues and prophecy through the laying on of hands rather than through tarrying meetings.

As Riss shows in "The Latter Rain Movement of 1948," the movement saw itself as a fulfillment of the prophecy given during the Azusa Street revival of 1906 that a great revival would begin in Northern Canada (p. 38). God was seen as moving in a "strange new manner." Prophecy operated differently—minute details were provided in a supernatural manner. Some of the churches affected were Bethesda Missionary Temple in Detroit, MI, under pastor Myrtle Beall; Wings of Healing Temple in Portland, OR, with Pastor Thomas Wyatt; and the Elim Bible Institute in New York State. Latter Rain ideas were fed into the independent charismatic renewal (to be discussed later) by individuals such as John Poole, who was a frequent contributor to *New Wine* magazine. Together with Ern Baxter, he was also associated with the Christian Growth Ministries of Ft. Lauderdale, FL. These influences reemerged in the so-called Third Wave of the Charismatic movement. Another significant stream of Latter Rain ideas was disseminated through World Missionary Assistance Plan (World MAP), an international missionary service founded by Ralph Mahoney (pp. 40–44).

In the later development of the movement, teachers became more extreme. They saw themselves as "the Overcomers" who have attained fullness. They would dethrone Satan and bind him, ushering in believers free from the curse, sin, sickness, death and carnality (p. 45). Perfectionism had returned in a new and more radical form.

At the same time as the Latter Rain movement, a healing revival was taking place across North America. This movement had broader impact and lasted from 1947 to 1958. David Edwin Harrell's *All Things Are Possible: The Healing and Charismatic Revivals in Modern America* describes healing evangelists William Branham and Oral Roberts as the two giants of the movement. With tent crusades, coupled with radio and television broadcasts, they with others spread Pentecostal thinking across a wide spectrum of Christianity. This revival focused specifically on bringing salvation and bodily healing to the masses. The list of important healing evangelists of this era includes Gordon Lindsay, Jack Coe, T. L. Osborn, A. A. Allen, David Nunn, William Freeman, and Morris Cerullo. Several of them also traveled internationally. The healing revival did not develop new doctrines for the Pentecostal and Charismatic movements, but it certainly revitalized their awareness and expectation of the mir-aculous. However, the healing revival helped significantly to prepare the way for the next major movement—the Second Wave of the Spirit in the twentieth century, in which Pentecostal practices and teaching spilled over the entire spectrum of Christian churches and across the world.

Conclusion

In this chapter, the teachings of the first of the waves of the Holy Spirit awakenings of the twentieth century have been outlined. Doctrinal developments were formulated mostly in response to religious experiences and by interacting with the narratives of the book of Acts. The radical Wesleyan understanding of sanctification as the attaining of Christian perfection as a step initially characterized the movement but was seriously challenged by William Durham's view of the Finished Work of Christ. The theology of subsequence, however, was still maintained as the widespread experience of glossolalia was seen as the required gateway to life in the Spirit (or initial, physical evidence of Spirit baptism). In this way, the movement remained vulnerable to an elitist dividing of believers into two camps, one spiritually superior to the other. The New Issue brought the movement to the brink of heresy by rejecting the doctrine of the Trinity, and the New Order of the Latter Rain brought forth a number of doctrinal emphases that will be taken up again in the Second and Third Waves.

Nevertheless, the positive doctrinal significance of this First Wave is hard to overestimate. Furthermore, the maturing forces of inevitable self-correction were already in place in a movement in which love of God and of the Scriptures was paramount. Christianity itself was undergoing a self-correction, freeing itself from functional binitarianism through this global awakening. The thoroughgoing life in the Spirit, complete with the New Testament range of charismata, was being embraced again after many centuries of neglect. The occurrence of present-day healings was shaking the foundations of conservative Protestant theories of cessationism, and the miraculous was being reintegrated into normal Christian life.

In all confessional traditions, a period of maturation is usually required to bring the initial fervor and the often-unbalanced doctrinal deposit of this fervor into closer alignment with Scripture. Pentecostalism was no exception. Given the cultural milieu of modernism and its devastating impact on the whole Church—especially through the elimination of the supernatural dimension—it comes as no surprise that the a-rational or non-rational gift of tongues could be used by God to curb the arrogance of human intellectualism. Unfortunately, this led to this one gift's being elevated beyond biblical warrant. As the movement continued, this would become a major issue, as is seen in the reflections on the Second Wave. What remains paramount, however, was the return of evangelistic fervor, striving after holiness, the openness to all the gifts of the Spirit, and spiritual empowerment to live the Christian life. This is the unquestionable legacy of the First Wave.

5

The Second Wave: Denominational Charismatic Renewal

T he story of the denominational Charismatic Renewal has been told in many books, ranging from devotional literature, to personal testimony, to a few historical publications. The latter category includes the work of Vinson Synan, Peter Hocken, and Richard Quebedeaux. Only the briefest of outlines is pursued here, since this study intends rather to probe the doctrinal dimensions of these twentieth-century movements.

Precedents

The earliest stirrings of what is being dubbed the Second Wave (with Classical Pentecostalism as the First Wave) are found in a number of ministries of Pentecostal persuasion which began reaching those outside the Pentecostal fold. Leaders of the healing revival of the late 1940s and '50s (mentioned in the previous chapter) such as Oral Roberts, a successful and balanced preacher and healing evangelist, had the stature and integrity to appeal to a wider spectrum of society. Roberts was also an astute observer of the trends in religious culture in America. He used radio and then national television, founded a university, and built a medical center in Tulsa, Oklahoma. In March 1968, he left the Pentecostal Holiness tradition of his up-bringing and joined the United Methodist Church. This momen-tous step was, in itself, a symbol of wider trends among Chris-tians in the USA. The isolation and anti-intellectualism of Pente-costal thinking was being broken down, and a neo-Pentecostal movement was emerging, in which divine healing was slowly being accepted into mainstream circles.

The Full Gospel Business Men's Fellowship International, led by California businessman Demos Shakarian, also did much to spread awareness of the work of the Holy Spirit via conventions and prayer breakfasts through the laity of various Protestant denominations. Also significantly influential was the indomitable Mr. Pentecost, David du Plessis, a roving ambas-sador of sorts for Pentecostal teaching in ecumenical circles, including the World Council of Churches, the International Mis-sionary Council, and the Vatican in Rome. His denomination, the Assemblies of God, withdrew his accreditation because of these involvements, but he was later honorably restored. Du Plessis rendered an invaluable service to many denominational and confessional groups by emphasizing that they needed to explore and develop the work of the Holy Spirit within their own doctrinal heritage or, as Kilian McDonnell would phrase it, within their own ecclesial cultures. Du Plessis, aware of the societal and educational differences between the various constituencies, made it clear that mainline Protestant, Catholic, and Orthodox believers did not need to become Pentecostal in their styles of worship or even in their theology. Insightfully, he did not want the work of the Spirit and its reception to be hampered by what he termed "Pentecostal baggage."

Other forces helped prepare the way for the denominational Charismatic renewal. Camps Farthest Out founded by Glenn Clark, the "Jesus People" revival of the 1960s, the "inner healing" teaching of Agnes Sanford, the healing Order of St. Luke, and books such as David Wilkerson's *The Cross and the Switchblade* and John Sherrill's *They Speak with Other Tongues* all played a role. It has been estimated that by the year 2000 this Second Wave movement had affected 60 million Protestants and 80 million Roman Catholics.

Beginnings

The precipitating experience later recognized as the land-mark of the denominational renewal movement was an an-nouncement on April 3, 1960, by Dennis Bennett, Episcopal priest at St. Marks, Van Nuys, California, to his parish. He told them that he had experienced the power and fullness of the Holy Spirit in his life and that this included the gift of unknown tongues. This caused a great stir and led to his resignation. Nevertheless, he took the ecclesiologically significant step of deciding to remain within his denomination. Up to this point, those in mainline churches who had received the gift of glossolalia either kept it to themselves or chose to become Pentecostals. The publicity surrounding Dennis Bennett's announcement and the popularity of his book, *Nine O'clock in the Morning,* in which he related his Pentecostal experience, triggered a wide response, and many in mainline churches who had previously experienced tongues were now emboldened to share this with others.

The Charismatic awakening that followed touched nearly every denominational tradition within Protestantism. It is gen-erally assumed that at least 15 percent of the membership of various mainline denominations in North America had some or other charismatic experience in the 1960s and 1970s. At the massive Kansas City, Missouri, conference in July 1977, Protestant denominational tracks included Baptist, Methodist, Lutheran, Episcopalian, Presbyterian and Reformed, and Mennonite believers. This conference of 50,000 people concluded the formative and more ecumenical phase of the Charismatic Renewal. Later, the grassroots unity would be superseded by a new focus on doctrinal distinctives and denominational identity, in order to reach out to the non-Charismatic constituencies of each denominational and confessional grouping. This conference at the Arrowhead

Stadium also included Roman Catholics, who had joined in the Protestant movement in 1966/67, Messianic Jews, some Classical Pentecostals, as well as a very large section of Third Wave independent Charismatics—including both supporters and critics of the Discipleship-Shepherding-Submission movement (which the next chapter discusses).

The Episcopalian Charismatic renewal in California received support through a wealthy lay member, Jean Stone, under whose auspices the quarterly periodical *Trinity* was published and an association called the "Blessed Trinity Society" formed. By July and August 1960, both *Newsweek* and *Time* had had cover stories on the events at Van Nuys. The significance of the titles "Trinity" and "Blessed Trinity Society" should not be missed. From the very beginning there was an understanding that the Charismatic movement was not a foreign import or *Fremdkörper* to Christianity, but rather the development of something intrinsic to orthodox teaching—the reclaiming of a fully Trinitarian perspective. The name Blessed Trinity Society certainly sounds more Episcopal or Anglican than Pentecostal.

Mixed Receptions

While the development of the movement from Episcopal to American Lutheran, American Baptist, and United Presbyterian Churches and further afield is not outlined here, it is significant to note that the movement encountered varying degrees of opposition. Although the Episcopal bishop of Los Angeles discouraged the movement, Bennett was welcomed by the bishop of Olympia, and he became vicar, or priest, of St. Luke's in Seattle, Washington. Catholic ecumenist and specialist on the Charismatic movement, Father Kilian McDonnell, documented the responses of churches worldwide to the Charismatic renewal in three volumes, *Presence, Power, Praise: Documents on the Charismatic Renewal.* Broadly speaking, the responses were initially somewhat negative but moved gradually to a more supportive stance in the 1970s, in most confessional groupings. Early documents tended to discount contemporary miracles as being spurious and counterfeit. Behind this view was a dispensational legacy that had become widespread in many Protestant circles. As a result of exegetical work done in the fifties by Catholic biblical scholars such as Otto Pesch in Germany and Protestant theologians such as G. C. Berkouwer in the Netherlands, the dispensational tenet that the miraculous came to an end at a particular point of time in history was thoroughly discredited. Cardinal Suenens of Brussels opposed cessationism powerfully in a debate with Cardinal Ruffini during the Second Vatican Council in Rome. Reformed theologians also came to realize that limiting the era in which supernatural occurrences could take place went against deeply-held Calvinist convictions regarding the majesty or sovereignty of God. As a result, most denominational statements became gradually less negative as the fledgling Charismatic movement entered its second decade.

It is noteworthy that it was the most conservative denominations that usually remained the most critical of the movement, since the denominational Charismatics often came to represent the most biblical and conservative segments of their denominations. Southern Baptists and Missouri Synod Lutherans were most strongly anti-charismatic. In 1971, the Charismatic renewal touched Eastern Orthodox Churches as well. Leaders include Zabrodsky, Eusebius Stephanou, and Athanasios Emmert. It needs to be said that whereas Roman Catholicism proved to be remarkably open to the Charismatic renewal and supplied it with exceptional theological leadership, most Orthodox priests in the renewal have over time withdrawn from it under pressure from their bishops. Most Eastern Orthodox theologians, who see Orthodoxy as in direct continuity with apostolic Christianity and as the true Church, saw little need for any renewal and tended to discredit the Charismatic movement as being intrinsically Protestant and therefore theologically suspect.

Southern Baptists tolerate the Charismatic renewal better today. A Texas-based movement using the term "Fullness" articulated the renewal within the Southern Baptist Convention.

The renewal reenergized James Robison as a leader, and many Baptists became involved in it on foreign mission fields. In Methodist, Episcopal, and Presbyterian circles, the term "charismatic" was, over time, generally replaced by the term "renewal" to lessen any association with Pentecostalism. The first denominational Charismatic group organized was the Presbyterian Charismatic Communion, formed in 1966. It later renamed itself the Presbyterian and Reformed Renewal Ministries International and continues today, headquartered in Black Mountain, NC, but it has now dropped even the word "Renewal" from its title.

As with Classical Pentecostalism, the denominational Charismatic renewal soon became a global movement, spreading especially to Europe and Latin America. It was characteristic of the Roman Catholic tradition that its interaction with Charismatics led to intense theological activity concerning the teachings of the renewal movement. The Catholic Pentecostals, as they were first called, grew mostly out of events on university campuses—Duquesne in Pittsburgh, Notre Dame in South Bend, IN, and the University of Michigan in Ann Arbor, MI.

The major doctrinal development of the Charismatic movement was the theological reflection that occurred when Pentecostal teaching met Protestant and Catholic traditions. This interaction led to a variety of interpretations of the central tenets of Pentecostal thinking, to which we now turn.

Interpretations

When the first generation of Charismatic Christians sought to make sense of the fresh experiences of God in their lives that came through the awakenings of the 1960s and 70s, they at first naturally gravitated towards the easily accessible Pentecostal interpretations of their experiences. The first group of Protestant Charismatic leaders held a view of Spirit baptism (the primary experience of God that was being attested to in the renewal movement) that could be termed neo-Pentecostal. Their contribution was a slight modification of the Pentecostal model of the Christian life, downplaying the issue of subsequent stages and the pivotal experience of baptism in the Holy Spirit as being necessarily accompanied by the "initial evidence" of speaking in tongues. This issue is discussed in more detail below. The supernatural worldview, however, was readily embraced, as well as an openness to the full range of the charismata (or so-called gifts of the Spirit) mentioned in the New Testament. Generally speaking, becoming involved in the Charismatic movement also led to a more evangelical or conservative stance regarding the authority of Scripture and morality. It would soon become apparent that significant differences remained in ecclesial culture—to use Kilian McDonnell's term. Issues such as the use of alcohol, tobacco, and forms of entertainment still divided the constituencies, as did their varying political commitments. The differences in social practices and moral stances between Catholics and Pentecostals are beautifully captured in the amusing title of a booklet that was published in the early Catholic Pentecostal movement: *Father McCarthy Smokes a Pipe and Speaks in Tongues.*

More important to our purposes, however, are the theological discussions that developed over time. Now entering into the world of Pentecostal experience and the miraculous signs of God's power were Christians from a wide variety of denominational traditions. The Charismatic renewal movement in the United States was the first truly nationwide revival. The First and Second Great Awakenings had affected only Protestantism (and not even the full range of Protestant denominations). Here was a renewal movement that included virtually every branch of Protestantism, influenced American Catholicism significantly, and also touched Eastern Orthodox Churches. It spread rapidly from coast to coast. As the influence of this denominational renewal movement increased, many theologically trained believers also became involved.

An unexpected by-product was a good deal of serious theological interaction—especially during the 1970s. Catholic theologians such as Edward O'Connor reflected on the Catholic Pentecostal movement, as it was then called, within the realm of traditional Catholic spirituality and mystical experiences. Different Protestant traditions engaged in a novel endeavor of (re)discovering charismatic elements within their own heritage. The early life of Luther provided Charismatic Lutherans with some "legitimacy." Bengt Hoffman developed this argument in his academic dissertation. Luther's first publication was an editing of the early German mystical writings titled the Theologica Deutsch. The awareness of the supernatural, specifically interaction with the demonic, is evident in Luther's writings and hymns. The popular hymn "A Mighty Fortress is Our God" speaks of "this world with devils filled."

Church historians soon discovered traces of charismatic manifestations throughout the history of Christianity, especially in times of awakening and among fringe groups. John Wesley was most favorable in his evaluation of Montanism and was aware of supernatural phenomena occurring in several of his meetings, especially among the so-called French prophets who had found refuge in England after persecution across the channel. Charles Wesley testified regarding a woman whom he claimed "gobbled like a turkey cock." To modern-day Charismatic Methodists, this was an early evidence of glossolalia. Presbyterians in the Renewal discovered that John Calvin advocated praying with arms raised in the "orante" position that had become popular among Charismatics. He refers to this six times in his writings, both in the longest chapter in the *Institutes of the Christian Religion*, which is on prayer, and in his biblical commentaries. The raising of the arms signifies surrender and devotion to the majesty of the Lord, but Calvin does caution that it should not become a hollow gesture. He states that unfortunately it is possible to leave your heart on the ground while raising your hands. These examples illustrate the attempt by the denominational Charismatics to legitimize their charismatic experiences within their ecclesial cultures. This process, of course, was significant in attempts to propagate the Charismatic renewal within their own traditions, often in the face of much skepticism and criticism from the mainstream denominational and theological leadership.

The Charismatic renewal, however, not only resulted in a fresh look at history and ecclesial tradition. There was also the more serious grappling with doctrine. The central theological teachings of the renewal movement presented various obstacles to new "initiates" in the Charismatic renewal. What is Spirit baptism, and how does it relate to baptism? It was in this area that a great deal of innovative reflection and writing occurred in the 1970s and '80s. We now focus on the different interpretations of the central Charismatic doctrine of "baptism in the Holy Spirit."

Views about Spirit Baptism

Broadly speaking, the views fall into three basic categories, which may be identified by the terms Neo-Pentecostal, Sacramental, and Integrative. The last includes a wide variety of positions that have in common only the goal of presenting a way in which Spirit baptism may be more fully integrated into the rest of Christianity, whether evangelical or mainline.

Neo-Pentecostal

As one would expect, the first generation of Charismatic writers relied heavily on Classical Pentecostal thinking. These neo-Pentecostals had inherited a conceptual framework and did little more than make some minor adjustments. The basic evangelical critique of Pentecostalism had been expressed clearly by New Testament theologian Frederick Dale Bruner. As we saw in chapter 4, Bruner's widely-used *A Theology of the Holy Spirit* (based on his Hamburg doctoral dissertation) attacked Pentecostalism on three fronts. He rejected (1) their theology of subsequence, (2) their doctrine of glossolalia as the "initial, physical evidence" of Spirit baptism, and (3) their concept of "conditions" to be met in order to be Spirit-baptized. Most neo-Pentecostal Charismatics accepted the theology of subsequence, which maintained that there were distinct experiential stages in the Christian life and that Spirit baptism is necessarily subsequent to conversion and should be seen as separate from it. On the point of "conditions," however, they provided a helpful corrective. There were no extra requirements needed to be baptized or filled with the Holy Spirit. Faith in Jesus Christ as Lord and Savior is all that is needed for access to the gifts of the Spirit.

Restating my argument again in a little more detail, it is my personal contention that Pentecostalism had not ever meant to use the word "conditions" as a form of "works righteousness" to be added to the work of Calvary. One arrives at such an evaluation only when one interprets Pentecostal statements without understanding their various genres. Devotional literature, sermons, even fund-raising letters, may contain expressions and statements that have to be interpreted within their contexts. Classical Pentecostals had produced very little systematic theology up to that point. As a result, Pentecostals often mentioned the need for so-called "conditions," such as worship, intense desire, obedience, fervent prayer, restitution for past wrongs, joyous faith, baptism, praise and thanksgiving, etc., as they prepared themselves for God to work in their lives. Researchers would interpret Pentecostal statements more graciously and charitably if they acknowledged that one should not expect terminological precision from the largely inspirational and exhortatory writings of a fledgling Pentecostal revival movement.

On the other hand, the Charismatic writers of the Second Wave generally came from churches with a long tradition of seminary-educated leadership. The theological pitfalls of requiring "conditions" for Spirit baptism were readily recognized and thus avoided. At the same time, the "ecclesial culture" of Pentecostalism was also changing. The earlier practice of "tarrying meetings" had fallen into disfavor. The "Latter Rain" revival of the 1950s had emphasized the laying on of hands as a way for imparting God's gifts. In the denominational Charismatic renewal of the 1960s, people wishing to be filled by God's Spirit generally were filled unexpectedly, or through individual prayer, or through communal prayer. In prayer meetings, people gathered around a person seated on a chair and prayed while placing their hands on the person's shoulders. They prayed sometimes in glossolalia and also in the vernacular. When the emotionally-charged tarrying meetings ceased (which had often lasted for hours into the late night or the wee hours of the morning), the idea of fulfilling certain "conditions" also became unimportant.

With regard to Bruner's critique of evidential glossolalia, neo-Pentecostals made some minor adjustments. It became increasingly difficult to support the doctrine of "initial evidence" because the New Testament never states that tongues constitute an absolute *(sine qua non)* requirement for anything, nor is it clear that tongues needs to be the first "evidence" (cf. "initial, physical evidence"). As a result, neo-Pentecostal writers often stated their position with some ambiguity. They viewed glossolalia as part of a "package deal." It was not so much that one must or needs to speak in tongues but that one usually does as a matter of course. Some neo-Pentecostals, wanting to back off from what had derisively been called "the law of tongues" by British charismatic author Thomas Smail, pointed out that prophecy, bold witnessing, or healings could also be biblically valid evidence of Spirit baptism. Tongues, nevertheless, remained prominent in neo-Pentecostal Charismatic spirituality. If one had not received this gift, it was not viewed as ideal, and the individual was patiently encouraged to continue seeking it without drawing the conclusion that such a person was not yet Spirit-filled.

On the matter of subsequence, there was stronger agreement. Not only were biblical arguments presented, but there was almost universal support for a two-stage position based on widespread personal experience. Most leaders of the neo-Pentecostal Charismatic movement had been sincere practicing Christians before their Charismatic breakthrough experiences. They now testified to new freedom, enthusiasm, love for Scripture, increased joy and faith, etc. It seemed clear that one could be a believer but still be missing something significant in one's spiritual walk with the Lord. Those outside the movement found this very aspect to be the most threatening. Although it was seldom stated bluntly, many traditional church members were convinced that these "new" Charismatic worshipers doubted their salvation and/or Christian commitment. Without wise leadership and a generous dose of 1 Corinthians 13, this attitude led to much divisiveness and, sometimes, to schisms in local congregations or even in denominations.

Neo-Pentecostals supported their theology of subsequence also on the Classical Pentecostal pattern. It consisted of two major arguments. As has been outlined above the first argument was that a two-stage pattern was discernible in the life of Jesus and in the lives of the apostles or disciples of Jesus. The analogy based on the life of Jesus was never very convincing and was consequently not widely used. The argument went as follows: Jesus was conceived through the power and overshadowing of the Holy Spirit. Before He embarks on His public ministry, however, He has a subsequent encounter with the Spirit and a resulting enduement with power at His baptism in the Jordan. These two experiences of Jesus were seen as correlating, first, with a believer's regeneration through the Spirit and, then, second, the believer's baptism in the Spirit. The argument (expressed in a question) would then be that if the Son of God needed this subsequent experience for ministry, how much more would we, as his followers?

The analogy based on the lives of the apostles was more widely used. It still remains a somewhat tenuous argument pressed by a number of difficulties. The first difficulty is that there is no actual indication of a conversion experienced by the apostles of Jesus in the Gospels. Some consider their response to the call to discipleship as constituting a conversion—at least with regard to the eleven (excluding Judas).

Second, the uniqueness of their position as people living between the two eras or testaments makes analogical conclusions less than helpful. The disciples' lives stretch across the salvation-historical milestone of the Cross and the Resurrection. They belong to both major dispensations, straddling the Old and the New Covenants. This fact alone should caution the New Testament believer not to seek too strict an analogical relationship. In the quest to determine when the apostles were converted or became regenerate, some argued that their conversions must have taken place after the salvific events of the Crucifixion and Resurrection. John 20:22 provides the best possibility, but many commentators do not find the argument convincing. Jesus breathes on the disciples and says: "Receive the Holy Spirit." This action is then seen as their conversion. The context seems to suggest that the imparting of God's Spirit and life abundant at this junction was rather part of an enabling or commissioning. New Testament scholar H. Ridderbos finds it much more natural to see this receiving of the Spirit in the context of the mission and authorization of the disciples, referring to the transmission of the Spirit in a broader sense of an equipping for service. If it could be seen an indication of regeneration, it would be certainly be unique and unparalleled. The very next phrase of the text addresses the authority of the disciples to forgive and retain sins.

To return to the basic argument: After the "conversion" of John 20:22 the events of the Day of Pentecost described in Acts 2 would then provide the second crucial event for a two-stage paradigm based on the experience of the disciples.

Apart from these two analogies, the second and more common argument from Scripture for "initial evidence" is the so-called five cases from the book of Acts: chapter 2, 8, 9, 10, and 19 (Pentecost, Samaria, the conversion of Saul, the household of Cornelius, and the disciples in Ephesus). This actually represents the classic apologetic for glossolalia as initial, physical evidence given in Classical Pentecostal circles. As we saw, although neo-Pentecostal Charismatics did not insist on tongues as the necessary sign for Spirit baptism as the Classical Pentecostals, they usually found the concept of subsequence convincing. Very briefly stated, the line of reasoning is that each of these chapters illustrated that Spirit baptism comes at a stage after conversion. In three cases, glossolalia is specifically mentioned (chapters 2,

10, and 19). Regarding chapters 8 and 9, proponents argue that glossolalia may safely be assumed to have occurred. Most of the exegetical debate has focused on chapters 8 and 19, which present the strongest case for subsequence. Expositions by New Testament scholars abound, both pro and contra the neo-Pentecostal Charismatic argumentation. Without now entering into this debate (which I discussed in a previous publication, *Treasures Old and New),* I would like to contend that in any case no universally applicable or pattern may be generalized from any of these cases.

Acts 2 presents us with a number of disciples who experience the definitive salvation-historical milestone and unrepeatable first outpouring of the Spirit with tongues of fire on the fledgling Church. For many (or all?), it could have come as a second experience after their initial decision to commit to following Jesus as the Messiah. Acts 8 is clearly an exceptional situation in which the strange delay in the coming of the Spirit (v. 16) needed to be rectified. Acts 9 relates Saul's conversion and being filled with the Spirit, both occurring within a matter of days (no specific mention of tongues, but certainly a healing—the restoration of sight). Acts 10 describes the unified experience of Cornelius' household, where Peter preaches the gospel, and household members suddenly and unexpectedly manifest tongues and praise, followed then by their water baptism.

Acts 19 is again unique, since the twelve or so disciples in Ephesus had previously been baptized into John's baptism and then manifested glossolalia and prophecy after receiving Christian baptism and the laying on of hands. It seems as if one may safely conclude that God's transforming presence generally evokes or calls forth an experiential response, that the work of the Holy Spirit is thus made manifest, and that tongues is often part of this glorious experience. Fear of downplaying this newly reclaimed experiential aspect led most of the early neo-Pentecostal Charismatic leaders to teach a theology of subsequence. This teaching caused a measure of contention within their respective denominations and this, in time, resulted in further attempts to interpret and reinterpret theologically what had undoubtedly been a vivid and transforming encounter with God in the lives of millions of people. Neo-Pentecostal Charismatic authors representing this perspective include Dennis Bennett (Episcopal), Stephen Clark (Catholic), as well as Larry Christenson (Lutheran), and Rodman Williams (Presbyterian) in their earlier writings.

Sacramental

The sacramental Charismatic perspective presented a new understanding of Spirit baptism. When Christians from historic sacramental traditions such as Eastern Orthodox, Roman Catholic, Anglican/Episcopalian, and Lutheran began experiencing the Charismatic renewal, tensions in doctrinal heritage and terminology became very apparent. The terminology "baptism in the Holy Spirit" was a major stumbling block. This language was now used for a distinct experience, unrelated to and in some tension with the established practice of infant baptism. Traditional Catholics and mainline Protestants would ask: Were we not already baptized in the Holy Spirit when we were baptized in water? In some European circles, the term "baptism in the Holy Spirit" was replaced by such terms as "effusion" to avoid misunderstanding, but in English the usage was already so firmly established and entrenched that it could not be dislodged. Other ways of referring to the paramount Charismatic experience that did not seem to pass the test of time were substitutes such as "baptismal renewal" and "renewal of confirmation" (German: Firmerneuerung).

From the very beginning, the Catholic Charismatic movement profited from competent theological advisors. They included American theologians Edward O'Connor, Josephine Ford, Kevin Ranaghan, and very significantly, a philosopher of religion, Donald Gelpi. René Laurentin in France, as well as Simon Tugwell of England, offered similar support to sacramental views of interpreting Spirit baptism.

The major contribution, however, came from Kilian McDonnell, a world-renowned ecumenical theologian from the Benedictine St. John's Abbey and University in Collegeville, MN. McDonnell, who has published widely on the Charismatic movement, worked closely with Leon-Joseph Cardinal Suenens of Brussels, Belgium, to provide ecclesiastical guidelines for the Catholic Charismatic movement. The series of booklets called the Malines Documents were the result. Cardinal Suenens, one of the four moderators of the Second Vatican Council, had been an advocate for the theological position that the present-day occurrence of the charismata could not be ruled out. For him this had been more of a theoretical argument due to the lack of biblical evidence for any form of cessationism (or dispensationalism).

Soon after the close of the Second Vatican Council in 1965, however, he was faced with the practical challenge of hundreds of American Catholics' claiming experience of such charismata as tongues, prophecy, and divine healing. Together with Cardinal Suenens, Kilian McDonnell worked out a radically different way of understanding the experience that was transforming the lives of so many Catholics in the late 1960s and '70s. They interpreted Spirit baptism as a "release of the Spirit." According to orthodox doctrine, Christian initiation involves the work of the Holy Spirit. In the Catholic tradition, this primary conviction is expressed as follows: the Spirit is imparted to the believer in and through the sacraments of initiation—baptism, confirmation, and the Eucharist. It is possible that, in the believer's subjective awareness, experiences may occur that signify a later "flowering" of the initial reception of baptismal grace. Theologically, the Spirit was imparted in His fullness at Christian initiation, but one may experience a release later in life. This interpretation breaks from the two-stage heritage of Pentecostal and neo-Pentecostal thinking. Sacramental baptism (of infants) is considered the valid and irrevocable baptism in the Holy Spirit. Further experiences of God's grace are merely a becoming aware in a new way of God, who is already present and resident in the individual's life.

Kilian McDonnell and George Montague, two eminent and orthodox Catholic scholars, wrote the major work *Christian Initiation and Baptism in the Holy Spirit: Evidence from the First Eight Centuries,* in which they pursue this matter further. With solid scholarship, they uncover, in both the New Testament and early Church history, a rich legacy of life in the Spirit evinced at Christian initiation. Major patristic writers from a wide geographical area and representing various languages and ethnic groups expect an experiential dimension in the process of becoming a Christian.

McDonnell illustrates this expectation well with his fascinating discussion of Tertullian. This description emanates from the earlier and undeniably orthodox phase of Tertullian's writings, long before he came in contact with Montanism. The experience of becoming a Christian in second-century Roman North Africa involved an initiation expressed spatially by moving between three rooms. First, there is an architecturally separate room, a baptistery in which initiates descend by steps into a large circular pool for baptism and then ascend on the opposite side. Second, in the adjoining antechamber, the new believers are anointed with oil and blessed by the laying on of hands by the church leadership. It is here that the atmosphere is fraught with charismatic expectation. At the end of his treatise *On Baptism,* Tertullian encourages the new believers, "When you come up from the most sacred bath of the new birth, when you spread out your hands for the first time in your mother's house with your brethren, ask your Father, ask your Lord, for the special gift of his inheritance, the distributed charisms, which form an additional underlying feature (of baptism)" (p. 108).

Tertullian exhorts the believers with a confidence that seems bolstered by personal experience. He declares: "Ask and you shall receive," and then adds, "In fact you have sought, and you have found" (p. 108). In the third larger room, the newly baptized and initiated believers join the local body for a Eucharistic celebration. In this little vignette from early church history, charismatic expectation and realization integrate with sacramental practice (baptism and the Lord's Supper). In time, especially due to the practice of infant baptism, there was a delay between the rites of initiation and the experiencing of the charisms. With this sacramental interpretation of Spirit baptism as the release of the (dormant) Spirit into experiential manifestation, we have an understanding of charismatic experience that is clearly not foreign to Roman Catholic ecclesial culture and tradition.

This sacramental interpretation, which testifies to later experiential release of the Spirit, has influenced many Catholics, but writers from other confessions have also espoused it, such as Lutherans Theodore Jungkuntz and Larry Christenson (in his later writings), John Gunstone and James Jones (Anglican/Episcopal), and such Greek Orthodox thinkers as Eusebius Stephanou and Athanasios Emmet.

On the other hand, others have expressed several reservations about this interpretation. Catholic theologian Francis Sullivan of the Gregorianum in Rome has argued that the Spirit is seen here almost as a kind of commodity that can be stored away for many years. This interpretation has also been likened to a "time bomb" or "alarm clock" set to go off at some time in the future. In one's Christian walk, one inevitably appropriates aspects of God's truth long after they were first acknowledged or received. There is a coming into conscious awareness of God's previously given grace. Perhaps the analogy of a seed planted and then growing to full bloom later is more apt. With regard to the charisms of the Spirit, the first Malines Document advocates openness to the full spectrum of biblical gifts. Whereas the gifts from A through P may already be operative in the Church at the present time, the rest of the range, the charisms Q through Z, need also to be incorporated. No one charism is seen as having a gateway function, giving access to all the others. This interpretation succeeded in incorporating the experiences of the Charismatic renewal into the theological culture of sacramental churches. It also avoided the dangers of both elitism and event-centeredness.

Successfully integrating a vibrant renewal movement with the established theological heritage of a large sector of Christianity is a remarkable theological achievement. Success was due to at least two forces: the grace and wisdom of Church leadership and theological advisors, and the generally accommodating attitude that Roman Catholicism has over time developed toward renewal movements—its penchant to embrace and include rather than to exclude. The establishing of the Franciscan order is an example of this approach. In the next section, it will become apparent that even within Roman Catholicism there are also other interpretative models available, but the sacramental model enabled the integration of the Charismatic movement across a very wide spectrum of Church traditions.

For the first time in Christian history, all three major branches of Christianity, albeit to differing extents, were influenced globally by the same religious awakening or renewal movement. The Charismatic renewal also influenced Church traditions beyond those that could be termed sacramental and liturgical. It is to the broader range of these predominantly Protestant churches that we now turn.

Integrative

The integrative interpretations of Spirit baptism do not present as unified a front as the neo-Pentecostal and sacramental positions. Broadly speaking, they share a desire to interpret Charismatic experience within established mainline or evangelical churches and to integrate such experience into their theological cultures. There seem to be at least four distinct ways in which the experience of Spirit baptism was interpreted in a more integrative framework among writers in the 1970s and '80s. In many ways, these were faltering attempts that did not always have lasting impact. Their merit lies in making clear that the transforming work of the Spirit may be understood in more than one way and that the "human factor" cannot be eliminated from theological interpretation.

Several British Charismatics from the Anglican tradition sought to integrate Spirit baptism by describing it as the "final stage of Christian initiation." The process of becoming a believer was seen as including a series of overlapping concepts, such as justification, adoption, conversion, and receiving the Spirit. Where the integral nature of Christian initiation is maintained this may be helpful, but viewing Spirit baptism as the final stage leaves this position open to the conclusion that those without it are then "incomplete" Christians. This view smacks of elitism, and for this reason it did not survive long or gain wide support.

Another line is followed by Norwegian Lutheran Tormod Engelsviken. He seeks to identify the experience—incorrectly designated as "Spirit baptism"—with the terminology of being "filled with the Spirit" rather than with the language of being baptized in the Spirit. Infilling, he says, is not necessarily initiatory, definitive, or complete. Difficulties, however, appear in attempts to distinguish the experiential and the ethical overtones of this biblical usage. Does being filled relate to sanctification or charismatic manifestation? Engelsviken sees it as encompassing both, but how this operates practically is not really clear.

A step towards fuller integration of Spirit baptism into the life of the Church universal is found in a middle European model with German Catholic, Lutheran, and Free Church support. Here the Charismatic dimension is simply called "Geisterneuerung" or simply renewal in the Spirit. There is a particular concern here not to separate the charismatic from the non-charismatic segments of Christianity. Catholic theologian Heribert Mühlen wants to present "a spirituality for every Christian" that includes openness to the Holy Spirit and His charisms. A crisis experience may occur, but that is not considered necessary for all.

This wide variety of interpretations feeds into the last group, in which charismatic experience is seen as an "outpouring" of the Spirit or a breakthrough or growth experience—one of many that are possible. In *Charisms and the Charismatic Movement: A Biblical and Theological Study,* Catholic theologian Francis Sullivan formulates another clearly Catholic interpretation as an alternative to viewing Spirit baptism as the "release" of the Spirit—as mentioned above. He maintains that the Christian experience of God's grace does not need to be tied to any sacrament. It seems psychologically unsatisfactory to tell people who have just had a powerful experience of God's presence that the change that they experienced actually took place many years ago at their infant baptism and what they are now going through is merely a release of the already indwelling Spirit, a gift previously given.

Sullivan prefers to express the change that is taking place in terms of a "new outpouring" of the Spirit. It is not just the manifestation or appropriation of a bygone sacramental event. It is a fresh coming of God to the person. Sullivan points out that no one less than the major Catholic theologian of all times—the thirteenth-century thinker Thomas Aquinas—used the concept of new comings or outpourings of the Spirit in the sense of real impartings of grace to people already inhabited or indwelled by God's Spirit. Aquinas discusses such impartings under the mission of the divine Persons in the *Summa Theologiae*. These are invisible sendings of the Spirit that result in growth in virtue, increase in grace, and enablement for suffering or the working of miracles and prophecy. Sullivan sees the Spirit baptism experiences of the Charismatic renewal as such fresh outpourings or surprises (innovations) of the Spirit. They lead to a new way of the Spirit's indwelling in the soul and a real innovation in the person's relationship with God.

It is important to note that there is no note of ultimacy or definitiveness in these experiences. They are fresh outpourings. They may be, and probably will be, followed by other missions or new sendings of God's Spirit. In a similar vein, a number of Protestant, especially Reformed, theologians have developed interpretations of Spirit baptism that facilitate the integration of the Charismatic movement into churches from a wide variety of doctrinal and confessional backgrounds. Presbyterian Renewal theologian Barbara Pursey, for example, points out that spiritual breakthrough experiences have characterized all ages of the

Christian Church. They often have a different focus and the terminology changes. They have in common a new level of awareness of God and a new effectiveness in Christian service and discipleship. Pursey observes that the operation of the charismata can occur with or without such breakthrough experiences as a prelude. She emphatically denies a necessary correlation between spiritual breakthrough experiences and the specific practice of glossolalia. She considers tongues to be helpful in many ways but not as a requirement for the infilling of the Spirit. The book of Acts presents prophecy, healing, powerful witnessing, and fervent prayer as other illustrations of the Spirit's working.

Sullivan and Pursey have provided new ways for denominational Charismatics to embrace what they have found valid in Pentecostal and neo-Pentecostal experience and to integrate that doctrinally into other confessional communions or families of faith. Spirit baptism as a fresh outpouring or repeatable coming of God's Spirit or a spiritual breakthrough experience leading to deeper levels of relationship with God and service to others can readily be incorporated into almost any Christian tradition.

In my own doctoral dissertation, published in 1988 I outlined a rather similar approach in which I accept the validity of Pentecostal and Charismatic experience and the present-day occurrence of all the charisms of the Spirit in the New Testament—and even ones not specifically mentioned there including prayer and deliverance ministry. However, I reinterpret what is known as Spirit baptism, not as an event that sets one apart or opens up the life in the Spirit, but as a dimension. What the renewal movements have rediscovered and need to bequeath to the rest of Christianity is the realization that normal Christian life has an experiential dimension to it that may be manifested through the gifts or charisms of the Spirit. What has become known by the designation Spirit baptism is in fact a major part of the experiential or charismatic dimension of normal, vibrant

Christian living that includes more direct experiences with God, His direction, and the operation of the gifts.

The denominational Charismatic movement of the 1960s and 1970s was an unprecedented move of God, and it influenced a very broad spectrum of people. The fundamental conviction of Dennis Bennett had been not to leave the Episcopal Church. This ecclesiologically significant decision had both advantages and disadvantages. An advantage had been a widespread openness toward the movement because it was not seen as a new, rival denominational tradition. Its focus was renewal within established churches and, thus, it tried to forestall members' transferring from their churches to a new and perhaps more vibrant alternative. It is true that the Charismatic renewal did, in fact, split a number of congregations into charismatic and traditional factions. Even whole denominations were affected similarly in some instances, but by and large, the renewal movement built up the congregations in which it operated, guiding them to greater maturity.

The disadvantages of the strategy to renew from within also became apparent over time. Even when renewal participants prepared thoroughly doctrinally, much opposition to the Charismatic movement remained. It became clear that the renewal, as it increasingly came to be called, would become eventually nothing more than an ecclesial subculture—an alternative style of worship and spirituality within denominational bodies that increasingly exhibit a growing pluralism of forms and traditions.

Another disadvantage was opposition from leadership. Different patterns of church polity also played a role. The whole spectrum from Episcopal to Congregational forms of polity (church government) is represented in both Pentecostal and Charismatic circles, as well as a variety of intermediary patterns. In terms of the denominational Charismatic movement, the polity structures both aided and hindered the growth of the renewal. Centralized and more hierarchical structures sometimes impeded the Charismatic movement when, for example, local parishes and priests or ministers experienced stifling control from an unsympathetic bishop. In an independent or congregational system, it was easier for individual congregations to incorporate a Charismatic style of worship or a ministry pattern that included the flowing of the charisms of the Spirit. Denominational conventions or general assemblies do not have doctrinal control over churches in "Free Church" traditions, in which each local church is sovereign and retains full authority, despite belonging to a convention of like-minded congregations.

However, the converse pattern also occurred. In an Episcopal structure, a sympathetic superior could also be instrumental in bringing about a change in attitude toward denominational Charismatics in a large area. A classical example of this was the ministry of Anglican Archbishop Bill Burnett in South Africa. When he became a participant in the Anglican renewal movement, the whole country's Anglicans were affected—of course, to differing degrees. In congregational systems—although there may generally be more local freedom or tolerance—it may also occur that congregations or groups of congregations are disfellowshipped by regional or national bodies. This has occurred several times within the Southern Baptist Convention in the United States. Strategies differ, and most often leadership tries to avoid schism at all costs, and the Charismatics tried to keep a "low profile." Over time the renewing of the denominations charismatically proved to be an unattainable ideal that could not be sustained. Millions of Charismatics became what the demographers now call post-Charismatics.

Conclusion

In this chapter we have probed the theology of the Second Wave—the denominational Charismatic renewal. The reflection on the teaching of Classical Pentecostalism continued unabated. While embracing the evangelistic fervor and openness to spiritual experience and the charisms of the Spirit, there was an increasing distancing among denominational Charismatics from some core elements of Pentecostal theology. The present-day empowerment of the Spirit and the awareness of the supernatural dimension were never questioned. The teaching of Spirit baptism as an experiential "release" of the Spirit became the most influential interpretation among Catholics. Protestants preferred seeing this pivotal experience as renewal in the Spirit for every Christian, a new outpouring, spiritual breakthrough or milestone, or just evidence of the experiential dimension of normal Christianity. Some Classical Pentecostal leaders revised their views and came to remarkably similar conclusions, viewing the biblical sign of the fullness of the Spirit more broadly as love and power, as well as the gifts and fruits of the Spirit, rather than as one specific charism.

Within Classical Pentecostalism, there has also emerged a new tendency to re-evaluate their doctrinal heritage. In "Making Sense of Pentecostalism in a Global Context," a paper presented at the 1999 Annual Meeting of the Society for Pentecostal Studies, a leading Assemblies of God theologian, Cecil Mel Robeck, illustrated the wide-ranging diversity within Pentecostalism itself. He describes seven different Pentecostal paradigms which all claim to represent authentic Pentecostalism. They range from the first Wesleyan-Holiness Pentecostal teaching of Parham in which tongues had to be xenolalia (an existing but unlearned human language), through "Finished Work" (Durham) and Jesus' Name (Oneness) positions, to convictions that dancing, visions, and prophecy are evidences equally valid as glossolalia and, finally, a merging of Pentecostalism with the evangelical subculture so that Pentecostals view themselves as nothing more than evangelicals who also happen to speak in tongues (pp. 6–18).

It is notable that a minority tradition within Classical Pentecostalism has always expressed convictions contrary to the "initial evidence" doctrine of the mainstream. It was William Seymour himself who broadened his understanding of the "baptism of the Holy Ghost" to include an ethical dimension. He saw divine love and the fruit of the Spirit as the real evidence of receiving the baptism. Especially his experience with racial prejudice convinced him that the occurrence of tongues alone was insufficient evidence. Seymour also maintained that God is free to choose whatever manifestations He wishes and God is not limited to glossolalia for evidence of baptism in the Spirit. It is due to this shift in position from Parham's original teaching that Robeck concludes that Seymour should perhaps be seen as a forerunner of the modern Charismatic renewal or the founder of a more broadly defined Pentecostalism (McGee, *Initial Evidence,* p. 88).

The early Swiss Pentecostal pioneer Leonhard Steiner also spoke out against the theology of subsequence, which he called the Zweistufentheorie (two-stage theory) at the European Pentecostal Conference way back in 1939. The same is true of German Pentecostal leaders Jonathan Paul and Christian Krust. Prominent Assemblies of God theologian Gordon Fee, who has written a major work on the Spirit in the epistles of Paul *(God's Empowering Presence)* and teaches at Regent College in Vancouver, Canada, abandoned the theology of subsequence in a paper before the Society of Pentecostal Studies in 1972. He warns against a tendency for individuals to interpret or exegete their own experience rather than Scripture.

A more recent but very significant example of this minority position within Classical Pentecostalism, in which there is a convergence between some writers in the First Wave and the integrative viewpoint of the Second Wave, is Jack Hayford. In his book *The Beauty of Spiritual Language,* he indicates a shift he underwent regarding glossolalia. He describes it as honoring historic landmarks while still broadening boundaries. With pastoral insight, he recognized that the "spirit of debate" regarding initial evidence was controlling the interchange so that arguments merely tended to deepen the chasm between good people. While never doubting the value or desirability of tongues, he became convinced that no one could make a categorically conclusive, airtight case (for initial evidence) from Scripture. Hayford writes that God never intended spiritual language as a proof but that He has offered it instead as a provision—a resource for readiness in prayer and praise (p. 94). It appeared to him that there were just too many people he considered to be living Spirit-empowered lives who had never spoken in tongues. In pursuing the question, "What is the biblical sign of the fullness of the Spirit?" his conclusion was threefold: love, power, and the nine gifts of 1 Corinthians 12:8–10, as well as the nine fruits of Galatians 5:22–23 (p. 98).

6

The Third Wave: New Independent Charismatic Churches

*T*he third major movement of the Pentecostal-Charismatic segment of Protestantism distinguishes itself from the First and Second Waves in two important ways. First, as we have just seen, it led to *new structures* being formed. Although the word "denomination" has remained suspect in these circles, and the idea of tradition is usually also viewed rather negatively, these new Christian groups are, in fact, already new denominations in the making, rapidly forming their own traditional patterns of organization and church life. It has been estimated that over 3,000 of these new independent Charismatic groups or denominations have been established globally. Second, in the teaching of these Independent Charismatic Churches, a whole spectrum of *innovative doctrinal emphases* emerged. There has been much debate about some of these teachings. Usually there is some continuity to be found within the Pentecostal-Charismatic heritage with these new teachings. Some of their teachings have remained contentious, especially in the wider circles of Christianity. The fact is, however, that most of these innovations had their roots in the classic spiritual writers of the nineteenth century. This fact will be pursued later.

The term "Third Wave" will now be used as synonymous with the Independent Charismatic Churches. Here the primary slogans and metaphors were not "Hang in there," "Be salt and light," "Renew from within," as in the Second Wave, but rather, "Go out from among them," avoid "unequal yoking," seek "new wineskins" for the new wine. The universally pervasive conviction was that "the Cloud has moved on" and God's pilgrim people need to launch out and chart a new course. The people who make up this new move include both converts to the Christian faith and many believers who transferred from other churches. A significant number of the latter group came from both the First and the Second Waves. Classical Pentecostalism provided a large number of leaders in the Independent Charismatic movement.

Some believed that the Pentecostals had themselves fallen prey to denominationalism and had become too formal or traditional. The Latter Rain movement expressed this in a scathing critique of Pentecostal churches that led to an equally swift denouncing of the Latter Rain as a heretical movement. Although the Classical Pentecostal denominations continued to experience growth, some of their members left to join the new Independent Charismatic ministries. The same applied to the Second Wave. It has been estimated that at least 50% of mainline denominational Charismatics gave up on their program to renew their churches from within and left for what they considered to be greener pastures. They had a hunger for a church where Spirit-empowerment and Charismatic gifts and ministry could be more visible or regular. Some naturally found a home in major Pentecostal denominations, such as the Assemblies of God. A larger section of the discontented, however, pursued the pathway of the non-denominational or Independent Charismatic Churches.

First a word needs to be said about the term "Third Wave." It was, I believe, first coined by C. Peter Wagner, at that time from the School of World Missions at Fuller Theological

Seminary in Pasadena, California. He believed that the "Second Wave," or denominational Charismatic movement, influenced the larger mainline Protestant churches that were of a more liberal background theologically. I disagree with this analysis and maintain that more conservative and evangelical Protestants were also deeply involved in this movement from the very beginning. Wagner further stated that the Second Wave writers, who preferred to identify themselves as Charismatics rather than as being of a neo-Pentecostal persuasion, nevertheless still remained within the theological tradition of a theology of subsequence with a heavy emphasis on glossolalia. The more integrative understandings of Spirit baptism, as developed in the global Charismatic awakening, especially in England and Germany, were less prominent in the United States than in Europe, and their unique contribution may have escaped his notice. As a result, the awakening of charismatic gifts—especially of healing and prophecy—among more conservative Protestant groups was heralded by Wagner as constituting a "Third Wave," while others, like myself, still considered them as an integral part of the whole denominational Charismatic Renewal, or Second Wave.

A significant aspect among the evangelical Charismatics, which Wagner was accentuating, is a fresh openness and acceptance of all the charisms of the Spirit without requiring any initiatory crisis experience. In these circles, the major hurdle to clear was the theory of cessationism, which still held sway in many conservative Protestant groups. Cessationism teaches that at some point in early church history all miracles ceased. In this study, Wagner's third wave is discussed loosely under the third subsection of the Third Wave (Empowered Evangelicals). The term Third Wave is here more broadly understood as the whole Independent Charismatic movement.

To my mind, the primary objection against designating this group of more conservative denominational Charismatics as a separate Third Wave is the limited size of this movement. Whenever illustrations of this approach are given, the examples seem to come from the Vineyard movement associated with the ministry of John Wimber. The Vineyard movement, however, is *not* structurally parallel to the renewal movement within conservative Protestant Churches, such as Southern Baptists or conservative Congregationalists, because it is clearly a new denominational grouping. It took the major ecclesiological step of forming a separate structure. The renewal among conservative Protestants has been an arduous journey. The Southern Baptist Convention, for example, has a long history of disfellowshiping local congregations that become overtly charismatic, and it objects to glossolalia being practiced among its missionaries—even as a private prayer language.

As a result, this researcher chose to use the term "Third Wave" for a much more prominent and sizeable movement that has taken place in the last two decades of the twentieth century. I am referring to the *Independent Charismatic churches* that grew to become a global phenomenon in the eighties and nineties. They are structurally distinct from the renewal movement *within* established churches and have become known for specific doctrinal emphases. There is, nevertheless, a very broad spectrum of theological views represented in this group.

For this chapter, no thorough written history of the development of this movement is available, as was the case with the First and Second Waves of the Spirit. The tentative analysis of the major groupings presented here is the result of my own taxonomy that was published in 1990. Due to the paucity of sources, some attention will be given to the development of the movement itself. The Third Wave—used in this particular way to designate all Independent Charismatic churches—has at least four subsections or currents (to maintain the analogy of waves). These currents range from the faith emphasis found in the Rhema Bible Church to the more "laid back" West Coast style of the Vineyard movement. Some of these Independent Charismatic churches or ministries are rooted in Classical Pentecostalism or, more especially, in the Latter Rain movement of the late 1940s and early 1950s. Others more clearly have a *post*-denominational renewal stamp to them, being born of the dissatisfaction that arose when traditionalists in many churches resisted Charismatic emphases and the renewal movement was stifled or sidetracked by denominational leadership.

The Third Wave has produced a large number of strong and dynamic leaders. While many Independent Charismatic groups over time felt the need to form loose networks and some even opted for clearly defined Episcopal structures (such as the International Communion of Charismatic Churches), others formed local congregations with no formal links to any other believers at all. Churches of this latter category are usually generically named according to locality, e.g., Middleton Family Church, Laketown Fellowship of Believers, and Westville Worship Center. The term "non-denominational" has sometimes been used to describe the whole Independent Charismatic movement, but "non-denominational" applies only to the unconnected type of churches referred to in the previous sentence. Most Independent Charismatic groups have tended to seek some form of mutual accountability, association, and networking with those of similar ministerial focus and teaching. The trend toward forming links has been made more urgent by the unfortunate circumstances of several prominent Charismatic leaders going astray morally when too much influence and control were concentrated in the hands of an individual. "Non-denominational" or unconnected churches may initially still have a strong sense of theological heritage, communality and connectedness to Christian tradition, simply through the heritage and training of the current leadership.

The Independent Charismatic movement is a global phenomenon. Firmly established in the United States and Canada, it has spread internationally, with significant concentrations in England, Sweden, France, the Netherlands, South Africa, Nigeria, China, Russia, South Korea, Singapore, and India.

Four Third Wave Currents

We move now to a description of the doctrinal distinctives of the four main currents of the Third Wave, seen as the Independent Charismatic churches, or networks of churches. As pointed out above, in contrast to the previous two chapters, this chapter will be based largely on my own research.

The first two groups are both kingdom-focused, but will be dealt with separately, since the first has a premillennial approach and the second a postmillennial one.

Restorationist (Premillennial)

The first Independent Charismatic group to be dealt with may be designated as the *Restoration* movement. In many ways, the Restorationist current of the Independent Charismatic movement is merely the latest expression of a perennial trend that can be observed in church history. The early church, as described in the book of Acts, has been viewed as the ideal model throughout the centuries. The vibrancy of Christianity under persecution in the first three centuries has also been somewhat romanticized. The dream is to build a New Testament church—one that is truly *apostolic* in the sense of being like that of the first apostles. Most major renewal movements in church history have expressed something of this passion to restore the Church to the way things were, but inevitably become the victim of the same tendencies against which they were protesting. A striking example in North America was the movement led by Barton Stone and Alexander Campbell in the nineteenth century. They were against any form of denominationalism, wanting merely to be known as Christians, disciples, or churches of Christ. Nevertheless, in time they took on structural form, got organized, experienced internal dissension and have now added another three denominations to the American landscape of churches.

Within the whole Independent Charismatic movement, this Restorationist vision plays a significant role. It goes hand in hand with an insistence that "denominations" are not in the plan of

God. Like the Irvingites, the Brethren, and the Disciples of Christ, they are striving to restore the New Testament pattern of early Christianity. A special characteristic of this ideal among Independent Charismatics is *the restoration of the fivefold (or fourfold) ministry of Ephesians 4:11–12*. The charismatic offices of apostle and prophet need to be restored to the church, in addition to the more common offices of evangelists, pastors, and teachers. (According to many exegetes, the office of pastor and teacher actually forms one office. This is why views vary as to whether there are four or five primary offices in the Church.)

The Restorationist wing of the Independent Charismatic movement significantly influenced England, where it was originally called the British "House Church" Movement—a name that did not apply long, since the increase in numbers soon moved the gatherings out of private homes. The underlying conviction was that the Church should invest in relationships rather than in buildings.

Authoritarian Undercurrent

There is a strong authoritarian undercurrent in this movement, coupled with some influence from the Exclusive Brethren Church. Leadership is placed in the hands of apostolic teams which have oversight and supervision over regional geographical areas (like bishops). This oversight, however, is not considered formal or hierarchical but rather relational in nature. Authority is upheld through relationships nurtured with local pastors by the traveling apostolic teams. The emphasis is not on formalized structures, as may be found in an Episcopal polity or church government in the hands of bishops. Restorationism has generally seen itself as radical and engaged in preparing the bride of Christ as a church "without spot or wrinkle." The history of Christianity is viewed very negatively. Historic, established churches are part of the apostasy of denominationalism and staid tradition. This view was advocated by William Branham in the Latter Rain movement as well. In parts of the restoration movement, freedom and openness have been marred by authoritarian leadership. Although rejecting the hierarchy of bishops, some leaders assumed authority that may, in practice, be greater than any Episcopal authority found, for example, in the Church of England, which has developed over the centuries a system of checks and balances for the exercise of power. Restorationist groups in the Independent Charismatic movement have sometimes fostered intentional communities and covenantal extended households. This practice became a worldwide phenomenon in the 1970s, but it has not stood the test of time. Many large communities experienced problems with authoritarian styles of leadership (usually all male), leading them to fragment and eventually disband.

Strong Link to Israel

Another dimension of the Restorationist movement is its strong link to the nation of Israel. This is also shared more widely in the Independent Charismatic circles, for example, well known Charismatic leader, Pastor John Hagee of Cornerstone Church in San Antonio advocates unwavering support for the state of Israel and the Jewish community. In broader theological circles, some have emphasized and (re)discovered of the Jewishness of both Jesus and Paul since the 1960s.

The Christian Embassy in Jerusalem and the annual celebration of the third great Jewish festival, the Feast of Tabernacles, by evangelical and Charismatic Christians are also indications of this focus. In line with this is an exuberant style of worship found among Independent Charismatics, including dancing, rhythmic hand clapping, and joyous praise. By this style of worship, some claim the Tabernacle of David is being spiritually restored, ushering in the rapture. David's way of worship is seen as paradigmatic for New Testament church believers because it was not centered on animal sacrifices like the temple worship; and worship centers like the International House of Prayer in Kansas City have had ongoing worship led by musicians and prayer leaders around the clock (24/7) for almost a decade.

The biblical basis presented for the "Tabernacle of David" trend in worship is found in Acts 15:16, where James quotes Amos 9:11–12 concerning the restoration of David's tabernacle. Other more common interpretations are that the reference is to the restoration of Israel as a nation or to the restoration of the Davidic kingship in the eternal kingship of the Messiah. However, to these Restorationists, the renewal of a perfect pattern of exuberant praise and worship is seen as a pivotal step in restoring God's glory to the Church, which will then usher in the return of Christ. This form of worship is sometimes called "warfare praise" and is linked to doing battle with demonic forces. Bill Hamon speaks of the "Joshua Generation" which has crossed over the spiritual Jordan to march around Jericho in order to take the land. The term "Eagle's Nest" for a network of congregations also represents this military language of conquest.

Shepherding & Discipleship

In the United States the whole Charismatic world was rocked just prior to its largest gathering ever—some 50,000—at Arrowhead stadium in Kansas City in 1977 by the controversy which centered on the so-called "Shepherding" movement associated with such leaders as Bob Mumford, Derek Prince, Don Basham, Charles Simpson, and Ern Baxter. They were leaders in a Restorationist style group called the Christian Growth Ministries. These popular Bible teachers and evangelistic preachers gathered a large following through speaking at Charismatic conferences, circulating audio tapes, and their primary publication, *New Wine* magazine. At the heart of this Shepherding movement was a concept of discipleship involving submission to Christian leaders that challenged both American individualism and the style of evangelism represented in the frontier revivalist heritage of American evangelicals. The discipleship teaching of Argentinean evangelist, Juan Carlos Ortiz, seems to have been influential in developing the theological concept of the Church found in both the British and American forms of restorationism. His 1975 book *Disciple* sold well internationally. Leaders in the Shepherding movement, which was centered geographically in Fort Lauderdale, Florida, and later in Mobile, Alabama, emphasized that the Christian life necessitated ongoing discipleship and character development. Leading someone to Christ made one responsible to provide follow-up teaching and guidance. Here the controversial term "shepherd" was introduced. New converts were to submit to their shepherds.

In time, problems were bound to surface. Some shepherds abused their authority and saw themselves as mediators between the "sheep" and the Lord. Some also challenged the authority of local pastors. When suggestions were made that tithes may be paid to shepherds rather than to local congregations, a showdown became inevitable. The underlying tension erupted at gatherings arranged to discuss ways to resolve the issues and maintain unity in the fledgling Charismatic movement. Most denominational Charismatics (Second Wave) as well as many Classical Pentecostals (First Wave) questioned the Fort Lauderdale teaching on submission. Independent Charismatics, with unexpected support of some Catholic Charismatics, aligned themselves on the other side. The underlying fear was that popular and widely influential leaders, such as Derek Prince and Bob Mumford, might form a new denomination and that most denominational Charismatics would then leave their churches and flock to it. The "Fort Lauderdale five" of the Christian Growth Ministries were stung by the criticism they received and were adamant about rejecting the option of a new denomination. A large number of Second Wave denominational believers did eventually leave their more traditional churches and formed new structures of an independent nature within the Third Wave.

S. David Moore's *The Shepherding Movement: Controversy and Charismatic Ecclesiology* is the definitive history of the American movement. He traces its origins as a distinct stream to 1974—a few years before the public controversy—when many denominational Charismatics started leaving their traditional churches. To counter a lack of moral discipline and character among new converts, individual believers were being taught to submit to a shepherd and develop covenant relationships that could foster growth in spiritual maturity and integrity. Leaders also needed to be linked to one another for mutual accountability and "covering."

Those remaining in the Second Wave feared a virtual take-over of the whole Renewal movement by these Independent Charismatics. David du Plessis, also known as Mr. Pentecost, who—as has been pointed out above—had been very instru-mental in bringing people from a wide range of established churches into the Charismatic movement, expressed the opposition of many to this non-denominational movement. Against the idea that Christians need to submit to a shepherd, he stated publicly and in a dramatic way: The Lord is my Shepherd.

Between 1973 and 1975, three annual Shepherds' confer-ences consolidated a network of churches under the leadership of the five Fort Lauderdale leaders. *New Wine* magazine became the most widely circulated Charismatic journal in North America. Churches that related to the Shepherding/Discipleship move-ment adopted new structures, often in accordance with the writings of Ortiz. Relationships were seen as crucial. When these churches became large, they often adopted the following pattern. The smallest unit was the regular weekday house church or cell group gathering in homes for Bible study, fellowship, and worship, under a local shepherd. Next came a Sunday congre-gational or district meeting in a hall or other facility, under a pastor. The largest meeting would be a Sunday celebration of the whole group of several thousand, perhaps bi-monthly, under the leadership of a Charismatic senior pastor who often was also an apostle with translocal authority.

Kilian McDonnell, the prominent Roman Catholic ecumenist and scholar, who has been referred to several times, gathered the documents describing the heated Discipleship controversy that developed in 1975–76 and included them in his three-volume study on the global responses to the Charismatic movement entitled *Presence Power Praise*. In his doctoral study, Moore describes the meeting in Minneapolis, called to bring leaders of different emphases together, as the "Shoot Out at the Curtis Hotel." The independent, or non-denominational, movement's teaching on submission was severely criticized, and the Shepherding leaders were shocked and hurt by the vehement attacks by their Christian brothers. The movement actually reached its peak only in 1982 with 100,000 members and 500 associated churches. However, by then their teachings had been widely discredited, and internal problems also led to the dissolution of the movement by 1986. Much later Bob Mumford publicly declared contrition and admitted that he had been wrong in some of his views. Only a small group continues under the leadership of Charles Simpson in Mobile, Alabama, now called the Covenant movement.

With the advantage of hindsight, it is probably true to say that the differences that existed between the proponents and detractors of the shepherding/discipleship/submission teaching belong well within the parameters of acceptable diversity within basic evangelical Christianity. Had a new church grouping been formed, it is probable that the extremes which were being evidenced on the fringes (shepherds claiming too much authority, manipulation, etc.) would have been corrected within the movement over time.

Perhaps the reasons why this greatly feared "new denomination" was not formed and momentum and support for this whole movement was lost could be summarized as follows: (1) There was still a deep theological aversion to forming new "denominations." This tendency had been more recently illustrated in 1948 by "the New Order of the Latter Rain" and its across-the-board rejection of Catholicism, Protestant denominations, and even Pentecostalism. In these Restorationist type movements, organized, institutional structures and personal relationships were seen as mutually exclusive. (2) The overreaction of, especially, mainline Protestant Charismatics and some of their Classical Pentecostal allies unnerved the Fort Lauderdale Restorationist leaders. Their motives and personal integrity had been questioned. Their growth was said to be largely by transfer of believers, and the reproach of "sheep stealing" was leveled. The forming of a national network of churches would have confirmed the worst fears of their detractors. (3) There seemed to be theological differences on the nature of the church, as well as practical issues like unbridled individualism, lack of moral accountability, pride, and authoritarianism that muddied the waters.

Apart from the Fort Lauderdale movement, which was then called the Christian Growth Ministries (but renamed itself several times), there are many other examples of Restorationist style groups in the USA. A typical example may be Silver Spring Community, also known as the People of Destiny International (PDI), under the leadership of C. J. Mahaney and Larry Tomczak. These two young evangelists, coming originally out of the Jesus movement, formed a network of churches in which relationships, communal living, and exuberant worship were of pivotal importance. The movement started in 1977 in Wheaton, Maryland. Tomczak's background was in the Catholic Charismatic renewal. He later left PDI and was for a time connected to the Brownsville Revival in Pensacola, Florida. Mahaney's background is Reformed, and the official stance of PDI expresses this with its new name "Sovereign Grace." The designation PDI has been retained as an acronym: *P*roclaiming God's grace, *D*eveloping local churches, and *I*nfluencing our world with the gospel. The ministry is now led by an apostolic board of six men, with headquarters in Gaithersburg, Maryland. Catholic scholar Peter Hocken discerns an influence on PDI from the Bradford (Harvestime) group of restorationism in Britain. There is a similar focus on an end-time restoration of the New Testament church and the concept that spiritual gifts are to be used in mission and ushering in God's kingdom rule.

In his 1985 study on restorationism titled *Restoring the Kingdom: The Radical Christianity of the House Church Movement*, Andrew Walker explored the influence of the Catholic Apostolic Church (associated with Edward Irving) and the Christian Brethren (associated with John Nelson Darby) of the nineteenth century on the contemporary restoration movement in Britain. Walker distinguishes two factions, which he dubs Restoration 1 and 2, after their separation by 1976. The first group is identified more clearly by its apostolic teams, involvement in the annual Dales Bible Week, and the magazine *Restoration*. Restoration 2 is more loosely structured and contains many who have distanced themselves from Restoration 1. Leaders in the second group include John Noble, Gerald Coates, and David Tomlinson, while Arthur Wallis, David Matthew, and Bryn Jones and, later, Terry Virgo of New Frontiers, placed their stamp on Restoration 1. The connection between the British and American Restorationists came about through contacts between Bryn Jones and Canadian Pentecostal Ern Baxter, who was part of the "Fort Lauderdale five." Together with the Vineyard Association, which will be referred to below, these Restorationist groups are called the New Churches and number about a half million in Britain.

Restorationist Independent Charismatics are widely diverse. Some have more rigid leadership styles while others are more flexible. Theologically, they espouse believer's baptism and generally have an Assemblies of God approach to baptism in the Spirit and glossolalia (i.e., support the view that tongues is the initial, physical evidence of Spirit baptism), although they do not focus much on speaking in tongues in their preaching. What holds the remaining Restorationist grouping together is a vision for restoring apostolic leadership—including prophets and apostles—and a rejection of "tradition." As a current, it has passed its heyday, and some of the larger churches have realigned themselves and formed new networks.

Dominion (Postmillennial)

The second major group of Independent Charismatics is also characterized by its view of the kingdom of God. The distinctive teaching is known as Dominion theology and has been described by its pre-millennialist detractors as "Kingdom Now." The recently deceased Earl Paulk, perhaps the most significant representative of this new thrust, became the Archbishop of the International Communion of Charismatic Churches, a global network representing at its zenith some 10 million members. The ICCC, however, may not be totally identified with Dominion theology. The ICCC was formed in 1982 by Bishop John Meares of Washington, DC, and Bishop McAlister of Rio de Janeiro, Brazil. Later, Bishop Idahosa of Benin City, Nigeria, and Bishop Paulk of Chapel Hill Harvester Church in Atlanta, Georgia, joined. They were all part of a global Pentecostal denomination named the International Evangelical Church, which, interestingly enough, joined the Geneva-based World Council of Churches in 1972 and was the first Pentecostal denomination to participate officially in the Roman Catholic-Pentecostal dialogue.

The origins of Dominion theology, however, do not lie within the Pentecostal-Charismatic arena but outside it in classically Reformed theology. (This is illustrated in the ICCC Handbook, which lists the Presbyterian Westminster Confession in its creedal statements that provide the proper interpretation of the Bible.) Dominion theology is the product of the Christian reconstructionist movement, which developed in the 1960s and '70s around the publications of scholar Rousas John Rushdoony. In order to understand their influence on the Dominion movement some reconstructionist views will be now outlined briefly. Rushdoony, an Armenian American, established the Chalcedon Foundation in Vallecito, California, in 1965. Another center is the Institute for Christian Economics in Tyler, Texas, founded by Gary North, who has also published widely. Central to the reconstructionist vision is the acknowledgement of the all-embracing cosmic headship of Christ, who has dominion over every dimension of reality, and the ensuing ideal of transforming society in accordance with God's divine laws. Rushdoony had studied presuppositional apologetics with Cornelius van Til, who taught for many years at Westminster Theological Seminary. It is widely believed that in his book *Theonomy in Christian Ethics*, Christian reconstructionist theologian Greg Bahnsen argues that the laws of Moses should be applied directly to contemporary public life. The vision is, first, to reclaim the United States as a Christian nation and then to work in a gradual postmillennial strategy to establish the kingdom rule of God over all the earth. This would, in fact, be theocratic rule, with obvious parallels to Puritan thinking. The moral decline in the Western world is seen as the direct result of forsaking the eternal laws of God.

This vision is radical and goes far beyond a mainstream Reformed understanding of the transformation of culture under the Lordship of Christ. Christian reconstructionists hold to a theonomy (law of God) which considers Old Testament laws to be normative for all times. That would entail such extremes as capital punishment for adultery, bestiality, homosexuality, and even for incorrigible children! Critics of this movement go so far as to allege that some reconstructionists condone slavery, and exhibit racist tendencies.

Reconstructionist advocacy starts with the regeneration of individuals, who are then restored to fulfilling God's purposes and remade in God's image, receiving His cultural mandate and dominion over the earth. In the political and economic realm, this vision is worked out along clear, free-market principles— limited government, decentralization, and a strong focus on private enterprise and individual rights.

Dominion theology is unswervingly committed to postmillennial eschatology. The Church is seen as the instrument of God, aggressively reoccupying the world in the name of Christ. The kingdom is already established and is advancing. The Second Coming of Christ does not break into world history suddenly in an apocalyptic fashion but only after the Church has fulfilled the Great Commission and established global dominion.

Gradually Dominion thinking also started to influence a number of leaders in the Independent Charismatic movement. This aggressive and encompassing vision for the transformation, not only of the Church but of all of society, proved to be attractive to them. Originally Classical Pentecostalism had aligned itself to anti-cultural tendencies, withdrawing from secular society. Premillennialist and dispensational views with a pretribulation rapture of believers tended to discourage any active involvement in societal and, especially, political matters. Later initiatives, however, such as the Moral Majority of Jerry Falwell and the Christian Coalition associated with Pat Robertson, decisively changed the attitude of many evangelical Christians towards involvement in the public sphere and political life. Rushdoony's influence even reached the Reagan White House.

Bishop Paulk caused a stir in Pentecostal circles when he defected from the traditional cause of premillennial eschatology, denied the doctrine of the rapture, and questioned the relevance of the nation of Israel to biblical prophecy. He taught that the Church is the spiritual Israel and has replaced the Jews, and that current events in the Middle East have no bearing on prophetic fulfillment. The fact that an imminent return of Christ is not expected is reflected in the title of his 1985 book *Held in the Heavens Until. . . .* Christ must remain until the restoration of all things—a reference to Acts 3:12. The Church needs to accept its responsibility first to attain unity and maturity as the bride of Christ. The doctrine of the rapture is also reinterpreted: the new hope of the church is achieving victory *in* this world. Paulk maintains that his "Kingdom Now" principles transcend traditional millennial categories, but there is an unmistakable postmillennial slant to his teaching. God is effecting restoration through His Church, and we now have to assume the dominion that was lost in the Garden of Eden. It needs to be noted that Bishop Paulk's church is well integrated racially and heavily involved in outreach to the African-American community in Atlanta.

The vision of cosmic societal restoration has had a broader impact among Charismatics than the sphere of Bishop Paulk. Bob Mumford, one of the "Fort Lauderdale five" of the Restoration movement, was also attracted to it and gradually incorporated dominion perspectives into his public teaching. At the same time, these ideals also influenced people very critical of the Discipleship movement, such as Pat Robertson. The university he founded in Virginia Beach changed its name from CBN

University to Regent University, thereby reflecting the idea of Christ's regency over the world. Dominion thinking, in a more general and balanced sense than the rigid theonomist views of Christian reconstructionists, pervades the whole University as it seeks to train Christian graduate students in a variety of disciplines such as law, education, global leadership, psychology, divinity, and government. The ongoing influence of this perspective can be seen in initiatives such as the legal advocacy of the American Center for Law and Justice (Jay Sekulow) and the Republican presidential primary race in 1988 of Pat Robertson—although unsuccessful, he surprised many by winning the Iowa caucuses.

Maranatha Ministries, under the leadership of Bob Weiner, had also propagated a postmillennial vision of societal transformation to thousands of college students before it disbanded in 1989.

An intriguing aspect of the whole Independent Charismatic movement is the fact that influence from the "Latter Rain" movement keeps reappearing. Although this brief revival was snuffed out by vehement opposition by Classical Pentecostals, its seminal ideas seemed to go underground and resurface time and again. The Latter Rain has also come to be known by other names such as Sonship, Manifested Sons of God, or the Body of Christ. Leaders such as Bill Britton and Sam Fife continued to propagate their ideas through publications and meetings in Lubbock, Texas. Their major teaching of the restoration of the five-fold ministry was viewed as a threat to the authority of denominational leaders and local pastors. Another key concept of the New Order of the Latter Rain that resurfaced in the whole Third Wave was a high view of prophecy, sometimes including predictive and personal prophecy—the ongoing revelation of truth to apostles and prophets. Some critics attacked Paulk for his concept of revelation, which was viewed as equating revelation gained through contemporary prophecy with the Bible. Paulk denied this and affirmed a closed canon.

Personal prophecy also occurred in the Latter Rain circles. Bruce Barron's study *Heaven on Earth: The Social & Political Agendas of Dominion Theology* notes that George Hawton of North Battleford supposedly rejected the concept of the imminence of Christ, teaching that Christ could only return after the restitution of all things (Acts 3:21; p. 76). It was said that Earl Paulk taught the very same thing. Barron declares that Paulk "mainstreamed" Latter Rain ideas, presenting them in a more respectable form (p. 78). Bishop John Meares, who founded the ICCC, also represented a clear link to the Latter Rain through Bethesda Temple in Detroit, which was a leading Latter Rain church.

While Paulk reshaped traditional premillennialism into a postmillennial vision with a societal involvement, the "Christ against culture" stance (as expressed in H. Richard Niebuhr's classic *Christ and Culture),* or otherworldliness of early Pentecostalism, has been retained by Bill Hamon, who, for a time, was also a Bishop of the ICCC and who authored *The Eternal Church* (p. 76). It presents a very negative view of church history reminiscent of Restorationism.

Since Bishop Paulk, who died in 2009, had been sidelined due to accusations of immoral conduct going back several decades, this grouping and its teachings have unfortunately lost influence in the public arena and in Independent Charismatic circles.

Empowered Evangelicals

The third major group of the Independent Charismatic movement is quite different. It is closely connected to the ministry of John Wimber and the Association of Vineyard Churches and is said to consist of about 1,000 churches worldwide. It is sometimes called the Power Encounter movement or the Signs and Wonders movement. The term "power encounter" comes originally from use in missiology and refers to the force of the supernatural in spreading the gospel; often the references are to victory over demonic spiritual forces. "Signs and Wonders" highlights the role of the miraculous and the fact that churches seem to grow rapidly, especially in the Majority World, based on testimonies of dramatic healings and powerful signs. This is sometimes called Power Evangelism. More recently, some have preferred to use the designation "Empowered Evangelicals." It is this category that C. Peter Wagner identified with the term Third Wave. (In this book, Third Wave is used to designate the whole Independent Charismatic movement.) The term Empowered Evangelicals captures the essence of this current well. This group is self-consciously not Pentecostal or Charismatic. It represents those evangelicals who have become open to the present-day occurrence of the full range of the charisms of the Spirit. (An important book by several scholars that is a kind of progress report showing Empowered Evangelicals grappling with the ideas discussed in this section is *The Kingdom and the Power: Are Healing and the Spiritual Gifts Used by Jesus and the Early Church Meant for the Church Today? A Biblical Look at How to Bring the Gospel to the World with Power,* edited by Gary Greig, J.I. Packer, and Kevin N. Springer, with a foreword by C. Peter Wagner, published in 1993.)

Worldview

The distinctive core of this second grouping of Independent Charismatics is made up of *three interrelated concepts*. First is the awareness of the importance of *worldview* and philosophical presuppositions. The Empowered Evangelical movement has become profoundly aware of the role of naturalism, materialism, and rationalism in the heritage of the Western Enlightenment. This insight has its origins in academic circles and missiologists such as Paul Hiebert and Charles Kraft, who have published along these lines and have strongly influenced the leadership of the Vineyard movement. Nevertheless, the concept of worldviews and their impact on how we perceive reality is profoundly practical. It is through a rejection of rationalist modernity that the dimension of the miraculous is often discovered and reclaimed. More so than any other group, the Power Encounter movement has opened our eyes to the role played by these pervasive frameworks or mindsets in church as well as in culture.

Every-member Ministry

Second, the Vineyard Bible Churches have a unique focus on an *every member ministry*. This is a form of democratization. The usual way of referring to it is "equipping the saints." Although the principle of what Martin Luther called "the priesthood of all believers" dates back to the sixteenth century, most churches still maintain a rigid demarcation between clergy and laity, and they concentrate most of the "ministry" in the hands of ordained leadership. The Empowered Evangelical movement objects to this. For example rather than create "healing lines" in which one gifted individual would pray for all the sick, Wimber encouraged the whole body of believers to become involved in healing prayer. The practice of healing lines actually originated with the controversial healing evangelist William Branham. In concrete terms, the Vineyard approach was quite different. It usually started by asking people requiring prayer to stand up in a meeting, with those who happen to be sitting around them then simply laying hands on them, uniting in prayer for healing. The presumption is that God would grant gifts of healing across the congregation as needed. The Empowered Evangelicals emphasize the healing ministry.

Signs and Wonders

The third distinctive aspect of this grouping is quite simply the present-day reality of *signs and wonders*. The reclaiming of the miraculous is, of course, the heritage of a number of movements in the twentieth century. The Vineyard movement, however, has a different perspective on them. Healings and miracles are consciously seen as a means of evangelism and church growth. The concept of church growth, as developed by Donald McGavran of Fuller's School of World Missions, had a significant impact on John Wimber. It was the testimony of students from the Majority World that first opened the eyes of Charismatic leaders to the fact that healing can play a pivotal role in evangelism. This is certainly the case in many churches in Africa and Asia. What Wimber discovered was that the proclamation of God's kingdom needs to be accompanied by the demonstration of God's power. The concept of power was to become crucial, as can be seen from Wimber's book titles *Power Evangelism, Power Healing, Power Points*. Here was a new strategy—the growth of the church in numbers and in maturity is consciously and intentionally linked to the power and gifts of the Holy Spirit.

The Kingdom of God: Already but Not Yet

An important theological impulse behind this movement was an understanding of the kingdom of God. George Eldon Ladd, of Fuller Seminary, developed this as a central motif in his book *Jesus and the Kingdom*. The Lordship of Christ is of paramount importance and presents a challenge to the contemporary church, with its focus on meeting people's needs and fulfilling human potential. Equipped with kingdom power, the believer receives the authority to drive out demons in what has become known as spiritual warfare. Crucial to Wimber's understanding of the kingdom of God is the creative tension between the *already* and the *not yet*. This polarity was originally formulated by Geerhardus Vos, developed by Oscar Cullmann, and popularized in North America by George Eldon Ladd. The Christian life is lived out between the First and Second Comings of Christ. Certain aspects of God's rule are *already* apparent, such as salvation, fellowship in the Spirit, forgiveness of sins, and Charismatic manifestations, but others will only become evident at the final consummation of the kingdom. They are *not yet* manifest due to the fallenness of creation and include such things as the elimination of death, total healing, and moral perfection. Wimber argues powerfully that physical healing is affected by this tension. Against the traditional Classical Pentecostal doctrine of healing as included in the atonement, he advocates, rather, healing *through*, or as a result of, the atonement. With this formulation, he desires to break loose from an automatic guarantee of healing. Wimber also advocates a holistic under-standing of healing that includes an inner healing of the memories and emotions as well as deliverance of people who are demonized.

John Wimber was converted as an adult. He had an Evangelical Quaker background and was generally Reformed in his theological leanings. He was initially associated with Chuck Smith of Calvary Chapel and the Jesus Movement of the 1970s. He led the Vineyard movement from 1982 until his death in 1997. It was Wimber who gained notoriety by teaching the controversial course MC510: Signs, Wonders and Church Growth at the Fuller School of World Mission between 1982 and 1985. This course was eventually canceled due to widespread objections, including opposition by the theological faculty at Fuller. One of the concerns expressed in their report *Ministry and the Miraculous,* edited by Lewis Smedes, is that it is inappropriate to include the practice of healing within the academic setting of a classroom. (No such reservation seems to exist with regard to preaching in homiletics courses!) They furthermore argue that the answers to prayers for healing should not be called "Signs and Wonders" because that detracts from the uniquely revelatory events of salvation history (p. 28). The course had become immensely popular, and the demonstrations of healing in the laboratory, or practical, part of the class had an extensive impact. The cancellation of the course may have illustrated that the broader evangelical community has not yet fully moved beyond its heritage of cessationism and dispensationalism.

The fact that Classical Pentecostals were also critical of Wimber's approach illustrates the tension between the First Wave and this particular form of the Independent Charismatic movement. This tension is illustrated further by the whole concept of spiritual warfare, which has become as contentious as the concepts "faith" and "prosperity" in the Word of Faith grouping of Independent Charismatics. Classical Pentecostals generally have supported the conviction that Christians cannot be demon possessed and, consequently, have grave reservations about much of the deliverance ministry practiced in Empowered Evangelical circles.

Spiritual Warfare

John Wimber explained his approach in battling demonic spirits in *Power Points,* warning against a pre-occupation with the satanic realm. There is an age-old heritage of exorcism found within Eastern Orthodox and Roman Catholic churches and, to a lesser degree, in mainline Protestant churches, such as the Anglican and Episcopal communion. Usually specific priests have this as a designated ministry, and ritual formulas and prayers are used. In practice, however, little of this has remained in operation due to the Western scientific mindset and the preeminence of rationalism. It is mainly among some denominational Charismatics that this more liturgical ministry is being practiced. In evangelical Protestantism, however, there is a new a growing awareness of the importance of spiritual warfare that is quite independent of any Pentecostal or Charismatic influence. Often the focus of these groups is on preserving doctrinal truth. As with Wimber, there is an acknowledgement and interest among these non-charismatic evangelicals of the role that worldview plays in our thinking, but Neil Anderson, in his well-known book *The Bondage Breaker*, concentrates on spiritual warfare as a conflict between truth and error. For Wimber, it is not merely a "truth encounter," exposing the lies and false teachings of Satan, but also a power encounter, in which victory and liberation are demonstrated.

Independent Charismatics from the Empowered Evangelical movement deal with the thorny issue of Christians and demon possession by relying on a new approach among scholars that suggests it is better for Christians to change our terminology. The New Testament word usually translated as "demon possession" should rather be rendered "demonized." A Christian cannot be possessed by Satan in the sense of ownership, but a high degree of oppression or evil influence is possible as people give a foothold to demonic spirits through habitual sinful practices. It is appropriate to pray prayers of deliverance in such situations.

A further contentious issue is the concept of territorial spirits. With some humor, the question has been raised: Do demons have zip codes? Are they to be associated with specific geographical areas? Peter Wagner advocates this understanding and encourages Christians to do "spiritual mapping"—discerning the prevailing spirits over cities and nations according to the most prominent sins (such as drug abuse, prostitution, greed, racism, divorce, etc.), and doing battle against them in the Spirit. Although there are references in Scripture to demons exerting influence over specific locations, such as "the Prince of Persia" in Daniel 10, one needs to be cautious about generalizing this idea. The role of intercessory prayer and prayer walking as a practical strategy against these powers and principalities has been vividly illustrated by ministries in Argentina. Wimber himself cautions that it is God who sends angels into battle. Perhaps prayer for God to deploy angelic forces is more appropriate than intercessors commanding angels themselves.

The understanding of Ephesians 6 and the believer's battle against demonic forces is of pivotal significance in this understanding. Bishop Michael Reid of England, formerly of Peniel Church in Essex, England, who is a bishop with the International Communion of Charismatic Churches, has written a book whose title expresses his view: *Strategic Level Spiritual Warfare: A Modern Mythology?* Reid rejects this Strategic-Level Spiritual Warfare approach associated with C. Peter Wagner and George Otis, Jr. and warns against demon-phobia and quasi-pagan concepts. While Reid's view is supported by some senior Classical Pentecostals, it is clear that our struggle is not against flesh and blood, and I believe the Bible reveals a physicality to grace as well as to evil that our rational minds find difficult to accept and grasp. Response to such manifestations of spiritual evil may lapse into an animistic superstition, but that is not necessarily the case.

The Vineyard movement grappled with two contentious issues in the late 1990s, which caused it, at first, to reevaluate its identity as Empowered Evangelicals. Then, eventually, it recognized that it wished to retain its original identity and the ideal of a democratizing of ministry and so severed ties to two new movements that it had initially embraced.

Prophecy

The first was the encounter with a new style of prophecy. The Kansas City Fellowship joined the Association of Vineyard Churches in 1990. Prominent leaders with a prophetic ministry included Mike Bickle, Bob Jones, and, especially, Paul Cain. Cain had been involved in the New Order of the Latter Rain. Predictive prophecy as practiced by leading individual prophets introduced an element into the movement that threatened the thorough-going democratization of Wimber's original vision. Just as the healing ministry had been concentrated in the hands of prominent leaders in the 1940s and '50s, so prophecy was becoming concentrated in a small number of gifted prophets. The leadership of the Vineyard movement weighed the situation and decided to steer back to its more mainstream evangelical roots. Reservations were expressed about some of the prophecies as well as behavioral issues. Wimber did not come to reject the gift of prophecy, but ultimately he did not find the Kansas City Fellowship's expression of it in line with his vision.

Toronto Blessing

The encounter with the "Toronto Blessing" followed the same pattern of initial support, followed by a gracious, if contentious, parting of ways. The Toronto Airport Vineyard Fellowship had begun as a home group founded by John and Carol Arnott in 1990. It soon became associated with the Vineyard movement as it grew into a church. Then revival broke loose. What came to be known as the "Toronto Blessing," started on January 20, 1994. Arnott had invited Randy Clark, a Vineyard pastor from St. Louis, to come and minister at his church. Clark had recently been exposed to the ministry of Rodney Howard-Browne, a South African-born evangelist from Tampa, Florida, whose meetings were characterized by involuntary fits of laughter. Howard-Browne had been reared in the Word of Faith teaching at the Rhema Bible Church in Randburg, near Johannesburg, South Africa. This laughing revival drew much attention. Howard-Browne had led a revival at Karl Strader's Carpenter's Home church in Lakeland, Florida for fourteen weeks. He also ministered powerfully at Oral Roberts University, where students were so overcome by the Spirit that many still needed help walking in order to return to their dormitories three hours after the service had ended.

As Clark ministered in Toronto, similar manifestations of holy laughter and being "drunk in the Spirit" occurred. Wimber initially supported this awakening, but by December 1995, the Toronto Airport church was ousted from the Vineyard Fellowship. The reason given by the Vineyard leadership was not that they did not recognize this blessing as a genuine move of God but that they realized that they themselves were not called to give further leadership to it because of differences in style. The awakening continued. Membership has skyrocketed from 350 to 4,000, and it is estimated that 2.5 million people from all over the world visited Toronto Airport Christian Fellowship between 1994 and 2000. The Toronto Blessing touched several thousand churches in England, most notably Holy Trinity Church, Brompton, in London that later launched the Alpha courses for new believers that is now used across the world.

Criticism from traditional anti-Charismatic sources as well as from Classical Pentecostals has focused on some of the more unusual phenomena that have accompanied the revival, especially uncontrollable laughter and some animal noises. (Actually animal noises such as barking are not unknown in the history of revivals. As far back as 1801 there was a practice of barking, known as "treeing the devil," at the Cane Ridge revival in Kentucky!) According to their critics the centrality of Christ, sound preaching, and a discernment regarding miracles was judged to be somewhat lacking in the revival, but the 5,000 professions of faith and many more transformed lives have testified to the great impact of this movement. Theologian James Beverly has written about the Toronto Blessing and gives a balanced and helpful critique. Wimber was unwilling to go too far beyond the confines of North American evangelical culture, and so disassociated the Empowered Evangelical movement from the Kansas City prophetic movement and the exuberance of the Toronto blessing. The Vineyard churches are growing into an organized denomination, representing the more Reformed and evangelical sector of the Independent Charismatics. They have left behind the theology of subsequence and the requirement of tongues, but practice the full range of the charismata, acknowledging the supernatural dimension very clearly in their Power Encounters with the demonic.

Word of Faith

The fourth major grouping of the Independent Charismatic movement is known as Word of Faith or Faith Confession Churches. (This movement will be discussed again in detail in chapter 7 because of the prominent role it plays in the current situation.) It has probably been more misunderstood and maligned than any other part of the movement but surprisingly has retained its vibrancy and exhibits great potential for the future as it moves beyond some of the unfortunate excesses of the past. Other names for the movement reflect this criticism: the Health and Wealth Gospel, Prosperity Theology, Positive Confession teaching, or even the derogatory phrase "Name It and Claim It" movement. After an initial spate of knee-jerk reactions, such as critiques by Hunt and McMahon, Hank Hanegraaff and Dan McConnell, the movement itself seems to have undergone some self-correction. This current of the Third Wave has a lot of continuity with the Classical Pentecostal teachers and healing evangelists of the 1940s and 50s. What are the origins of this movement?

Although the father of the movement undoubtedly is Kenneth E. Hagin, founder of the Rhema Bible Church and Training Center in Broken Arrow, Oklahoma, the originator is seen as E. W. Kenyon (1867–1948). Essek William Kenyon grew up in New York State where he joined the Methodist Church. In 1892, he moved to Boston and enrolled in the Emerson School of Oratory, where he was exposed to New Thought and the Christian Science of Mary Baker Eddy, who also had her headquarters in Boston. Classical idealism was coming into vogue at this time, and the concepts of Plato and Ralph Waldo Emerson formed part of the curriculum. Mind was seen as superior to matter, and through mental attitudes and positive confession, circumstances could be transformed. McConnell, who evaluated the Faith movement with a degree of harshness, relates an anecdote about Ern Baxter (also a link between the Latter Rain and the Discipleship movements) once happening upon Kenyon engrossed in reading Mary Baker Eddy's *Key to the Scriptures*. When Baxter commented on that, Kenyon responded that a lot of good could be gained from her perspectives.

Kenyon was ordained as a preacher in the Free Will Baptist Church and traveled extensively. He often spoke in Pentecostal churches but clearly did not consider himself Pentecostal. He had serious reservations about the gift of tongues and the importance placed upon it. He was inspired by the work of George Mueller in Britain and ran his Bethel Bible Institute on the same "living by faith" principle.

Kenyon responded sharply to the higher criticism of the Bible that was fashionable in his day by firmly rejecting the claim that Paul had exaggerated the importance and stature of Jesus, making Him into the divine Son of God. Many scholars of that day (and in later so-called Jesus Quests as well) were seeking the "historical Jesus" behind the Gospel narratives, stripped of His divinity. Reacting to this, Kenyon, in fact, believed that the epistles were superior to the Gospels and built his thinking mostly on Pauline theology.

The major contribution of Kenyon to the Faith movement was distinguishing knowledge into two radically different categories: "sense knowledge," based on the physical world, and "revelation knowledge," which is vastly superior and is based on supernatural revelation from God through the Scriptures or through the guidance of the Holy Spirit, communicating with the human spirit. When these two kinds of knowledge conflict, the believer needs to transcend empirical understanding and act in faith upon God's Word. This action may even necessitate the denial of physical symptoms of illness. At this point, the danger of a radical Gnostic dualism between the natural and the supernatural as two mutually exclusive realms becomes apparent. The issue becomes even more troubling when the biblical tension between the flesh and the spirit is superimposed on this polarity. Kenyon found support in Hebrews 11:1—"Now faith is being sure of what we hope for and certain of what we do not see" (NIV). William DeArteaga points out that this faith-idealism is in line with the Christian Science healing practice which teaches "corresponding action." This practice entails acting upon the revelation knowledge even before the change has taken place. Scriptural support and illustrations of this are not hard to find—the ten lepers of Luke 17 were healed as they headed off in faith to go and show themselves to the priests. Kenyon considered the taking of medication after a prayer of faith for healing to be inappropriate.

Kenyon taught that through identification with Christ, the believer can approach God without guilt (DeArteaga, *Quenching the Spirit,* p. 219). Through this Pauline concept of identification (being in Christ, Christ lives in me), which is found abundantly in Paul's letters and is well expressed in Galatians 2:20, believers have the same power that Jesus did on earth. By exercising faith, believers can become "Christian Supermen" with power over diseases and demons. The only limitation that Kenyon recognized in his faith idealism was that one can ask in faith only for things that are promised in Scripture. They could be claimed and confessed without any qualification. In his teaching, Kenyon provided all the theological building blocks on which Kenneth Hagin would later construct his teachings.

Kenneth E. Hagin was born in Texas in 1917. He suffered from a congenital heart defect and was bedridden by the age of sixteen. He then had an experience that stamped his whole ministry. He had a revelation or vision from God (the first of several) and gained a new understanding of Mark 11:24: "Therefore I say to you, all things for which you pray and ask, believe that you have received them, and they will be granted you." Meditating on this verse, he realized that "the *having* comes after the *believing*." Previously he had been reversing it. One needs to believe you have it before you actually receive it. This led to his getting out of bed and being healed after some days of struggling with his paralysis. Total recovery took sixteen months.

Hagin did not receive formal theological training, but a number of amazing visions and personal encounters with Jesus form the foundation of his ministry. He considers his calling to be that of a prophet and a teacher. Because of its origins, there has long remained a critique of Word of Faith or Faith Confession teaching that it is implicitly anti-intellectual and somewhat anti-medical. (The genius of the ministry of Oral Roberts was to bring perspective into this realm of thinking by his building both a university and a hospital.) Today the objection of Faith teachers is not against scholarship as such, but only against a certain type of scholarship that exalts itself above God's revelation and denies the realm of the miraculous!

Hagin became well known through his radio program and the Rhema Bible Training Center, founded in 1974, where hundreds of thousands of students received Bible training—many coming from overseas. It seems that *when the Shepherding/ Discipleship movement ran into difficulties in the late 1970s, the momentum and growth among Independent Charismatics was passed on to the Word of Faith movement.* This shift of momentum led to a substantial growth in the ministries of Faith leaders, such as the Hagins, Kenneth and Gloria Copeland, Jerry

Savelle, Fred Price, Robert Tilton, and, further afield, Ray McCauley in Randburg, South Africa, Ulf Eckman in Uppsala, Sweden, David Yonggi Cho of Seoul, Korea, Benson Idahosa of Nigeria, and Hector Giminez of Argentina.

The pivotal doctrinal issue is how faith is understood. Nico Horn of Namibia describes the Word of Faith movement's concept of faith thus:

> It may be described as "a special emphasis on faith as a mechanism at the disposal of the believer to make him or her victorious; the belief that positive confession creates faith, and, linked with faith, changes circumstances; the belief that everyone who has faith can receive either healing from sickness or eternal health; and the belief that financial prosperity is, like healing, provided for in the atonement."

Here is a brief outline of three of the major teachings of the Faith movement (from Barron, *Health and Wealth*, p. 9).

Positive Confession

The doctrine of *positive confession* comes directly from the idealism of E. W. Kenyon. Perhaps it was inevitable that in the pioneering stage, the newness of this teaching would lead to unfortunate excesses. For many centuries, Western culture has been dominated by a realist worldview in which physical matter and the material world are seen as fixed and closed. The world is seen as a "space-time box" and is accessible to our knowing only through empirical investigation by the five senses and through analytical reasoning. Any involvement of a supernatural being, such as God, is at best *indirect* and, in line with the cessationist teaching of many conservative Christians, should be limited to "the age of miracles," which has passed. This doctrine of cessationism is based on a dispensational theory of God's using different strategies in different epochs of history. In our present Church age, God no longer operates with the miraculous but rather only through the Scriptures. William DeArteaga, in his book *Quenching the Spirit*, defines idealism as the philosophical position that mind and matter can interact, with mind having some influence over matter (p. 335). The classic expression of an extreme *idealist* view would be sorcery, magic, or alchemy, in which officiants incant formulae in order to change reality magically. DeArteaga himself argues rather for a moderate idealism, which he sees as being in accordance with Scripture. (More about this in chapter 7.)

In the face of the strong realist tradition of the Western Church, any ascendancy of idealist thought represents a radical shaking of the foundations. Knee-jerk reactions abound. Positive confession is portrayed as manipulating God, deifying humans, and disregarding God's sovereignty. It is possible to supply several quotations from Word of Faith teachers' sermons that are vulnerable to such portrayals. A fine line separates believing that what you say can have an impact on concrete reality from lapsing into claiming things just for one's own comfort and gratification. It is distressing when speakers "guarantee" material wealth seemingly in direct connection with contributing financially to a particular Christian ministry. Unfortunately, this is a perception that is widespread among people today, based both on limited exposure and on some unbalanced preaching on television. Reality has a way of catching up with those who distort the truth in such a way. It is possible that such overblown claims may seem to "work" for a season, but the ultimate fall and collapse of such extreme teaching is inevitable. We also know that God in His mercy is longsuffering and patient, wanting us to repent.

Nevertheless, the fact remains that the prayer of faith and the spoken word *do* have power and, when used in accord with God's purposes, they can miraculously change circumstances. Two Scripture references will suffice—Mark 9:23, "All things are possible to him who believes"; and Mark 10:27, "With people it is impossible, but not with God; for all things are possible with God." Naturally the danger exists that faith may be placed on particular historical promises in the Bible that are then auto-matically transposed to contemporary circumstances in a one-to-one relation (without any confirming quickening of the Spirit's guidance, often called a *rhema* word). Ultimately, faith rests securely as a trusting in Christ Jesus; in God the Father, who calls us to covenantal relationship and whose love is unfailing; and in the Holy Spirit, who is our Helper and dependable Guide.

Prosperity

The teaching on *prosperity* is also is an area fraught with potential pitfalls. In the Protestant Reformation, a spiritualizing tendency abounded. God's preeminent blessing was the forgiveness of sins, grace for the soul, and spiritual liberation from bondage. Long neglected was the rich Old Testament tradition of an encompassing shalom or peace that includes the promise of land, offspring, and material blessings—sitting under your own fig tree and vine, and the integral concept of salvation in the New Testament, which includes not only salvation for the soul, but physical healing for the body. As a result, money itself is often considered suspect, rather than just the *love* of money (1 Tim 6:10). Western asceticism and the monastic cult of poverty have further clouded the issue. The Faith movement bucks this trend by teaching that the blessings of Abraham may come to the Gentile peoples through Christ (Gal 3:13–14) and that these include material blessings. Usually, preaching of this nature also emphasizes tithing. Despite some extravagant portrayals, most Word of Faith teachers make it clear that giving from egotistical and selfish motives is unacceptable. Hagin himself denounces the type of faith that is focused on "getting Cadillacs" for oneself. Prosperity is defined as having sufficient for one's needs and the ability to bless the poor.

The ministry of Oral Roberts was revolutionized by the simple statement from 3 John 2, that God desires for us good health and welfare or prosperity. He later developed the concept of seed-faith, which underscores three principles: God (and not our abilities) is our Source and Provider; Give generously to others—the so-called law of seed time and harvest (or give and it shall be given to you); and, Be expectant in your faith—Expect a miracle! This is not the language of automatic manipulation or mechanical guarantees, although it can sometimes be twisted to sound that way. The reference in Mark 10:29–30 that selfless service in evangelism will bring a hundredfold return is preceded by Jesus' admonition to the wealthy man (the so-called rich young ruler) to sell his possessions and give to the poor. Human covetousness *can* take these verses out of context and turn them into a calculating attitude of giving one item in an attempt to receive a hundred back for oneself.

Remarkably, Faith teaching here shows a similarity with Liberation theology by acknowledging the importance of material possessions and rejecting an over-spiritualized salvation that focuses only on the soul and the life hereafter. Rightly understood, both stand in stark contrast to secular, materialistic culture and the narcissism of postmodern society.

The last central teaching of the Faith movement may be discussed under the rubric . . .

A Right to Healing?

With regard to the healing of the body, the Faith movement stands in direct continuity with Classical Pentecostalism. In fact, the recovery of the doctrine of divine healing in evangelical Christianity preceded the Pentecostal movement by a good fifty years, as has been pointed out above. On the fringes of Christianity, divine healing has probably never been absent. Through the Pietist and Holiness movements, physical healing became part of a crucial stream of Christianity. The first advocates were generally skeptical about medical work. In time, the anti-medical stance of such people as John Alexander Dowie of Zion City, Chicago, Illinois, was replaced by an integral or holistic approach in which medical, psychological, and spiritual aspects were all incorporated, as we see, for example, in the ministry of Francis MacNutt.

The Faith movement represents only one group of a broad spectrum that acknowledges the reality of divine healing today. There is a growing emphasis in all Three Waves of the whole Pentecostal-Charismatic movement that God desires wholeness and health for His children. Sickness and disease are of the devil, and Jesus came to liberate those under demonic influence and to destroy Satan's evil purposes. The term "Healing in the Atonement," which correctly links the biblical passages Isaiah 53:5, Matthew 8:17, and 1 Peter 2:24, was originally conceived in anti-medical circles and still carries that baggage. Today its focus is to emphasize that the death of Christ on the cross has consequences not only for our eternal salvation but also for our bodily healing. The reference is to the messianic prophecy in Isaiah that "by His wounds we are healed."

How this is worked out in practical details brings us to divergencies within the Pentecostal and Charismatic movements. The most radical form of the Word of Faith teaching claims absolute victory in this present life. Christians are entitled through Christ's atoning death to the blessings of Abraham, which include salvation, health, and material prosperity. Physical healing is considered a *right* of every believer that may be expected and claimed boldly after the devil has been rebuked. Sometimes it is even stated that praying is not necessary. The believer just needs to make a positive confession of faith. Most problematic are the situations in which people are taught that all lingering symptoms of illness are to be denied and not to be treated medically. Unfortunately, there have been examples where this has led to deaths that easily could have been avoided by timely medical treatment. (Denying symptoms is a more extreme approach than that of temporarily *disregarding* symptoms when one is convinced that this is what God is requiring.) One is often dealing with the hardness of human hearts that have difficulty focusing on the seen rather than the unseen dimension.

Inevitably, a one-sided focus on faith may lead to the loss of acknowledging God's sovereign freedom. It seems as if God has no choice but to respond to human proclamations and requests. Support for this view is offered from Isaiah 45:11, which in the King James Version states: "Concerning the work of my hands, command ye me." Modern translations capture the implied irony by rendering it: "Would you command me?" Once more it needs to be said that reality and experience soon trip up those who follow on this path. God, as a personal loving and responsive being, is our hope, not a particular key phrase from Scripture.

Examples of foolhardy and presumptuous faith in fact amount to over-realized eschatology. Claiming total healing as an absolute right in the here and now for every believer denies the element of mystery that remains in our fallen condition. There is a creative tension between the *already* and the *not yet,* as was explained above. The continued occurrence of death is a conclusive indication that some aspects of fallenness still remain and will be resolved only in the life hereafter.

Although this polarity or creative tension may bring some balance, it should nevertheless not come to function as a way to evade the biblical call to prevailing expectation and robust faith. The concept of the *already / not yet* tension itself is helpful, but the major episodes of salvation history illustrate that God works not only *from* the *already to* the *not yet,* but regularly does miracles—something totally new, that allows the power of the future to invade the present. Creation is a radical creation out of nothing. The exodus is encircled by the wondrous inflicting of plagues and miraculous deliverances. The incarnation, resurrection, and ascension of Jesus are all unexpected, apocalyptic events through which God reveals Himself and His majesty. The outpouring of the Spirit at Pentecost, the Second Coming, and even individual rebirth are the *not yet* becoming the *already* through God's inbreaking grace and sovereign rule. Paul states that we live by faith and not by sight (2 Cor 5:7). Life in the Spirit walks the fine line of ongoing openness to the miraculous on a daily basis.

These insights of radical biblical truth the Word of Faith movement presents to Christianity at large.

Conclusion

In this chapter the four major groupings of the Independent Charismatic churches have been discussed. The first two groupings Restorationism and Dominion-minded Charismatics have premillennial and postmillennial perspectives respectively. For differing reasons their impact has decreased. The third grouping, Empowered Evangelicals, has moved away from traditional Pentecostal and Charismatic distinctives but retains a strong ministry of the full range of biblical charisms and openness to the supernatural realm. They have moved into the position of a new denomination as a global Vineyard Fellowship.

The roots and fruits of the Word of Faith movement were probed in the final section. Despite some initial excesses which discredited the whole movement, it continues to grow internationally and challenges traditional Christianity with an innovative perspective on the role of faith and the spoken word. The pivotal position of these churches in the twenty-first century will be explored further in the next chapter.

7

The Future of the Spirit Movements in the Twenty-first Century

Over the last six chapters we have surveyed the conceptual and doctrinal developments of the "Three Waves" of the Spirit in the twentieth century after addressing some related issues. These included the unique contribution of Azusa Street to societal unity, the role of the modernist worldview in eclipsing the supernatural dimension and the ways in which various confessional groups responded to spiritual manifestations. *The underlying purpose of this journey has been to look toward the future.* What does God have in store for the Church of Jesus Christ in this twenty-first century, more specifically for the mushrooming Pentecostal and Charismatic movements? The Lord is the One who does "new things" and always surprises us, so no one should imagine that they have a crystal ball. At the same time, it is instructive to explore the growth points and take stock of what has happened.

Renewal movements have always been "messy." On the fringes of all the major awakenings in Christianity, unbalanced extremes and manifestations, or physical phenomena, have occurred that may have been more of the flesh than the Spirit.

However, it was Jonathan Edwards of the First Great Awakening of the 1740s who cautioned us not to be distracted by the external phenomena but rather to look at the transformed lives, growth in love for Jesus, the Scriptures, the body of Christ, and the lost. These are the true and lasting touchstones for revival. It is wise not to overreact and throw out the proverbial baby with the bathwater!

While discussing the failings of the Second Wave denominational renewal, two well-known European leaders had an informal evaluative conversation. One declared in exasperation, "It's two-thirds phony!" The other agreed, but then pointed out the immense value of the remaining one-third that was genuine. While I believe the proportion of the phony part was probably an overstatement, this little dialogue (I believe it was between Tom Smail and Arnold Bittlinger) well reflects my own approach: there is much to be appreciated in the Spirit movements.

Another helpful analogy is that only the river that is full to the brim will cast off brushwood and debris onto the riverbanks. The life and power of the raging river itself is more significant than the occasional littering of the banks. Perhaps this fact should make us less eager to judge one another's failings.

My Theological Testimony

In this context, it is only fair to the reader to include some autobiographical details. In the Preface of my published doctoral dissertation, *Treasures Old and New: Interpretations of "Spirit baptism" in the Charismatic Renewal Movement,* I outline something of my background:

> In January 1980 I had a vivid charismatic experience which caught me unawares theologically. My doctrinal apple-cart was overturned, and I spent a year or two trying to get my bearings again. I had been blessed "right out of my socks" and needed time to digest what God was now doing in my life and in my family. I had found a new dimension to my faith, which I experienced as deeply meaningful,

integrative, and transformational. Coming from a Reformed background with both evangelical and ecumenical roots, I sought an acceptable interpretive framework for the fresh upwelling of doxology in my heart. My seminary training seemed to have left me in the lurch. As I started charting my own course I discovered that a variety of contemporary theologians were grappling with the same issue, and I wanted to classify their differing interpretations and develop my own perspective. In time that endeavor led to my completing a doctoral dissertation on "Spirit baptism" at the University of South Africa in Pretoria. . . .

I came to realize that centuries of Western rationalism, individualism and naturalism had robbed the Christian church of many of its "old treasures." I found that I needed to delve deeper into my heritage as an ecumenical Christian. I rediscovered the devotional or "mystical" tradition in Christianity, and in my own Calvinist background. I could identify with Calvin's teaching on the Christian life and was overwhelmed by the beauty of the way in which the Westminster divines described the main purpose of our lives, namely: to glorify God and to enjoy Him forever.

In the global spiritual awakening of the sixties and seventies "old treasures" were being rediscovered; but at the same time many unacceptable and superficial theological theories were being constructed and imposed on the renewal movement in the churches, leading to experience and event-centered faith, spiritual elitism, and schism. The search for a meaningful interpretation of "Spirit baptism" has become crucial, and I tried all the various options that were being presented. In a sense I have now come full spiral (rather than full circle!) in my understanding of the charismatic movement. What I mean by that will become clear from the following chapters in which the neo-Pentecostal position is gradually superseded by attempts at a full integration of the legitimate elements of the renewal into historic Christianity. I believe this entails the recognition of the deeply experiential nature of normal Christian living and an ongoing openness towards an expectancy of the full range of charismatic gifts as a present-day reality which the Holy Spirit freely distributes in the congregations.

My dissertation was published in 1988 and I am thankful that several thousand copies were sold. In 1990, I emigrated from South Africa with my family to teach for a total of eight years at Oral Roberts University—an amazing laboratory for any theologian interested in the Three Waves of the Spirit. My current teaching position at a small, rural, evangelical liberal arts college in the Midwest affords me the opportunity to view the Holy Spirit movements at some distance and determine what I consider most valuable and most promising. The rather humbling and surprising thing about this whole process is that my evaluative resolution in the last part of this final chapter is counterintuitive and contrary to where my background and theological heritage would normally have directed me.

In Brief: The Movement's Status

Perhaps the most ignored or underestimated factor in the history of spiritual awakenings is simply the natural process of maturation and self-correction that sometimes occurs. Reality has a sobering way of catching up with people and straightening us all out, especially when our hearts are sincere. Practical circumstances and pastoral experience may affect the most doctrinaire advocates of specific teachings and agendas, (e.g., the strange teaching that Jesus was "born again" in hell). In many religious movements, there is a gradual, ongoing process of maturation. (I hope that applies to us as individuals, as well!)

Over the last thirty years or so, journalists have focused a lot on the personal failures of prominent leaders within the Three Waves, and these have discredited the whole movement in the public mind. Transgressions of the seventh, eighth, ninth, and tenth commandments are unfortunately all in evidence. Perhaps the number of people involved in this "clergy misconduct" is not disproportionate when compared to the general population, but it is tragically high when one contemplates the high calling of the gospel and the example that leadership in the Church is supposed to set regarding accountability and moral standards. These failures need to be humbly acknowledged, but in themselves they do not necessarily discredit the teachings espoused by the individuals concerned. People in the pews do yearn for transparency and genuineness in leadership. The younger generation of Charismatics deeply desire spiritually sound mentors, father and mother figures that they find trustworthy. This study, however, is ultimately not about ethical behavior but rather about doctrinal truth.

Veteran church historian Vinson Synan has called the twentieth century the "Century of the Holy Spirit," and prominent Classical Pentecostal pastor Jack Hayford has termed it the "Charismatic Century." The final balance on the Spirit movements of the twentieth century is, I would submit, incredibly positive. They have affected the whole Church of Jesus Christ, resulting in significant growth in numbers and even in maturity. After centuries of neglect, Pneumatology as a theological discipline has blossomed, and functional binitarianism has been banished to an ever-decreasing segment of the Church. Within a hundred years, the demographic picture of Protestantism has altered radically. In a near seismic shift, the mainline churches have been sidelined and the Pentecostal-Charismatic world has mushroomed to over 600 million adherents, second in size only to Roman Catholicism, with over a billion.

It is estimated that in the Majority World already two-thirds of Christians are Pentecostal-Charismatic. Philip Jenkins has documented the unprecedented shift of global Christianity towards the Majority (non-western) World. In the *Next Christendom: the Coming of Global Christianity* Jenkins states, "The day of Southern Christianity is dawning" (p. 3). By 2050 the six nations with the most Christians will not include Britain, France, and Italy, but rather the Congo (Zaire), Nigeria, Philippines, Mexico, and Brazil—in ascending order! The USA is still projected to have the largest number of believers. (Somehow Jenkins does not feature China in these calculations.) The movement is inexorably *towards the global South*, people of color, towards conservative morals and more literal biblical thinking, and towards a strong supernatural orientation. At the same time it is *away from the global North*, and away from the historic Protestant denominations with more liberal theological and social agendas.

After this brief introduction, I wish to present the agenda for this final chapter. It aims to cover three loosely related topics: First, a brief *overview* of the most relevant theological developments of the last twenty years, since the emergence of the Third Wave. Second, a further discussion on the central doctrinal theme of the whole movement, *Spirit baptism,* and an attempt to resolve the issue with a new approach. This will involve some of the discussion that came up in the Second Wave. Third, a more focused treatment of one current of the Third Wave that may be *the growing edge* of the Spirit movements of the twenty-first century.

Brief Overview of the Last Twenty Years

Vinson Synan has described the more recent state of the Pentecostal-Charismatic world in a chapter titled "Streams of Renewal at the End of the Century" in his book *The Century of the Holy Spirit.* In order to draw the theological conclusions at the end of this chapter, it is necessary to overview these developments briefly.

Media

Media have come to play a much more prominent role. The early pioneers in this field had been Oral Roberts and Pat Robertson. In time, Pentecostal and Charismatic evangelists came to dominate the religious Christian programming on the airwaves. Paul and Jan Crouch's Trinity Broadcasting Network and Marcus and Joni Lamb's Daystar grew astronomically. Successful television ministries include Benny Hinn, Kenneth and Gloria Copeland, Joel Osteen, Fred Price, Jack Hayford, Marilyn Hickey, Creflo Dollar, Joyce Meyer, T. D. Jakes, the late Billy Joe and Sharon Daugherty, Kenneth Hagin Jr., Reinhardt Bonnke, John Hagee and Andrew Wommack.

In the print media, the monthly magazine, *Charisma,* founded in 1975, published by Stephen Strang and ably edited by the courageous J. Lee Grady, established its dominance and today even rivals its evangelical counterpart *Christianity Today.* *Charisma* magazine and several of the other spin-off periodicals keep their readership up to date on the latest trends and "super-stars" of the movement but increasingly also sounds a note of caution concerning self-aggrandizing ministries. Moral failure and questionable financial decisions by the leaders of so many independent Charismatic ministries has led to a lack of focus in the movement as a whole.

Significant Developments

In Classical Pentecostal circles, there has been an unmistakable quest for academic and social "respectability" and acceptance within mainstream evangelical culture. This started back in the 1940s when Pentecostal denominations became part of the National Association of Evangelicals. In 1994 a measure of racial reconciliation was achieved when black and white Pentecostal denominations became united under one umbrella organization—the Pentecostal and Charismatic Churches of North America (PCCNA). This so-called "Memphis miracle" has been alluded to above. On the level of tertiary education, several significant seminaries, colleges, and universities were established. Some were denominational in nature (Assemblies of God, Church of God, Cleveland, Foursquare, etc). Prominent among the independent or interdenominational schools are Oral Roberts University in Tulsa, Oklahoma, and Regent University in Virginia Beach. Regent launched the first Ph.D. program in Renewal Studies in 2003. A clear sign of ecumenical commitment among Classical Pentecostals is the long-standing International

Roman Catholic—Pentecostal dialogue, started by David du Plessis and Father Kilian McDonnell of St. John's University in 1972. This scholarly conversation has continued for more than three decades, and Dr. Cecil M. Robeck of Fuller Seminary has played a pivotal scholarly role in this discourse from the Pentecostal side.

Revivals: From the Toronto Blessing to the Awakening

The section above on Empowered Evangelicals (largely the Vineyard movement) referred to the "Toronto Blessing." At the time when Wimber was starting to withdraw his support from the Toronto Airport Church, another revival was breaking out at the Brownsville Assembly of God in Pensacola, Florida—initiated on Father's Day June 8, 1995. This became known as the Pensacola Outpouring or the Brownsville Revival. Evangelist Steve Hill had previously been exposed to the Toronto Blessing, but here there was a more classical revival with a focus on repentance and holiness. Nevertheless phenomena like "going down under the power of God" (perhaps more accurately described as being overwhelmed by an intensification of God's presence), shaking, laughing, and jerking also occurred. As with Toronto, people flocked to Pensacola from all over the world. Large numbers were converted, and a Bible school was set up, the Brownsville Revival School of Ministry. Unfortunately, it seems as if fleshly divisiveness in leadership brought the revival to an end. In January 2000, Michael Brown, president of the School was fired, reportedly because he would not join the Assemblies of God. It was a classic struggle for control. Most of the faculty and students left with Brown to set up a new school known as FIRE (Fellowship of International Revival and Evangelism) in Concord, North Carolina. There has since been personal reconciliation between the leaders. From 1996 to 2000 a smaller revival impacted the village of Smithton, Missouri. In 2001 that congregation moved to Kansas City where Steve Gray and his wife now pastor World Revival Church.

Of more current origin (2008) is another Florida revival in Lakeland led by Todd Bentley. After four months of revival meetings Bentley stepped down after acknowledging moral failures. Once again the pivotal role of integrity in leadership in revivals is underscored. In 2010 Kansas City is the venue of an ongoing revival with many healing testimonies, known as the Awakening. It is linked to the International House of Prayer.

Two more movements of the 1990s and the first decade of the twenty-first century deserve brief mention although I believe neither of them have the potential of becoming doctrinally significant.

The Convergence Movement

The first came to be known as the *Convergence movement*. It was a fascinating but very limited phenomenon in which some evangelicals and Charismatics took what is called the "Canterbury Trail," seeking liturgical and aesthetical fulfillment in a journey to Episcopalianism, Catholicism or Eastern Orthodoxy. There was a yearning to integrate Catholic, evangelical and Pentecostal spirituality. Prominent British Charismatic leader, Michael Harper, a well-known evangelical, left the Church of England in protest over the ordination of women and became an Orthodox priest. The Charismatic Episcopal Church was formed by a former Pentecostal pastor who became a bishop. The movement seems to have run out of steam, but often attracts individuals who desire a more formal liturgy than the stark Word-centered and pulpit-thumping traditions of their fundamentalist upbringing.

New Apostolic Churches

The second movement became known as the *New Apostolic Churches*. It is the brainchild and creation of C. Peter Wagner. He noticed changes in the general ecclesial climate of upcoming postmodernism and was quick to categorize them. Unfortunately, as with his "Third Wave" category, which refers mostly to the Vineyard movement and leaves out the much more sizable Word of Faith and Restoration movements, this classification is not really helpful and will probably not endure. Noticing the changes, Wagner wanted initially to speak of post-denominational churches in the sense of churches under the influence of post-modernism. (This phenomenon of post-modern churches is in reality something quite different and largely coincides with that which is currently becoming known as the Emerging/Emergent movement).

In the end, Wagner rather chose the term New Apostolic Churches to reflect the new climate he was perceiving in a number of mega-churches in the USA and internationally. He describes them in his 1998 book *The New Apostolic Churches*. He refers to eighteen pastors whom he calls "Apostles". This terminology had, of course, already surfaced previously in the Irvingite movement of the 1830s and more recently in the New Order of the Latter Rain (1948), as well as in the Restorationist stream of the Independent Charismatic movement. Most of the examples Wagner provides are simply Pentecostal or Charismatic leaders and many (if not most) have never adopted the terminology "apostle". In his above-mentioned book, Wagner states on pages 19 and 20 that the most significant innovation of these churches is the "amount of spiritual authority delegated by the Holy Spirit to individuals." (With all the recent highly publicized abuses of authority among mega-church pastors this should give us pause!)

Other features of the movement which Wagner describes include the rejection of seminary education, new worship styles (keyboards and overhead projectors), new positive attitudes toward finances, new forms of concert (simultaneous) prayer, etc. This is a category largely of Wagner's own construction and lumps together many strange bedfellows.

It remains to be seen if this terminology or classification will endure. Synan in *The Century of the Holy Spirit* (p. 378), interprets it as an attempt to bypass Pentecostal distinctives. Hayford mentions Ted Haggard, previously of New Life Church in Colorado Springs, and Bishop T. D. Jakes of the Potter's House in Dallas as prime examples of what Wagner would call New Apostolic Churches. With discernment, Hayford prefers to call them Independent Pentecostals. In my classification, they would simply be referred to as part of the continuing Third Wave. Despite the forming of some networks for accountability, there is a lot of fragmentation in the movement and little inner coherence of vision.

Worship Music

Since the early 1990s, major changes have taken place in the *worship music* of American churches. Robb Redman speaks of the "Great Worship Awakening." Contemporary Christian music has become a significant industry, and contemporary worship music has become an international phenomenon. One can hear Worship Australia and Hillsong United songs by Darlene Zscheck, Joel Houston, Ruben Morgan, and Marty Sampson from Peru to Portugal to Polynesia. Chris Tomlin, Matt Redman, David Crowder, Michael W. Smith, Jared Anderson, Stephen Curtis Chapman, and Twila Paris are some of the best known artists. What is not always understood is that the Great Worship Awakening has deep roots in the Pentecostal-Charismatic movement.

The initial introduction of contemporary worship music into non-Charismatic churches has been documented by Joe Horness in his chapter in *Exploring the Worship Spectrum: 6 Views* (p. 108). He tells of how in 1982 Bill Hybels was looking for something different from traditional hymns to use in the mid-week services at Willow Creek Community Church in South Barrington, Chicago—the primary seeker-driven mega-church. These were his services for believers rather than "seekers." During a summer break he happened to attend a Charismatic service and discovered there the style of worship music he had been looking for. The transfer took place smoothly. Soon traditional evangelical churches were singing the same songs as their Pentecostal-Charismatic siblings. With wry humor some have called this "charismatic lite" or the "hands but no tongues" phenomenon. The raising of hands in worship has now been mainstreamed, but the practice of glossolalia in Contemporary Christian Music circles is still assiduously avoided. Synan speaks of the adoption of Charismatic worship music into all churches as a "Pentecostalization" of Evangelicalism.

24/7 Prayer Movement

Another intriguing aspect of the growth of interest in worship is the 24/7 prayer movement exemplified by the International House of Prayer in Kansas City. In this remarkable sanctuary, unbroken prayer and praise has gone up for a decade. Mike Bickle is the leader of the movement but in various cities across the U.S. similar initiatives are developing. They latch onto the "Tabernacle of David" tradition that was alluded to above in the Latter Rain revival. Historical precedents of continuous worship in Church history include the Abbey at Bangor, Ireland from the sixth to the ninth centuries; and the Moravian community at Herrnhut's historic prayer meeting that continued uninterrupted for 120 years. Both these initiatives gave rise to unprecedented *missionary* zeal. The unique worship music style at IHOP is called "Harp and Bowl" (Rev 5:8). It includes Scripture readings, prayers of intercession, worship songs, and then spirited, innovative, and improvised lines of a new song, building to a crescendo and based on the biblical text. This pattern is repeated several times each hour.

This brief overview has supplied the backdrop for another hard look at the central teaching of the Three Waves of the Spirit and then the conclusion about the future of the whole movement in the twenty-first century. There seems to be a renewed call for clear teaching about the Holy Spirit. Many pastors avoid the area completely because of its more controversial aspects. As a result younger generations can grow up in Charismatic churches with very little understanding of the distinctives of the movement. In the second major section of this chapter our attention now moves to the continuing debate on the concept of Spirit baptism.

Spirit Baptism Revisited

Significant new books and articles have contributed to the ongoing debate. We will discuss some of the publications by Macchia, Ervin, Land, Yun, Hart, Palma, Gordon Anderson, and Allan Anderson. This will be followed by another look at my own conclusions on this topic in the light of an analysis of my perspective by contemporary German Catholic theologian, Norbert Baumert. In a concluding part of this second section of the chapter, I will offer a new approach, strongly influenced by the thought of some classic devotional writers.

Frank Macchia

In his 2006 monograph *Baptized in the Holy Spirit: a Global Pentecostal Theology*, Frank Macchia, Swiss-trained Assemblies of God theologian from Vanguard University, writes a Pentecostal pneumatology using Spirit baptism as his point of departure and prevailing motif. This is a fresh approach. In a way Macchia wants to return Pentecostal theology to its origins but he broadens the metaphor of Spirit baptism in an eschatological, kingdom-oriented sense. Referring to Romans 5:5, Macchia states that the gift of the Spirit is the gift of divine love. On page 60 he continues, "Our final conclusion will be that Spirit baptism is a baptism into the love of God that sanctifies, renews, and empowers until Spirit baptism turns all of creation into the final dwelling place of God." In his last chapter on the Spirit-baptized life and divine love, Macchia challenges traditional dispensational eschatology. He writes,

> Rather than a beleaguered little flock waiting to be raptured away, the Pentecostal dreams of a great flood of the Spirit in the latter days to unite and to empower the church to do great things in the world. Their belief in a proliferation of apostolic signs and wonders amidst an empowered church also runs contrary to dispensational teaching." (p. 275)

There is so much to appreciate in this transforming analysis. At the end of his study, Macchia addresses the traditional issues in the debate. He "embraces subsequence" (p. 281) when interpreted in the context of an ecstasy of love as the power to self-transcend and to give of oneself abundantly to God and others. Who would want to argue with that, except perhaps to ask if one could seek this self-transcendence without embracing subsequence?

He sees glossolalia as a symbol of empowered ministry that bridges linguistic and cultural boundaries. He maintains that tongues were characteristic in the New Testament and can be for us but, "Tongues cannot be turned into a law that governs how Spirit baptism must be received without exception within the actions of a sovereign God" (p. 281).

With mounting enthusiasm, Macchia affirms on the same page a statement by Russell Spittler that tongues is "a broken speech for a broken body of Christ till perfection comes." He considers this statement as one of the most significant ever given by a Pentecostal scholar. With his analogy, he likens it implicitly to the historic breakthrough of Karl Barth's *Letter to the Romans* in 1919. "It falls," he declares, "like a bombshell on one-sidedly triumphalistic Pentecostal spiritualities" (p. 281).

Macchia's study is a breath of fresh air. He actually agrees with the statement that the heated debate about subsequence is a *non-issue* since, "Pentecostals were more concerned with spiritual renewal than with creating a new *ordo salutis*"—another quote from Spittler (p. 24). This is a clever observation, and I agree with its basic intention. Nevertheless, I need to point out that the seventeenth-century disputes about the order of salvation were fundamentally different. They involved prescribing a pedantic chronological sequence for aspects like regeneration, faith, conversion, repentance, etc. pertaining to all Christians. The twentieth century debate about subsequence had a very divisive agenda and harbored the potential of classifying Christians into different categories such as the merely saved, the saved and sanctified, and the ultimate: the saved, sanctified and Spirit filled.

It is not always easy to determine where Macchia actually stands. In the end my conclusion is that he is more in line with the general thrust of integrative or sacramental Charismatic views rather than with the Classical Pentecostal position of "initial physical evidence." In this he aligns himself with Assemblies of God thinkers like Russ Splitter and Gordon Fee as well as with Gordon Anderson and Anthony Palma. The clearest statement by Macchia seems to be on page 77:

> The older tendency was to see Spirit baptism as a separate reception of the Spirit that functioned as a rite of passage to spiritual fullness and spiritual gifts. What I regard to be a more helpful trend, the tendency now among many Pentecostals is to accent the gift of the Spirit given in regeneration and to view the Pentecostal experience of Spirit baptism as empowerment for witness as a "release" of an already-indwelling Spirit in life. Under the influence of the charismatic movement, the language of fullness tends to be replaced with "release of the Spirit" as an "enhancement" or "renewal" of one's charismatic life.

Macchia draws the significant conclusion that this implies that all Christians are charismatic. He is still particularly appreciative of his own heritage and seems to distance himself from those scholars like Steven Land who, he says, practically ignore Spirit baptism (p. 24). Even when conceding "subsequence" to Third Wave churches, Macchia wants them to recognize their debt to early Pentecostalism for the spawning of a global revival. He also wants to broaden and revitalize the concept of Spirit baptism in an eschatological and societally relevant manner, renewing the earth.

As seems to be the case increasingly, Classical Pentecostal innovators are currently battling passionately to free themselves from the questionable heritage of escapist dispensationalism. I find this simply ironic because logically early Pentecostals should never even have embraced this legacy. The whole purpose of J.N.

Darby in the 1830s with his seven dispensations was to have a way of explaining why miracles no longer occur (cessationism) without having to explain them away as was occurring in liberal Protestantism of that time. Early Pentecostals somewhat naively embraced this premillennial "Trojan horse" from fundamentalism and merely adjusted it to accommodate the present-day occurrence of the charisms.

With regard to Macchia it is interesting to note that he chooses to use the language of "release the Spirit," that I identified as the sacramental approach in my study *Treasures Old and New,* rather than integrative terminology, such as new outpourings, milestones, experiential breakthroughs, or fresh comings of the Spirit. Macchia's study is indeed the first major Pentecostal treatment on Spirit baptism in almost twenty years—since the studies of Hunter and Ervin.

Howard Ervin

It is to the perspective of the recently deceased Howard Ervin (d. Aug. 12, 2009) we turn next, since his views have lately been taken up by younger representatives such as Pavel Hoffman and Daniel Isgrigg. Hoffman, who is a young theologian from the Czech Republic currently teaching in Uppsala, Sweden, wrote a Master's thesis at ORU in which he argues for a fresh look at the issue of subsequence. He rejects the idea of two *stages* to the Christian life, advocating rather two events or categories, an *ontological* conversion and a *functional* Spirit baptism. The former is necessary for salvation; the latter is supernatural empowerment for effective Christian ministry. They may happen simultaneously <u>or</u> in subsequence, but they cannot be reduced to each other or identified. The ontological dimension refers to the act of becoming a Christian and the functional dimension to the operations of the believer in ministry which the Spirit empowers. This insight of Hoffman I believe may be a sign of a new approach that is gaining momentum and integrating valuable insights from both Pentecostalism and evangelicalism.

Daniel Isgrigg, another younger Pentecostal scholar, takes the opposite route to Hoffman. In his 2008 *Pilgrimage into Pentecost,* he presents an apologetic for the Classical Pentecostal position of Howard Ervin. He does this clearly and fully supports Ervin's exegesis that has been widely critiqued. Isgrigg mentions that many scholars find Ervin to be irrelevant to today's discussion. He advocates that they re-examine that position and not simply dismiss it because it is old (p. 128).

Although Ervin's position is vintage Assemblies of God Pentecostalism, as attested to in the Foreword to Isgrigg's book by William W. Menzies, Ervin also has some unique features in his Pneumatology, which he taught at ORU for several decades. For interest's sake I list a few of them:

1) The "birthday" of the Church is not Acts 2, but John 20:19–23 (when Jesus breathes on His disciples).
2) At least for Luke, baptism in the Spirit is synonymous with being filled with the Spirit. The terms are used interchangeably.
3) Tongues are not sub-rational but supra-rational.
4) There are *seven* Pentecosts in the book of Acts: (1) Acts 2:4—Disciples; (2) Acts 4:31—Jewish new believers; (3) Acts 8:14–17—Samaritans; (4) Acts 8:38–39—Ethiopian Eunuch; (5) Acts 9:17—Paul; (6) Acts 10:44–46—Roman; and (7) Acts 19:1–6—Ephesians.
5) The translation spiritual *gifts* in 1 Corinthians 12 is unfortunate. They are not gifts in the sense of permanent endowments or possessions, but rather manifestations.
6) *Signs* are for the world and create faith. *Gifts* are for the Church and build up the body.
7) Ervin is the only scholar who espouses the One Baptism —One Filling view. He rejects the idea of a refilling based on Acts 4:31. The Spirit is seen as baptizing us into a state of lasting fullness that does not fluctuate.

In his last publication (2002), *Healing: Sign of the Kingdom,* Ervin includes a brief chapter on Jesus and the Spirit.

Here he makes the distinction (that Hoffman suggests) between *functional* and *ontological*. He states that Luke's pneumatology is functional and John's ontological. The ontological work of the Spirit pertains to the new birth. The functional work is empowering and is inseparable from the phenomena that accompany the baptism in the Spirit, such as tongues, prophecy, healing, etc. Ervin does not draw the same conclusion from this distinction that Hoffman does, namely that the ontological and functional work of the Spirit may occur simultaneously. It is precisely at this point of distinguishing between the functional and ontological work of the Spirit that Archer Torrey, grandson of the famous evangelist, R. A. Torrey, and his protégé, Brad Long, cast new light. Here the terminology *internal* and *external* is used to refer to the ontological and functional (or phenomenological) aspects of the work of the Spirit respectively. More about this presently.

Steven Land

Steven Land, professor of Pentecostal Theology at the Church of God School of Theology in Cleveland, Tennessee, (recently renamed Pentecostal Theological Seminary) wrote a major study, titled *Pentecostal Spirituality: a Passion for the Kingdom* (1993), in which he says very little about tongues or Spirit baptism. He disagrees with F. D. Bruner's designation of the theological center of Pentecostalism as being "pneumato-baptistocentric." The term itself is linguistically monstrous at best, but it is probably in line with the majority view that Spirit baptism is the central Pentecostal distinctive. Land identifies that instead in eschatology, in the "apocalyptic affections" that integrate beliefs and practices—the passion for the coming (premillennial) kingdom. Referring to the seminal idea of New Testament scholar, Ernst Käsemann, that "Apocalyptic was the mother of all Christian theology," Land readily acknowledges the turn to the apocalyptic as the adopted mother of Pentecostal theology. It is interesting to note in passing that Charles Parham believed that the experience of Spirit baptism provided assurance to believers that they would escape the dreaded coming tribulation (by the rapture) before the advent of the millennium. It is, of course, possible to recognize the apocalyptic framework of New Testament thinking *without* accepting the dispensational view of the rapture. Adrio König, a South African systematic theologian is an able representative of this position, which I also support.

Koo Dong Yun

Koo Dong Yun, in his 2003 dissertation *Baptism in the Holy Spirit: an Ecumenical Theology of Spirit Baptism*, discusses thoroughly different "constructs" of Spirit baptism—Classical Pentecostal, Charismatic, Dispensational, as well as the views of Donald Gelpi (under whom he was studying), Francis Sullivan, and Karl Barth. Since he has a Classical Pentecostal background, it is noteworthy that Yun questions the initial evidence doctrine. However, he maintains that it "no longer remains a primary concern for present Pentecostals" (p. 134). When answering the question what the most distinctive feature of twentieth-century Pentecostalism may be, he does reply, "the doctrine of the verifiability of Spirit baptism," but the essence of the Pentecostal movement lies in its "pragmatic" method (p. 154). Perhaps expressing something of the postmodern climate of his generation, Yun avoids a prescriptive conclusion. When asked about the best or most biblical construct of Spirit baptism, he replies that it depends on one's ecclesial context or horizons. On page 161, he insists that the main role of theology should remain descriptive (perhaps succumbing to a prescriptive strain himself in that very statement!)

He ends on a note that asks the same question with which this current chapter grapples: How will the Pentecostal movement meliorate or improve in the future? Yun asks, "In what direction, then, is the Pentecostal movement heading in the twenty-first century? Will Pentecostals be absorbed in mainstream Christianity or continuously keep the sectarian impetus of the first Pentecostals? Answers to these questions still remain to be seen" (pp. 161, 162). My question in this chapter relates to all Three Waves (not just to the First Wave), and at this stage I would like to state that neither of the alternatives Yun mentions seems likely or attractive!

Larry Hart

In a 2004 publication *Perspectives on Spirit Baptism*, Larry Hart of ORU presents the Charismatic perspective. He calls his view *dimensional, which* he sees as a newer approach, a developing consensus among some Charismatic scholars that seeks to build bridges between evangelicals and Pentecostals (p. 108). Spirit baptism is a metaphor that includes various dimensions, such as eschatology, Christian initiation (rebirth), Christian life (holiness), and empowerment for mission and ministry. On page 123 he further states that "most Pentecostals would endorse a virtual 'law of tongues,' viewing speaking in tongues as the 'initial physical evidence' of Spirit baptism." On the other hand he warns against an arrival syndrome—"I got it all when I was saved, Brother!" (p. 124). Hart sees the work of the Spirit as revealing three fundamental dimensions. With the alliteration of an accomplished Baptist preacher, he calls them Paschal, Purifying and Pentecostal. They include respectively salvation, sanctification, and service, or (switching to Cs): conversion, consecration, and charisma. Back to Ss, they enable us to "get started, get straight, and get strong" (p. 128). In the same order, they are founded on the writings of John, Paul and Luke.

With unusual candor, Hart points out that it is not only the Pentecostals and Charismatics that are empowered and growing. He points to mega-churches such as Rick Warren's Saddleback Community Church (he could have included Bill Hybels and Willow Creek) as well as Southeast Christian in Louisville. He asks, "If Charismatics corner the market of the Spirit's power, then why are many non-Charismatic congregations outstripping them in growth?" (p. 158).

Anthony Palma

At the same time as Charismatics seek more integrative and holistic approaches, it is interesting to notice similar tendencies *within* Classical Pentecostalism. In the *Enrichment Journal* of the Assemblies of God (volume 10:1 of 2005), which I consulted online, there are several very irenic articles on the issue of tongues. Anthony Palma starts by referencing the high percentage of believers in Pentecostal churches who have not been baptized in the Spirit (according to the Assemblies of God understanding). Trying to avoid past misunderstandings he stresses that the Spirit already indwells all believers. A subsequent coming upon or infilling does not presuppose that the Spirit had left. These are "only figurative and graphic ways of portraying." Palma states that "the Lord certainly responds to believing prayer and praise, but . . . His timing may not coincide with our wishes."

Again to counteract widespread misperceptions he points out that the disciples were involved in healings and "demon expulsions" *before* Pentecost. He points out that spiritual gifts have been manifested by Christians in all epochs of Church history. Without addressing it directly Palma is redefining traditional Pentecostal teaching. There is little of the "initial" in "initial, physical evidence" left. He also emphasizes the need for those who are Spirit-baptized to "experience an ongoing fullness of the Spirit as well as periodic enduements in times of special need."

This statement revises the definitiveness of the experience. Palma concludes, "Baptism in the Holy Spirit must be more than enshrined doctrine; it must be a vital, productive experience in the life of believers and their personal relationship with the Lord, their interaction with other believers, and their witness to the world."

Gordon Anderson

Perhaps even more astounding is the article in the same periodical by Gordon Anderson, president of North Central

University in Minneapolis. He very artfully walks the fine line of affirming traditional Pentecostal positions while critiquing what he calls the *overstatement* of the Pentecostal position. The overstated views are the very ones that have regularly been seen as stumbling blocks by Charismatics and, especially, evangelicals. The so-called "overstaters" teach that tongues must precede an enduement with power in ministry and service. Anderson points to examples of the significant ministries of Hudson Taylor, Chuck Swindoll, Charles Stanley, Billy Graham, and others who have not spoken in tongues. Article VII of the Statement of Fundamental Truths expresses the Assemblies of God position on Spirit baptism. The ambiguity lies in the sentence that reads (concerning the baptism in the Spirit): "With it comes the enduement of power for life and service, the bestowment of the gifts. . . ."

Anderson argues that it could not possibly mean that *all* power and *all* gifts follow the baptism, but just *some*. A 2000 position paper of the Assemblies of God uses the language of more, of something additional or extra being imparted, "with the baptism come overflowing fullness . . .deepened reverence . . . intensified consecration . . . more active love." There is a dramatic increase, significant additional power.

Anderson even addresses the extravagant claim of some Pentecostals that a person must speak in tongues to be saved. This position has *never* been officially taught by mainstream Classical Pentecostalism. It does apply to the non-Trinitarian "Jesus' Name" Pentecostals who also deny salvation to everyone who has not been baptized (or rebaptized) in the Name of Jesus. Nevertheless, Anderson divulges that some Pentecostals have lapsed into this sectarian position (my wording, not his) by their application of the parable of the wise and foolish virgins, awaiting the coming of the Bridegroom (Matt 25). If the oil in the lamp is seen as referring to the Spirit, then those who are excluded could be seen as the non-tongue speakers. This would hold true where Spirit baptism is viewed as always accompanied by glossolalia. Anderson finds this preposterous. Most would probably concur, but it is alarming how widespread the false perception is in mainline and evangelical circles that Pentecostals teach that you must speak in tongues in order to be saved. This, of course, makes it so much easier to dismiss Pentecostals as misguided and unbiblical in their thinking.

Anderson also refers to the statistic of the demographer David Barrett that currently only 35% of Pentecostal church members actually speak in tongues. The practice has in fact become a minority even within denominations where it is highly valued and sometimes is required of office bearers. Anderson also alludes to an argument presented by veteran Pentecostal historian, Vinson Synan, that comparative statistics regarding the growth of churches in the twentieth century illustrate that, "Pentecostals have been dramatically more successful in planting and growing churches than those who have rejected the Pentecostal understanding of the baptism in the Holy Spirit and the necessity of speaking in tongues."

Synan makes the same point in his 1994 article on "The Role of Tongues as Initial Evidence" in the Rodman Williams Festschrift (or honorary collection of essays) *Spirit and Renewal*. He points to the growth of the Church of God in Christ in comparison to the Church of Christ (Holiness). But in the same article, Synan acknowledges that Bishop C.H. Mason of the Church of God in Christ did *not* accept the "initial evidence" position on tongues. They also accepted other manifestations as evidences equal to tongues. How can one determine whether the rapid growth of COGIC was not perhaps due to their more flexible position on tongues? In the USA, they actually outnumber the Assemblies of God, which holds to the stricter initial evidence position.

One can certainly pay attention to the statistics presented, but many factors play a role in Church growth: societal circumstances, quality and wisdom of individual church leaders, economic factors, as well as spiritual issues such as obedience to divine leading, courage, perseverance, character, etc. To link a particular doctrinal insight to the actual growth statistics seems more than a little tenuous. Larry Hart makes the argument cited above that in some areas in the U.S. the evangelical churches outstrip the Pentecostal ones in growth and size. An argument seeing a causal relationship between particular doctrines and growth statistics would for example make one vulnerable to counterarguments such as attributing the global success of Roman Catholicism to its teachings on Mary, the Pope, or priestly celibacy; or the dominance of Southern Baptists in the South to their position on the ordination of women or on eternal security!

Allan Anderson

In the chapter on "A Theology of the Spirit" in his important study *An Introduction to Pentecostalism: Global Charismatic Christianity*, Allan Anderson of Birmingham, England uses the phrase "the doctrine of *consequence*" instead of "initial evidence." Speaking in tongues is the consequence or primary evidence of Spirit baptism. He points out that consequence (like subsequence) has often been challenged—even from *within* Classical Pentecostalism. On page 193, Anderson gives a number of international examples: Minnie Abrams of the Mukti Mission in India maintained back in 1906 that tongues usually but not necessarily follow Spirit baptism. This amounts to the "normal but not normative approach" toward tongues taken by many contemporary Charismatics. Even William Seymour of Azusa Street later questioned initial evidence. The same applies to Willis Hoover who founded the large Chilean Pentecostal movement.

I added a few more examples of this minority position in Classical Pentecostalism in my book *Treasures Old and New*. South African Pentecostal leader G.R. Wessels concurred with this position in a paper at the 1955 International Pentecostal conference in Stockholm. Jonathan Paul, founder of German Pentecostalism also denied the initial evidence doctrine, as did Christian Krust of the German Mülheim Association. The pioneer Swiss Pentecostal Leonhard Steiner, one of the initiators of the first International Pentecostal conference in Zurich in 1947 questioned both subsequence and consequence. In Britain the Elim church accepted both tongues and prophecy as signs of Spirit baptism.

In the USA there were also the detractors. F.F. Bosworth, known for his groundbreaking publication on healing, and one-time executive member of the Assemblies of God resigned from the denomination in 1918 because he insisted that tongues was only one of several possible evidences of Spirit baptism. More well known examples today are present-day Pentecostal scholars such as New Testament theologians Gordon Fee and Russ Splitter and most probably also systematic theologian Frank Macchia—all of the Assemblies of God.

Allan Anderson finds the main characteristic of the movement not in subsequence or consequence but rather as expressed by Daniel Albrecht in *Rites in the Spirit* and by Steven Land. He cites the latter on page 203, where he locates the Pentecostal distinctive in

> The dimension of praise, worship, adoration and prayer to God . . . [and] the abiding, decisive, directing motives and dispositions which characterize Pentecostals . . . this depth of conviction and passion . . . a steadfast longing for the Lord and the salvation of the lost . . . a continuous, joyous, exclamation of the inbreaking presence and soon to be consummated kingdom of God.

When he expresses his own position, Anderson uses similar language:

> In spite of the inevitable dissipating of this early Pentecostal vision through institutionalization, for most Pentecostals and Charismatics today this experience of the imminence [perhaps Anderson means immanence?] of God through prayer, worship and gifts of the Spirit enabling believers to evangelize is still their main characteristic. The fullness of the Spirit is always encountered in the abiding presence of God through prayer and worship." (p. 196)

Looking toward the future, Anderson concludes that Christianity has received a new vibrancy and relevance through the pervading Holy Spirit in Pentecostalism, "The whole Christian church may be thankful that this is the case, for it may mean the salvation of Christianity itself in the next century from decline and eventual oblivion" (p. 286).

Norbert Baumert's Response to Treasures Old and New

It is now time to revisit my own conclusions from my 1988 publication *Treasures Old and New*. I have been gratified by the reception afforded to this study and the numerous references to it in the ensuing literature. With the exception of the more extensive use made of it by Charles Hummel in his second edition of *Fire in the Fireplace: Charismatic Renewal in the Nineties,* most mention of my work has been appreciative but brief. Roman Catholic New Testament scholar, Norbert Baumert of Frankfurt, Germany, however, has paid me the ultimate compliment of dealing with my arguments extensively in his two-volume work *Charisma-Taufe-Geisttaufe* (Charisma-Baptism-Spirit baptism). Although his main focus is to challenge the findings of fellow Catholic scholars G. Montague and K. McDonnell, his last chapter devotes a subsection of seventeen pages to my book, which he describes as the standard work covering the last fifty years. His conclusion about my own position was critical but very helpful and has actually led me to revise my position.

My position in *Treasures Old and New* was basically that the Pentecostal-Charismatic experience was valid and should be embraced by all Christians. It was the normal Christian life. However the doctrinal packing within which the experience was being wrapped proved to be a stumbling block. Neither subsequence nor initial evidence was exegetically sound. I attempted to evolve a new interpretation of Spirit baptism, after discussing and classifying the views of about forty authors on the topic. My view was that Spirit baptism was not a stage or step in the Christian's life but merely "the experiential dimension of normal Christian living" which we needed to reclaim after the inroads of materialism, naturalism, and rationalism in the secular era of modernity. In this way, the Charismatic Renewal would be compatible with all sections of Christianity. One simply needed potentially to incorporate all the charisms of the Spirit and acknowledge the role of experience and specific spiritual experiences. I advocated that the concept of charisms be broadened even to include ones not mentioned in Scripture. Seeing that the various lists in the Bible hardly overlap and thus are merely giving examples, one may be allowed to lengthen the list. Examples on page 228 include intercession, promoting justice, deliverance ministry, and rearing children.

Baumert, after following my whole argument with care and precision for more than 200 pages, declares in conclusion that "one is somewhat dumbfounded at the simplification that has been made on the conceptual level" (my translation from the German). He agrees that the experiential dimension of the Christian life has been suppressed and is fundamentally important to us but disagrees that the term Spirit baptism could be used to refer to the experiential dimension as such. It is only *one* among many possible types of experience. He also points out that the experiential dimension would more accurately refer to the human side of what happens, while Spirit baptism is rather to be described as God's action. In his final overview some 30 pages later, Baumert explains more fully what he means by different forms of being filled with the Spirit. On page 366, he refers to mystical experience (unio mystica—mystical union), Spirit baptism (tongues), and other experiences, such as the unique experience of Ignatius of Loyola at the Cardoner River.

Baumert is a Jesuit, so it may be helpful to describe briefly something of the experience of the founder of his order to which he here refers. The classic contemporary description of Ignatius's experience states that on the banks of the Cardoner River, something like the following occurred: the eyes of his understanding began to open and, without seeing any vision, he understood and knew many things, including spiritual things and things of the faith. This took place with so great an enlightenment that everything seemed altogether new to him. Surely this was a unique and most valuable encounter with God.

Without the encumbrance of the pervasive modernist/rationalist legacy of a Reformed Protestant, Baumert stands more comfortably in the long Catholic tradition of religious experience and more easily makes these distinctions than one (like myself) who was trained at seminary to distrust the notion of all religious experience and to be ever wary of *all* forms of "subjectivism, mystical experiences and emotionalism." I would nevertheless maintain that it was not entirely accurate of Baumert to describe my position in *Treasures* as *identifying* Spirit baptism with the experiential dimension itself (although I should have written more carefully). I do in fact state that the "experiential dimension of normal integrated Christian life" includes not only charisms, however broadly conceptualized, but also "a wide range of spiritual experiences" (p. 233). I then give examples of such particular experiences, noting among others, crisis experiences, doxological praise, the gift of tears, infused contemplation, and spiritual growth experiences.

What I should have said is that all Christians may discover or reappropriate the legitimate role of religious experience in their lives. *Life has this experiential dimension to it and the charisms of the Spirit are included in that.* They are imparted in Christian fellowship (or koinonia) and become manifest through prayer and are given for the upbuilding of the Body. The Spirit movements of the twentieth century burst onto the scene with the recovery of a number of long-neglected biblical charisms, as well as transformative experiences of encountering God in a deeply personal way. These became milestones in people's lives, mountain top experiences, and were often followed by prophetic ministry, anointed witness, miraculous healing, and/or tongues. In the Lucan idiom typified by Jim Shelton's dissertation, believers became "mighty in word and deed." This is the treasure that the Pentecostal-Charismatic movements unearthed, and it still has the potential to continue to influence global Christianity. This treasure is what Classical Pentecostals like Land, Anderson, and

Fee describe as the main characteristic of their movement. I maintain that the Pentecostal "ecclesial baggage" of consequence and subsequence places non-essential barriers in the way of transmitting this precious legacy. The doctrine of tongues as the required initial, physical evidence of Spirit baptism (which I maintain cannot be adequately supported from Scripture) forms a major stumbling block in this process.

Baumert is right to call the identification of the Pentecostal doctrine of Spirit baptism with the experiential dimension per se an oversimplification. At the onset of the Catholic Charismatic movement, one of its early theological writers, Edward O'Connor, actually makes the same point in *The Pentecostal Movement in the Catholic Church*. Writing about Pentecost and traditional spirituality, O'Connor denies that baptism in the Spirit is substantially new. As "an experience of the presence and action of the Holy Spirit," it is part of the "normal flowering of the life of grace" and "a fulfillment of our status as sons of God" (p. 216).

Significantly, he then goes on to say on the same page, "But I do not mean to imply that any religious experience whatsoever can be identified with the baptism of the Spirit." He underscores that it is a turning point in one's spiritual development—the entry into a "new regime of life in which one is led and strengthened and enlightened by the Holy Spirit much more effectively and manifestly than before."

He raises the question why this grace (of Spirit baptism) is now apparently being given much more lavishly and frequently in the twentieth century than in previous centuries. My own response to this question has been that glossolalia breaks down the grip of the rationalism of modernity on the Church so effectively. It humbles the intellectually arrogant and lifts up the lowly. O'Connor speculates (p. 219) that it has to do with the communitarian value of the experience—the breaking down of our individualism and establishing what we now increasing call the spirit of koinonia or community, "to a degree not seen since the primitive Church." Those words were published back in 1971. The communal motif was probably characteristic of the early Catholic Charismatic movement but sadly has been pushed into the background in the subsequent development of the Three Waves of the Spirit.

Interim Summary

At this stage a quick bird's-eye view of the whole historical development may give us some perspective. Classical Pentecostalism was the launching of a new religious awakening. There was a focus on preaching the gospel and winning the lost in preparation for Christ's return. Salvation was primary. The Wesleyan-Holiness tradition added a "second stage" to this in order to emphasize sanctification and then Spirit baptism, representing empowerment, came as a subsequent crisis experience that was evidenced by the supernatural sign of tongues.

The Second and Third Waves carried this revival further across the globe and the spectrum of denominations, questioning just a few of the theological parameters as drawn. They influenced virtually every branch of Christianity, recovering the full range of biblical charisms and the directness of the working of the Spirit in authoritative word and deed, confession, and healing. Today, participants and observers sound the cry for moral accountability and holiness, as well as transforming power.

As we look to the future, we members of these movements will necessarily continue "drinking from our own wells," to use a metaphor from classical spirituality. The triadic legacy of salvation, sanctification, and empowered service for ministry is part of our DNA. It also includes as ever relevant the call for our theological emphasis and ministry to rest on a biblical basis. However, the debate around evidential tongues has become tired and cumbersome. I am reminded of a reference by Tom Smail that I quoted in *Treasures* (p. 71), about the exegetical debate concerning 1 Corinthians 12:13:

> In that basic conflict many others joined till the terrain around the verse became so soft and soggy, after being trodden by the hooves of so many war horses, that many of us despaired of ever being sure precisely what it meant.

Toward a New Paradigm of the Spirit

In an attempt to provide a different framework and foundation for the *impartation* of the dynamic life in the Spirit and the *manifesting* of the charisms and power of the Spirit, I will now develop a new paradigm. Let me try and present a somewhat different approach to the doctrinal issues we have been pursuing. This new framework is based not so much on exegesis as on *systematic-theological* reflection. It is my contention that it is truly biblical in the sense of employing *broader scriptural themes* rather than being based on what the Germans call "Einzelexegese"—detailed exegesis or interpretation of specific texts. The ongoing skirmishes over the meaning of "being baptized in the Holy Spirit" in its context has been clouded by attempts over many decades to justify preconceived notions, denominational agendas, and even personal experiences. The intention of the biblical authors is proverbially difficult to deter-mine in these matters. The academic arguments back and forth between highly qualified experts in Greek can lead the interested laity or "person in the pew" to despair.

Over some thirty years of teaching courses in systematic theology on doctoral, master's, and undergraduate levels, I have personally evolved a diagram or schema to summarize the work of the Three Persons of the Trinity. It is not comprehensive and there will probably always be some debate about the terminology selected. I have nevertheless found it helpful in broadening the understanding of several generations of students.

My focus here will be only on the Third Person of the Trinity—and not on what is known in systematic theology as the *Person* of the Spirit, but on what is known as the *Work* of the Spirit. I distinguish between the *foundational, teleological,* and *culminating* work of each member of the Trinity. The terms "foundational" and "culminating" are self-explanatory. "Teleo-logical" refers to the purpose or aim of something. Let us now consider this in more detail.

The Foundational Work of the Holy Spirit

First, we note that the external, or economic, workings of the Persons of the Trinity (to use the terminology of classic Trinitarian theology) are unified and inseparable. The prominent Church father of the fourth and fifth centuries, Augustine of Hippo in North Africa, stated: Opera Trinitatis ad extra indivisa sunt (the external workings of the Trinity are indivisible). By economic, or external, he meant the work of God relating to the world and our salvation. The internal, or immanent, work, on the other hand, refers to the intrapersonal activity between Father, Son, and Spirit. Thus, there is no action or task on earth that the Holy Spirit does in isolation from the other two members of the Trinity.

The first work of the Spirit is based on the Father's loving plan to redeem His fallen creation through the atoning death of His Son, Jesus Christ. The Spirit is the Agent of the *new birth*. Those who receive Christ and have faith in Him become children of God, born of the Spirit. This initiates a new existence and is termed *ontological*—a new state of being as a believer.

We are regenerated by God's Spirit, born from above, or born again. The first chapters of John's Gospel are filled with this terminology of rebirth. In the evangelical, Pentecostal and Charismatic understandings the new birth, salvation or conversion is primary—the start of the Christian life. This focus is found throughout the New Testament, but it focuses especially on the Spirit's work in the individual believer and his or her relation to Jesus in the Fourth Gospel.

The Teleological Work of the Holy Spirit

In the second and third sections of this brief analysis, the matters become more complicated. Here we are dealing with *functionality* rather than ontology. (Compare the use of these terms by Pavel Hoffman above.) The purpose (or *telos*) of the Spirit's work is defined as indwelling or *inhabitation*. It is in the nature of spirits to indwell. This is an astounding teaching—the climax of God's involvement with human beings. In creation, God *makes* us; through Christ's atoning death, God *redeems* us; and now in the third act of the divine drama, after the Cross and Resurrection, God comes at Pentecost *to live inside* us. As Ephesians 2:22 explains, as the Church, we "are also being built together into a dwelling place of God through the Spirit." Paul uses the same analogy in 1 Corinthians 3:16, "Do you not know that you are a temple of God and that the Spirit of God dwells in you?" In 6:19 the metaphor becomes more individual, "Or do you not know that your body is a temple of the Holy Spirit who is in you, whom you have from God, and that you are not your own?" This means that God is in us and we belong to Him.

This invisible indwelling of the Triune God through the Holy Spirit is an operative, dynamic inhabitation. It makes us holy. As we yield to the sanctifying work of the active Spirit in our lives, we bear the fruit of the Spirit—"love, joy, peace, patience, kindness, goodness, faithfulness, gentleness, and self-control." Although they may understand *sanctification* somewhat differently, evangelicals, Pentecostals, and Charismatics all agree that it is the work of the Spirit. Few would still see it as a precondition for God's empowering work (see the next section) or as something that may be achieved in an instant. Most would see it as a necessary, ongoing work that continues throughout our lives and that there is *reciprocity*—we are involved in it ourselves as co-laborers with God.

Different from the gracious work of Christ on the Cross, which was in our place, for our sake, and to which we can add nothing at all, the work of the Spirit is, in the words of Dutch theologian A.A.van Ruler, "to set us to work" (p. 35 in *Calvinist Trinitarianism and Theocentric Politics*). This work of the Spirit is captured beautifully in the paradoxical language of Philippians 2:12, 13: "Work out your salvation with fear and trembling; for it is God who is at work in you, both to will and to work for His good pleasure." This work by believers is not a meriting of their redemption but the strenuous work of sanctification, involving spiritual growth, obedience, and perseverance. The epistles of

Paul include the whole wide range of the Spirit's work. Theologians enumerate the following aspects:

- soteriological (Rom 8:9);
- charismatic (1 Cor 12—14);
- prophetic (1 Cor 2:10–12);
- eschatological (Rom 8:15–17);
- communal (Eph 4:3);
- sapiential (1 Cor 2:6–10); and
- ethical (1 Cor 6:9–11 and Gal 5:22).

In contrast to *John* and *Luke*, however, Paul is the writer who underscores the *ethical* aspect of the Spirit's work. The Holy Spirit makes us holy by His indwelling.

The Culminating Work of the Holy Spirit

These three divisions are not watertight and do overlap somewhat. The work of the *Father* clearly culminates when He will be shown to be all in all (1 Cor 15:28), and *Christ's* culminating work is the Second Advent (however and whenever we conceive that to happen). The third aspect of the *Spirit's* work is *transformation,* working toward the new earth that will be filled with the knowledge of the glory of the Lord, as the waters cover the sea (or sea-bed; Hab 2:14). This work is not the gradual, sanctifying indwelling that starts in the New Testament only *after* the historic event of the atoning death of Christ. It is the dynamic and powerful, enabling work of the Spirit of God by His presence throughout all of salvation history (from creation on to the present). The Spirit comes upon us and empowers us to testify boldly and do the concrete, visible work of the ministry. These actions and events occur day by day, *building for God's kingdom*, to use an expression of N.T. Wright, or erecting signs of hope for the emerging of God's new creation. The role of the Spirit is to help—as the promised Paraclete, the One who comes to stand with us and speak on our behalf. He will empower us through the spiritual manifestations or enabling charisms of the Spirit. He makes us mighty in word and deed (like Jesus, in

Whose steps we follow; Luke 24:19 and 1 Pet 2:21). This work is a discernible *empowerment*: "You will receive power when the Holy Spirit has come upon you; and you shall be My witnesses. . . ."

Evangelicals, Pentecostals and Charismatics all recognize this pivotal empowering aspect of the Spirit's work but interpret it differently: some unfortunately believe that the more dramatic enabling charisms have ceased; others believe we have access to them all only through the gateway experience of one gift, tongues; while still others see all the charisms as directly available and operative in believers (and, I would argue, for them as a regular part of the experiential dimension of the normal Christian life, imparted in Christian fellowship and manifested through prayer for spiritual upbuilding and the achieving of God's purposes).

It is significant that the external empowering works of the Spirit are a special feature of Luke—Acts but can be illustrated throughout the Old and New Testaments. It is interesting to note that this same triadic or threefold division—foundational, teleological, culminating—is developed quite independently by my fellow systematic theologian, Larry Hart, who uses different terms, as referred to above (including conversion, consecration, and charisma), but says pretty much the same!

Behind this schematization of the two functional aspects of the Spirit's work as indwelling/sanctifying and empowering/transforming lies a little-known tradition in Pneumatology (the doctrine of the Holy Spirit) that goes back to the nineteenth century revivalists and holiness writers, such as D. L. Moody, R. A. Torrey and Watchman Nee. This tradition arises from observant study of the New Testament Scriptures rather than from academic scholarship. It expresses what I have above called the teleological and culminating work of the Spirit as the *internal* and *external* workings of God's Spirit. This teaching has influenced the Presbyterian Renewal ministries of Dr. Z. Brad Long from Black Mountain, North Carolina, through his now deceased mentor, Archer Torrey, a missionary in China, who was the grandson of the famous evangelist, R. A. Torrey. Here is a systematic exposition of this view that I have put together myself, based on some unpublished teaching of Brad Long and used with his permission:

> With regard to the *external* work the above-mentioned Archer Torrey states, "The Holy Spirit *upon us,* or *with us,* anointing us, or moving us, or leading us, is like the tools which a team of carpenters has to have for its work, but which tells us nothing about the inner attitudes or character of those who use them."
>
> With regard to the *internal* work Torrey states, "When the Bible speaks of the Holy Spirit in terms which make it clear that the Holy Spirit is *in one's inner being,* it also speaks of salvation, of character, of fruit-bearing, of life, of wisdom to know God's will, and the will to do it."
>
> To clarify this distinction further it is helpful to notice that in Scripture the prepositions "on" or "upon" are regularly used to designate the *external* work of the Spirit. On the other hand the prepositions "in" or "within" often occur when the reference is to the *internal* work of the Spirit. (These distinctions are not absolute and there may be some overlap in usage.)

The External Work

Let us consider a few biblical references to the external work of the Spirit (all NASB; emphasis mine).

Acts 1:8: But you will receive power when the Holy Spirit has come upon you; and you shall be my witnesses both in Jerusalem, and in Judea and Samaria, and even to the remotest part of the earth.

Acts 10:45: All the circumcised believers who came with Peter were amazed, because the gift of the Holy Spirit had been poured out *on* the Gentiles also.

Luke 24:49: And behold, I am sending forth the promise of My Father upon you; but you are to stay in the city until you are clothed with *power* from on high.

Note that the coming of the Spirit upon people is linked with power and action. The idea of being clothed underlines the *external* working. We wear our clothes on the outside of our bodies.

Acts 10:38: You know of Jesus of Nazareth, how God anointed Him with the Holy Spirit and with power, and how He went about doing good and healing all who were oppressed by the devil, for God was with Him.

The analogy of anointing refers to the outward placing of oil upon someone—again an external image. Anointing is associated in both the Old and New Testaments with equipping for action and service.

A pattern seems to be emerging: *the Holy Spirit comes/ falls/moves on or upon someone and this leads to some type of action.* This happens in the short term.

This pattern occurs in the Old Testament, in, for example, Saul the first king of Israel:

1 Samuel 10:10, 11: When they came to the hill there, behold, a group of prophets met him (Saul); and the Spirit of God came upon him mightily, so that he prophesied among them. It came about, when all who knew him previously saw that he prophesied now with the prophets, that the people said to one another, "What has happened to the son of Kish? Is Saul also among the prophets?"

This external coming of God's Spirit *upon* people, seems to be short term, intermittent, or episodic. It comes and goes. It leads to action—usually with power and often causing astonishment. It can happen again and again. Whereas in the Old Testament the Spirit came mostly upon kings, prophets and judges—leaders of the people—after Pentecost the Spirit comes upon all believers. The episodic working is the same. It is an endowment with power leading to a specific action—people become enabled in a fresh way and operate "mighty in word and deed."

It is interesting to note that the NT references to the external work of the Spirit appear overwhelmingly in the writings of Luke, the Gospel and Acts.

The Internal Work

Let us now consider a few biblical references to the internal work of the Spirit (all NASB).

Ezekiel 36:26–27: Moreover, I will give you a new heart and put a new spirit within you; and I will remove the heart of stone from your flesh and give you a heart of flesh. I will put My Spirit within you and cause you to walk in My statutes, and you will be careful to observe My ordinances.

Romans 8:8, 9: And those who are in the flesh cannot please God. However, you are not in the flesh but in the Spirit, if indeed the Spirit of God dwells in you. But if anyone does not have the Spirit of Christ, he does not belong to Him.

2 Corinthians 1:22: (God) who also sealed us and gave us the Spirit in our hearts as a pledge.

Ephesians 3:16, 17: (I pray) that He (God) would grant you, according to the riches of His glory, to be strengthened with power through His Spirit in the inner man, so that Christ may dwell in your hearts through faith. . . .

Here we see a different pattern emerging: *the Holy Spirit comes to indwell someone and this ongoing presence leads to deepening of relationship with God and the increase of virtue and character.* This is a long-term phenomenon.

This inhabitation by the Spirit is something new. It comes only after the Cross and Resurrection. John 14:17 seems to allude to this shift. Before His crucifixion, Jesus speaks to His disciples of the Paraclete (Helper, Advocate)—the Holy Spirit, whom the world does not know, "but you know Him because He abides *with* you and will be *in* you." This may refer to the impartation of the Spirit in John 20:22.

This internal working is long-term and ongoing. It does not lead to specific dramatic actions but to character traits like holiness, love, and wisdom. The New Testament references come primarily from John's Gospel and the writings of Paul.

Many theologians have pointed out that there are different emphases with regard to the Spirit in the New Testament authors. Examples include Charles Hummel, James Shelton, and Max Turner. Donald McKim expresses this varying emphasis:

> The Gospel of John does not so much emphasize the outward expressions of the Spirit (Luke—Acts) or the more inward experiences of the Spirit by Christians (Paul's writings). [John's] focus is on the immediate relation of the individual disciple to Jesus through the Spirit. (*Introducing the Reformed Faith*, p. 100)

This table summarizes these two motifs:

Works of the Holy Spirit		
	External	*Internal*
Location	Upon or on	In or within
Temporal Dimension	Starts in the Old Testament and continues through the New Testament and the Church.	Starts in the New Testament after Pentecost and continues in the Church.
Effects	Results in powerful action that advances the kingdom of God. Evidenced in spiritual manifestations, or gifts (Rom. 12:6–8; 1 Cor. 12:7–11).	Results in salvation, sanctification, and virtue. Evidenced in fruit of the Spirit (Gal. 5:22).
Occurrence	Repeatable and episodic.	Constant and continuous.
Time Span	Short-term	Long-term

This same basic insight appears in the way different Greek verbs express different senses for the phrases "filled with the Spirit" and "full of the Spirit." In English, two sets of Greek verbs are translated as "filled." The contexts make the meaning clear.

The *first set of verbs* is *plēthō* and *pimplēmi* (πληθω, πιμπλημι). Here are some biblical examples of these words that are *unrelated* to the Holy Spirit (all NASB; emphasis mine):

Matthew 27:48: A sponge filled with liquid. "Immediately one of them ran, and taking a sponge he *filled* it with sour wine and put it on a reed, and gave Him a drink."

Luke 4:28: People filled with rage. "And all the people in the synagogue were *filled* with rage as they heard these things."

Luke 5:7: Boats filled with fish. "So they signaled to their partners in the other boat to come and help them. And they came and *filled* both of the boats, so that they began to sink."

It is pretty clear that this type of filling was episodic—short term. The sponge can be emptied of the wine. The rage of people can come and go. The boats will be emptied of fish and may be refilled later.

These same verbs *pletho* and *pimplemi* also express filling *related* to the Spirit:

Luke 1:41, 42: When Elizabeth heard Mary's greeting, the baby leaped in her womb; and Elizabeth was filled with the Holy Spirit. And she cried out with a loud voice and said, "Blessed are you among women, and blessed is the fruit of your womb!"

Luke 1:67: And his father Zachariah was filled with the Holy Spirit, and prophesied. . . .

Acts 2:4: And they were all filled with the Holy Spirit and began to speak with other tongues, as the Spirit was giving them utterance.

Again it is apparent that this filling is short-term and leads to specific action—prophetic proclamations and manifestations of power, often through the charisms of the Spirit.

The *second set of verbs* that are translated as "filled" are the Greek words *pleroō* and *plērēs* (πληρόω, πληρης).

Here is an example from the Gospels *unrelated* to the Spirit:

Luke 2:40: The child continued to grow and become strong, He was *filled* with wisdom; and the grace of God was upon Him.

This surely refers to an abiding, ongoing filling—a long-term development of character. The same is true in the expressions *related* to the fullness of the Spirit described by these Greek words.

Acts 6:3: Therefore, brethren, select from among you seven men of good reputation, full of the Spirit and of wisdom, which we may put in charge of this task.

Acts 6:5: The statement found approval with the whole congregation; and they chose Stephen, a man full of faith and of the Holy Spirit. . . .

Ephesians 5:18: And do not get drunk with wine, for that is dissipation, but be *filled* with the Spirit.

Here the fullness is ongoing, describing a condition or state rather than activity. The reference is to character and ethical qualities—growth in wisdom, faith, and love.

From this analysis we may conclude that *plēthō* and *pimplēmi* are primarily used for the external, short-term, action-oriented working of the Spirit and that *pleroō* and *plērēs* are mostly used in a context of relationship with God and gradual, continuous growth in sanctification.

Another significant conclusion that flows from this distinction is the realization that individual Christians, churches, and even denominations can get out of *balance* with regard to the internal and external workings of the Spirit.

A believer may strive after the outward demonstrations of bold witness and giftings while still exhibiting a strong lack of patience and maturity and good character traits. It is not an effective ministry that moves in power but neglects holy living.

The other extreme also occurs. One may have advanced in the fruit of the Spirit but be closed to God's empowerment in charismatic gifts due to tradition, fear, or timidity. Both the inner and outer workings of the Spirit are needed for the edification of the body of Christ. Churches live below the New Testament standards for Christianity when they attempt to neglect either the external or internal work of the Spirit in their midst. Realizing that we may have this tendency may help us understand and gently correct others when they get out of balance. Every believer need to strive towards and be open to both these dimensions in their own individual and corporate lives.

Perhaps a somewhat muddled but helpful analogy may be that of a live "Christmas" fruit tree. *Internally* it is connected to the source of life by its roots—relationship—and it could bear fruit—character (long term). *Externally* one could hang from its branches special gifts, wrapped up for particular occasions (short term). Both the fruit and the manifestations are precious. They serve different purposes, but both kinds are needed. Most people would agree that, when forced to make a choice, the internal work is more important. Purity is more valuable than power. Jesus told His disciples that they should not rejoice that the spirits are subject to them but that their names are written in heaven (Luke 10:20). Nevertheless, for the advancement of the reign of God, the power and supernatural enablement of the Spirit is essential. We need a church reflecting God's love and holiness *and* being like Jesus, "mighty in word and deed" (Luke 24:19), to break down the deception of the evil one and transform lives and communities with the gospel of Jesus Christ.

It is not easy to determine where this distinction between the internal and external work of the Spirit originated or was used for the first time. D. L. Moody had a version of it in his sermons. In *Power from on High*, Moody simply states, "The Holy Spirit IN us is one thing, and the Holy Spirit ON us is another" (p. 36). The theme seems to have been more broadly developed by Watchman Nee (1905–1972), a well-known author and Chinese spiritual leader with a Plymouth Brethren background. He was imprisoned for his faith and died in custody after 30 years of incarceration. His books, especially the *Normal Christian Life*, were very popular in evangelical and Charismatic circles in the 1960's and 70's. In *The Communion of the Holy Spirit*, Nee concludes, "The Old and New Testaments show us that the work of the Holy Spirit is threefold: first, He gives people life; second, He dwells in people as life; and third, He falls upon people as power" (p. 49).

About five years ago, scholars discussed Nee's Pneumatology in some theological journals. Chinese scholar Archie Hui wrote a largely critical analysis of Nee's views, while Jim Batten responded to it, mostly agreeing with Nee and disagreeing with Hui. In our brief discussion of the debate, we will focus in the following presentation of their views on *one* issue only—the distinction between the two aspects of the Spirit's work. Hui explains Nee's view:

> He thinks that while the OT only speaks of the Spirit coming upon people, the NT speaks of the Spirit both coming 'upon' (epi) people and coming to dwell 'in' (en) them. For Nee, the external coming of the Spirit has to do with power and ministry, whereas the indwelling presence of the Spirit has to do with daily living, sanctification and holiness.

This seems relatively unproblematic. Hui, however, doubts whether these prepositional phrases are being used in a technical sense. He then finds a few exceptions in the Greek translation of the Old Testament and in Mark 1:10 where the upon/in distinction does not seem to be applied. Batten counters by pointing out that the three Septuagint exceptions provide a very flimsy basis for asserting that the Holy Spirit dwells *within* people in the Old Testament. They include references not by Israelite believers but by heathen rulers and a reference that could just as well refer to the human spirit as the divine Spirit. On the other hand, the Old Testament refers at least twenty-six times clearly to the Spirit *upon* people and another fifteen times to the Spirit's action upon people, without the preposition's being used. The reference in Mark proves to be equally unconvincing. The preposition is "into" (*eis*), and over 99% of Bible translations render it in this context as "upon" or "on." Even Hui acknowledges that that the Spirit's coming upon a person differs from His dwelling in the person. He prefers to express this as an inceptive/stative distinction, referring thereby to the beginning of an action—upon (inceptive)—or expressing an ongoing state—within or in (stative). This distinction supports the claim discussed above, based on the research of Long, that the Spirit's coming *upon* (external action) leads to human action, while the Spirit's dwelling *in* (internal action) denotes a condition or long-term development.

Jim Batten captures the excitement of Watchmen Nee in the midst of these theoretical distinctions when he quotes Nee's joy at the fact of the indwelling:

> I could shout with joy as I think, "The Spirit who dwells within me is no mere influence, but a living Person; He is very God, the infinite God is within my heart! . . . I would fain repeat it to you a hundred times—*the Spirit of God within me is a Person!* I am only an earthen vessel, but in that earthen vessel, I carry a treasure of unspeakable worth, even the Lord of glory."

In concluding his article, Hui agrees with Nee on a few points, one of them being that if one cannot have both giftedness and sanctification, priority should be given to the latter. Well said, but fortunately one never needs to choose between the internal and external work of the Spirit.

The major conclusion that one may draw from this section is that, despite the partisan debates over subsequence and initial evidence, there is possibly a growing convergence regarding the essential contribution and teaching of the Three Waves of the Spirit in the twentieth century, and an attempt to move away from more prescriptive, wooden requirements to more flexible and dynamic categories. Perhaps a focused dialogue along these lines could point the way ahead for the future of the Pentecostal-Charismatic movements in the twenty-first century.

Life in the Spirit: A Dimension with Events

In conclusion, I will venture a new and tentative contribution to carry this discourse forward. What then remains to be said about the perennial debate on Spirit baptism, regarding the issues of evidence and subsequence? I recently heard it described in a new way as the choice between *event* and *dimension*. That set me thinking.

Most Pentecostals would maintain that speaking in tongues is the unmistakable sign of entering into the life of the Spirit. This view is entrenched in doctrinal creeds and belongs to the collective consciousness of the Classical Pentecostal movement, even when the statistical evidence mounts that less than a third of Pentecostals actually practice this gift. It has become part of the DNA of the Pentecostal body politic that an *event* and experience is pivotal, and anecdotal support for this is found in the lives and testimonies of millions of sincere believers.

On the other hand, most Charismatics are less sanguine about the need for glossolalia. Their movements emanate from 1960 onwards rather than the start of the twentieth century. Many Charismatics experienced speaking in tongues and find it normal, but not necessarily normative. To them life in the Spirit is seen as a *dimension*—they acknowledge the present-day occurrence of the charisms but do not give *one* of them a pivotal gateway function. This view is also supported from authentic Christian experience. Charismatics, especially from the earlier denominational renewal, are perhaps more aware of the broader contours of church history. They find it hard to believe that prominent figures such as Augustine, Martin Luther, Jonathan Edwards, or John Wesley; and pioneer missionaries such as William Carey, Hudson Taylor, or David Livingstone were not Spirit empowered just because they did not speak in tongues. They also know evangelical Christian leaders such as Billy Graham, D. L. Moody, and R. A. Torrey who witnessed to the enablement of God's Holy Spirit without experiencing glossolalia. Nevertheless, they acknowledge that there is a dimension to Christianity that many believers disregard to such an extent that it often needs to be rediscovered, having been suppressed for so long due to the philosophical and cultural worldview of modernity.

It seems we have reached a *stalemate*. My own bias will already be clear to the reader. I have argued for a dimensional interpretation. This correlates well with my own experience, and we all have a tendency to want to generalize our own experiences. That has happened in both the Pentecostal and Charismatic positions. I experienced the charism of a word of knowledge, the gift of healing, as well as a deep encounter with prophecy many years before I ever experienced praying in the Spirit. My entrance into life in the Spirit in a more pronounced way was triggered by what I like to call an experience of *doxology*. I was lost in transcendent worship while singing the simple word "Hallelujah." I had an encounter with God that radically and permanently changed my life. There was no hint of tongues in the experience, although I was open to it at the time—and later even sought it actively because I was repeatedly exposed to the teaching that one was somewhat "second class" without it.

Apart from my individual experience, I also find it revealing that as the Church universal moved into the wider experience of the charisms of the Spirit historically in the nineteenth century, the widespread recovery of the supernatural gift of healing predated the eruption of glossolalia by at least forty years.

It was the unexpected publication of the study of Norbert Baumert (referred to above) that triggered something in my spirit to seek a way out of the tradition dilemma. One could say it took a Jesuit scholar to get through to a Reformed denominational Charismatic to see more clearly what the Pentecostals had been saying! Baumert understood the line of reasoning in my dissertation clearly but faulted me for equating Spirit baptism simply with the whole experiential dimension of Christian life.

I would now like to suggest a way out of our impasse. Could one avoid the dilemma of *event* or *dimension* by positing *a dimension with events and experiences* in it? I have now realized that is hardly credible to deny the event-character of the first occurrence of a particular charism. Who can forget the first time one was miraculously healed or saw someone else being healed? It is a milestone of the highest order. When a person breaks out in glossolalia or nervously delivers a first prophecy, it is a memorable *event*. On the level of experience, one may easily argue that such an event opened one up in a fresh way to the flow of the charismata and to life in the Spirit. It is only through the fullness of the experiences of the whole Christian community that one sees more clearly that although several may have an identical pattern of spiritual milestones or events, others may have a different sequence of experiences.

One can argue that both Pentecostals and Charismatics are *right*—Pentecostals because the experiential life in the Spirit usually starts with a dramatic and unusual *event,* Charismatics because one is thereby initiated into a whole new realm or *dimension* of openness to the supernatural in which one experiences God's grace more directly.

One can also argue that both Pentecostals and Charismatics are *wrong*—Pentecostals because the *event* that brings one into the flow of God's divine life and the empowering of Pentecost is not limited to *one* particular gift of the Spirit (i.e., tongues is not necessarily the "initial, physical evidence" of Spirit baptism but could very well be the most prevalent form of such evidence in this day and age). Similarly, Charismatics are wrong when they try to claim that there are no definitive events or experiences to the *dimension* of the Spirit. There may be differing levels of dramatic impact and emotional excitement, but life in the Spirit always affects the mind, the will, and the emotions. One could then legitimately use the metaphor of *Spirit baptism* for the release and functioning of the prototypical charisms of the Spirit (including prophetic word gifts, healings, and glossolalia) while acknowledging that every Christian believer's life has an experiential dimension to it. This dimension exhibits a combination of charisms and spiritual experiences or events that varies among individuals, some vivid and dramatic, some routine and repetitive, some quiet, some ecstatic. Our fault throughout the twentieth century has been the all-too-human tendency to universalize our own experience and then to attempt to regulate the unpredictable working of the Holy Spirit by prescribing the spiritual experiences and patterns of others. This faulty practice has led to our divisions and antagonisms. God works innovatively with each human at the point of his or her need and is infinitely creative in the variety of His dealings with us. We have already reflected on the way in which all of creation is charged with God's grandeur exhibiting myriad forms of diversity.

In summary then, let us embrace the events of our journey in the Spirit, the flowering of the charismata, without implementing the "law of tongues" (the phrase of Tom Smail). Let us acknowledge that every Christian is indeed potentially charismatic and should be encouraged to experience the Spirit vividly. As we have seen, the Spirit works *internally*, continually molding our character into conformity with Christ and bringing forth God's image in us relationally. The Spirit also works *externally* intermittently to enable and empower us to operate mightily in word and deed, evincing God's supernatural strength and love. This is the life in the Spirit, walking by faith and not by sight, a *dimension* that includes widely diverse experiences and *events*.

Growing Edge for the Future: The Word of Faith Movement

In our last section, we focus on the primary ecclesial bearer of the Spirit-awakening in the twenty-first century. I believe it is clear that constituent parts of *all* Three Waves should be bearers of the vision into the twenty-first century. The Classical Pentecostals have the most resources both intellectually and organizationally. They are in control of the major educational institutions. Their contribution will continue to be invaluable since they speak with a century of experience of life in the Spirit. The denominational Charismatic Renewal can also still play a role. They represent links to the non-Charismatic churches and the broader community. Their numbers have decreased significantly and this has lessened their influence. Many have now fallen into a new category that demographer David B. Barrett calls the post-Charismatics. Yet they have paved the way for the mainstreaming of the Spirit movements, and this process continues unabated. Cephas Omenyo of Ghana states (according to Allan Anderson, p. 279) that the Pentecostal experience is becoming "mainline" Christianity in Africa, "not merely in numbers but more importantly in spirituality, theology and practice." This phenomenon is repeated across the Majority World, with the movement growing most in Latin America, Korea, China, the Philippines, Indonesia, and sub-Saharan Africa. However, the cutting edge of this movement is no longer Classical Pentecostalism or the denominational Charismatic Renewal. *The momentum has shifted to the Independent Charismatic churches.*

Let us turn, then, to the role played by the Third Wave. The kingdom-oriented ministries, both the Restoration and Dominion movements, will continue to be a force, although they have also diminished in influence. The Empowered Evangelicals of the Vineyard movement continue to grow and make their contribution to the dialogue with mainstream evangelicals. *However, it is the contention of this researcher that the baton of global leadership has passed to the Word of Faith movement.* The mantle of leadership of the whole Pentecostal-Charismatic movement has fallen on these Faith ministries. I believe statistics will bear this out, although detailed information is still hard to obtain.

This stated position is remarkable in several respects. A mere twenty-five years ago it was this very sector of the Charismatic world that was being heralded as heretical and seen as proclaiming a "different" Gospel. Fortunately, that storm has died down. The overstated critique has been silenced, but a lingering doubt remains, especially outside the Pentecostal-Charismatic world. Word of Faith teaching and publications have matured, and the movement's continued growth and popularity worldwide has also given people food for thought. On a more personal, autobiographical level, I recall that while freshly inaugurated into the denominational Renewal in 1980 I was repeatedly warned in my travels against the "Copenhagen doctrine"—the reference I discovered was not to Denmark's capital, as I first thought, but rather to "the Copelands and the Hagins." In an early article on healing, I cautioned against the category of "demanding faith," but gradually I became convinced that there was a biblical basis for much that was being taught about the authority of the believer. In the heat of the fray and perhaps exacerbated by the unfamiliar and contentious tone of much of the argument, there were several examples of unbalanced teachings, extremism, and many overstated claims of healing. In 1994 in a Festschrift article for Rodman Williams, I ventured cautiously to defend a modified Word of Faith approach, using a definition of idealism gleaned from the writing of William De Arteaga's *Quenching the Spirit: Examining Centuries of Opposition to the Moving of the Holy Spirit*. The tension between realism and idealism will be discussed in more detail in the following paragraphs. It represents what I believe to be a pivotal contribution to Charismatic thinking.

Beyond Realism vs. Idealism

One of the most basic issues is our understanding of the universe itself. Centuries of Newtonian physics have conditioned us to consider the world from a realist vantage-point. It consists of hard and fast matter. It is the *object* investigated by the inquiring mind of the *subject*—the researcher. The Bible, however, has always viewed the world differently. It is the Lord's (Psalm 24:1). We are fearfully and wonderfully made in our mothers' wombs (Psalm 139:13,14). The heavens declare the glory of God (Psalm 19:1). The Jesuit poet Gerard Manley Hopkins captures this sense by declaring, "the earth is charged with the grandeur of God," and "there lives the dearest freshness deep down things." The Dutch philosopher, J.H. Diemer, spoke of the potential for the miraculous (potentie tot wonder) that was embedded in nature through creation. A miracle was not an action working against natural laws, but rather the unlocking of a potential in the created order for a different way of operating that scientists may not yet have discovered. The "New Physics" of Einstein, Heisenberg, and Bohr has started to uncover contingency, uncertainty, and complementarity in the functioning of the natural world. Quantum physics recognizes that light can behave as both particles and waves, and that the presence of an observer can change the results of scientific experiments. DeArteaga states that, "God intended the universe to be spiritual–from subatomic particles to archangels" (p. 157).

What we are really dealing with is the most basic polarity in all philosophical investigation: the (false) choice between realism and idealism that has haunted philosophy through the ages. DeArteaga recognized that this is the basic issue. He uses the definitions of Stanley Jaki, a Hungarian-born Benedictine scholar, to describe realism and idealism. *Realism* is the belief that matter exists completely independently of the mind, and *idealism* is the belief that the mind can influence matter.

The general definitions of these pivotal concepts are usually a little more wide-ranging. *Realism* is seen as the philosophical theory that reality is ontologically independent of our conceptual formulations: the external world has absolute existence prior to and separate from human consciousness. *Idealism* is the philosophical theory that reality is based on mind or ideas: the external world is ontologically dependent on our consciousness and perception. One may wish to tweak these descriptions a little, but they do express the basic difference.

It is noteworthy to see how the discipline of physics reflects these concepts. Newtonian physics posits the ontological independence of the material universe and the subject-object dichotomy of the researcher and the field of research. The new physics on the other hand is clearly more aligned to an idealist world where the researcher is not objectively isolated but relationally impacts what is being observed or studied.

It is not necessary to go into detail here concerning the pendulum swing in the history of philosophy between these two concepts. The conclusion I wish to draw from this is simply that the separation of realism and idealism into opposing camps reflects the loss of a biblical perspective. Contemporary German systematic theologian Eberhard Jüngel declares that *theology should never cease in its primary task of thinking through what it means to conceive of the world as the creation of God* (in his 1972 article"Die Welt als Möglichkeit und Wirklichkeit" in *Unterwegs zur Sache*, 220, 221.) In the true nature of this created order, we discover that both realism and idealism as independent ideologies are wrong simply because they have torn asunder what God meant to be one. God created matter and mind in a reciprocal relationship between the external and the internal. God created by speaking: Let there be . . . and there was! Jesus Christ is called the Word or Logos in the prologue to John's Gospel. To conceive of the world as God's creation is not to make reality dependent on human consciousness or ideas. Neither is it to declare that matter is ontologically independent and closed off in itself (like a space-time box). When we no longer see the world as God's creation, made ex nihilo (out of nothing), we inevitably fall into the polarity of mind and matter. This cleavage runs right through our understanding of reality. The Greeks distinguished form and matter (*morphē* and *hulē*). We divide our academic disciplines into the humanities and the natural sciences. We dualistically separate facts from values, laws of nature from human freedom.

Jüngel speaks of the world as possibility and actuality/ reality. He points out that, based on Aristotle, Western thought has largely given the primacy and priority to reality. Only the actual or real exists—the possibility is not yet. This is contrary to the biblical perspective. God justifies sinners, not based on their works of righteousness in the real world, but by declaration He makes them what they are not—just and redeemed. The dead are raised—Jesus triumphs over death. Paul speaks of God, "who gives life to the dead and calls into being that which does not exist" (Rom 4:17).

The Christian doctrine of creation sees the world not as *nature*—the material universe, but as *creation*, the created order that is charged with the grandeur of God. God's creation does not consist of two distinct realms, as Thomas Aquinas taught, Nature and Grace, but rather of "graced nature." Life in the Spirit is an expectant journey in which reality is not closed but open. Words of faith can influence circumstances; prayer can heal the sick. We walk by faith and not by sight (2 Cor 5:7). Faith is the assurance of things hoped for, the conviction of things not seen (Heb 11:1). We look not at the things which are seen, but at the things which are not seen, for the things which are seen are temporal, but the things which are not seen are eternal (2 Cor 4:18). Martin Luther defined faith similarly to these insights: "the nature of faith is to see that which you do not see, and not to see that which you do see."

A remarkably clear example of this "openness" of reality is found in Matthew 14, when the apostle Peter walks on the water of the Sea of Galilee. This event is also discussed by DeArteaga. It is only Matthew's Gospel that includes the episode of Peter's abortive attempt. The miracle of Jesus' walking on the water has been difficult to interpret in churches where modernist naturalism holds sway. In the realist tradition, science protests that the specific gravity of a human body is higher than that of water so sinking is inevitable. Demythologizing interpretations explain that Jewish thought sees the sea as the domain of chaos and evil, so the tale of Jesus walking on the water is merely saying metaphorically that He has authority over this realm. As previously cited, Scottish New Testament exegete William Barclay suggests a naturalist solution—perhaps there was a sand bank (or sand bar) that Jesus knew of and showed to Peter, who, in his fear, stepped off it and then had to be saved. Few evangelicals would take these "ingenious" theories seriously.

The narrative of Peter on and in the water illustrates the *reciprocity* of what we have come to call the real and the possible. Peter and the disciples in the boat encounter the rather terrifying situation of what they first thought was a ghost walking on the sea. Jesus identifies Himself and tells them not to be afraid. Peter responds with daring: "Lord, if it is You, command me to come to You on the water." Jesus speaks the word, and Peter walks on the water toward Jesus. *Matter responds to the divine word, but the human faith of Peter is also involved.* When Peter allows the visible phenomena of the wind and waves to dominate his thinking (instead of the divine word), he begins to sink. God's sovereign will and majestic control is above our comprehension. It incorporates a role for human response and faith (or the lack thereof) that is so significant that Peter's failing faith invalidates the miracle, and he actually begins to sink! We walk by faith and not by sight. There is an element of truth to realism and to idealism, but the truth really lies in understanding the world as God's creation that is not captive to either view.

Over against idealism, the chair that we do not see is really there, independent of our consciousness or perception. Over against realism, reality is more than what meets the eye. Possibilities are unlocked with the power of faith in the Lord who made and sustains the universe. Realism on its own degenerates into cessationism and then into materialism and naturalism that deny the supernatural and ultimately the soul and the existence of God. Idealism on its own degenerates into sorcery, witchcraft, and magic, in which reality is manipulated by incantations, orchestrated ultimately by the realm of the occult and the demonic. The task remains for us to conceive of the world as God's wondrous creation, within which the material and the spiritual can interact; but it is not the human mind or spirit but faith in the Creator's word of power (Heb 1:3) that opens up reality to the miraculous. Thus viewed, creation is open to that which is new. Jüngel actually argues for the priority of possibility over reality. De Arteaga speaks of a moderate idealism or faith idealism. Personally, I prefer not to choose either of the two poles but rather attempt to conceive of reality as God's creation. One could have called this creationism, but that term is already taken for debates about evolution and the age of the earth. In that context, creationism is used to designate the Young Earth perspective. Perhaps one could coin the term *creationality* to refer to this openness of the world, to the reciprocity of mind and matter "sub speciae aeternitatis" (from the perspective of eternity).

This creationality also aligns with a pneumatology that fully incorporates both the internal and external aspects of the Spirit's functional work. The long-term indwelling and sanctifying work of the Spirit expressed in the fruit of the Spirit is dynamically interdependent with the episodic and intermittent work of gifted empowerment. The powerful enablement is not a prized possession of the individual that works virtually automatically. Within this framework, there is no room for a wooden teaching that "guarantees" access to the supernatural on the basis of a single occurrence of a single charism. I believe that this dynamically open view of reality, beyond realism and idealism, rightly conceives of the world as God's creation, charged with His grandeur, and fits precisely that dimension of the Word of Faith teaching that we know as the authority of the believer.

When viewing contemporary culture, especially literature and film, it is telling to note the popularity of science fiction and fantasy literature. Where persons deny the genuinely supernatural and manifestations of the Spirit, the ready counterfeit will fill the ensuing vacuum. The human spirit rebels inwardly against the impoverishment of only a factual and cerebral realism. This fact leads us to consider anew the doctrinal innovations of the leading grouping of the Third Wave.

Major Word of Faith Themes

The Word of Faith (or Rhema) teaching has already been discussed above in the last part of chapter 6, which focused especially on E. W. Kenyon and Kenneth E. Hagin. That part analyzed three major doctrines briefly: confession, prosperity, and healing as a right. The summary statement of Nico Horn (given above, p. 148) may now once again serve as a typical expression of how the Faith movement has been portrayed. The pivotal doctrinal issue is how faith is understood. Horn gives the following description of the Word of Faith movement's concept of faith as

> a special emphasis on faith as a mechanism at the disposal of the believer to make him or her victorious; the belief that positive confession creates faith, and, linked with faith, changes circumstances; the belief that everyone who has faith can receive either healing from sickness or eternal health; and the belief that financial prosperity is, like healing, provided for in the atonement.

In fact this probably represents the way that many outsiders still view the Word of Faith distinctives. Horn is speaking as a Classical Pentecostal—who at the time of writing was radicalized by the erstwhile anti-apartheid struggle in South Africa—and may have considered the Word of Faith perspective as escapist or subtly aligned with the political status quo conservatism of white supremacy in the Southern African context.

In 2001 Dr. Paul L. King completed his impressive doctoral study on nineteenth- and twentieth-century "Faith Theologies," with Dr. Jacques Theron of the University of South Africa and me as co-promoters. This research was later published by Word & Spirit Press in 2008 as *Only Believe: Examining the Origins and Development of Classic and Contemporary Word of Faith Theologies.* In this study, King points out with the precision of a scholar versed in doctrinal history that the contemporary Word of Faith movements stands in remarkable continuity with highly esteemed, classical spiritual writers of the nineteenth century, such as Andrew Murray, E. M. Bounds, A. J. Gordon, A. B. Simpson, R. A. Torrey, George Müller, and Charles Spurgeon. The 1980s and 90s had spawned a whole collection of warnings about the cultic and heretical nature of the Faith movement: for example, *Seduction of Christianity* (1985) by Dave Hunt and T. A. McMahon, and Hank Hanegraaff's *Christianity in Crisis* (1993). With his Christian and Missionary Alliance background,

King was well situated to recognize that these are extreme overreactions, lacking in balance. Several of the early Alliance teachers who did not align themselves with Pentecostalism, such as F. F. Bosworth and John A. MacMillan, in fact taught the same doctrines. The teaching on the authority of the believer, which lies behind positive confession, is the seminal contribution of MacMillan. This doctrinal development is perhaps the most characteristic aspect of the Word of Faith movement.

King is aware that contemporary Faith teachers have sometimes not been careful and balanced in their formulations. Consequently, he concedes some validity to the objections leveled against them. He underscores some general hermeneutical principles, including these: first, the abuse of something does not preclude or invalidate its proper us (abusus non tollit usus); and second, the truth is elliptical. This statement claims that there are often two focal points (rather than one) to a doctrine, such as we see in the geometric figure of an ellipse. The creative tension between them must be maintained. King gives as an apt example God's sovereignty and human freedom.

The truth is that the formulations of Word of Faith tenets have matured slowly but steadily. The movement decided not to engage in public debate or the self-defense and damage control that characterize so much of secular confrontations. The cries of heresy were ignored, but silent self-correction ensued. In order to illustrate a) the biblical validity of strong faith teaching, b) the problems caused by overemphasis, c) the process of self-correction, and d) the continued need for balance, the following paragraphs will deal with four pivotal Word of Faith teachings. This discussion will also illustrate how it is appropriate, in my opinion, that the mantle of leadership—especially internationally—has fallen on the Word of Faith movement to carry the awakening of the Spirit movements into the twenty-first century. Historical continuity shown through the research of Paul King reveals that the balanced form of these teachings aligns nicely with some of the best evangelical and devotional writers of the nineteenth and twentieth centuries.

With the foregoing understanding of the world as God's creation, we now proceed to look at these foundational issues. (For a more detailed discussion, Paul King's book *Only Believe* is an excellent resource.) Here *four major themes* will be addressed: 1. the Believer's Inheritance; 2. the Authority of the Believer; 3. Positive Confession; and 4. Prosperity.

As King repeatedly points, out the difference between contemporary Word of Faith teachers and the classic evangelical writers of the nineteenth and twentieth centuries is mostly a matter of degree and, I may add, sometimes of common sense and ethical sensitivity. The overstated critiques that cry "heresy!" are out of line. There is also clear evidence that the Word of Faith movement is in the process of moving away from extreme presentations itself.

1. Claiming the Believer's Inheritance

First, then, *claiming the inheritance of the believer*. Paul refers to believers as being heirs of God and fellow-heirs with Christ (Rom 8:16–17). Galatians 3 argues that Christ has redeemed us from the curse of the Law so that the blessing of Abraham might come to the Gentiles (vv. 13–14). Some contemporary faith teachers go to extremes supposing that one may receive *all* of our inheritance now and that this is a matter of legal, almost automatic right, rather than flowing from a relationship with God our Father. The misuse of this concept should not preclude its legitimate application.

Writers such as Andrew Murray and Charles Spurgeon have similar teachings but are careful to express it within an ethical framework of abiding in Christ. They point out the spiritual content of our inheritance without denying material blessings as well. They regard physical blessings as enabling us to supply the needs of evangelism and ministries of mercy. Theologically, the ultimate issue is a matter of extent and balance.

The eschatology of the New Testament is stamped by the creative tension between what has come to be called the *already* and the *not yet* (discussed in chapter 6). We live in this tension, between the first and the second comings of Christ. We already experience many of God's blessings—salvation, fellowship, forgiveness, healing, guidance, prophecy, empowerment—the list goes on, but we do not yet have all the blessings we will experience on the new earth: perfect resurrected bodies, freedom from death, life without sin, absolute victory, etc. The danger exists that we may advocate an over-realized eschatology in which there is no creative tension left between the already and the not yet of the coming of God's kingdom. Yet this tension between already and not yet should not prevent believers from claiming their inheritance. After some initial excesses, I believe most contemporary faith teachers are claiming the promises of God in a balanced way. A good illustration is the ministry of Joyce Meyer.

2. The Authority of the Believer

Second, we come to the *authority of the believer*. This biblical teaching correlates very clearly with the understanding of the world as God's creation developed above. By exercising our God-given authority, life can be transformed and brought more into accordance with God's purpose. The miraculous dimension of reality can be unlocked and the desires of the evil one thwarted through the power of Christ. Five times in the letter to the Ephesians the unusual expression "in the heavenly places" occurs. We are described as currently seated there with Christ. We share in His exaltation and in every spiritual blessing. This authority enables us to do battle and reign through our union with the ascended Lord in the heavenly realm. This teaching has long been neglected and eclipsed by an almost defeatist attitude of believers considered to be nothing but miserable, unworthy sinners. Through the power of the Spirit, we can and are expected to advance in sanctification and grow in grace. We need to reign over the desires of the flesh and manifest our authority as children of the Most High God. Luke 10:19 speaks of authority to tread on serpents and wield influence over the power of the enemy.

In this area too, there have been extremes that are now being avoided. One may find a sound balance, for example, at the Victory Christian Centers in Tulsa and in Palm Springs. Some faith teachers initially even stated that believers are now in control, not God, and that He cannot do anything on earth unless we allow it. This clearly is presumptuous. As alluded to above, this may flow from an unfortunate mistranslation of Isaiah 45:11, which reads in some older translations, "Concerning the work of My hands command ye Me." More recent translations bring out the irony of the context with translations such as, "Do you give me orders about the work of My hands?" (NIV) or "Will you command Me concerning the work of My hands?" (NRSV). The classic faith teachers accepted the older translation but expressed it ever so cautiously. John MacMillan, who wrote the first major exposition on the authority of the believer, speaks of God's delight in working together with us. Surprisingly, Paul King still seems to favor the older translation but concludes that in order to avoid misunderstanding it may be better *not* to use the expression of "commanding God" today!

MacMillan maintains that the authority of the believer is a *delegated* authority, and it would be wise for contemporary Word of Faith teachers to underscore this insight. We command what God has already commanded. Other issues of debate regarding the believer's authority are the correct interpretation of binding and loosing (Matt 16:19 and 18:18) and the terminology "territorial" spirits. The latter has been discussed under Empowered Evangelicals in chapter 6. Although there are valid concerns when this teaching is expressed as if a human being has sovereignty over God, it is a very important biblical teaching. The exercising of the believer's authority by the Welsh intercessor Rees Howells during the Second World War is a classic example and a profound testimony to this teaching.

3. Positive Confession

The third topic is the matter of *Positive Confession*. Again we are faced with the danger of the proverbial baby that should not be thrown out with the bathwater. The Word of Faith movement has come into strong criticism on this score. Once again, people have been inclined, in the blush of the new discovery of a truth long neglected, to let the pendulum swing too far. There is much to commend a positive mental attitude. Philippians 4:8 exhorts us to let our minds dwell on that which is true, right, pure, lovely, excellent, and praiseworthy. Believers engage demonic forces in the battle for the mind. Proverbs 18:21 declares that life and death are in the power of the tongue, and James 3 warns us of the destructive power of the tongue. Mark 11:23–24, the reference to mountain-moving faith, is the pivotal scripture in this regard. Verse 24 reads in the NIV, "Therefore I tell you, whatever you ask for in prayer, believe that you have received it, and it will be yours." This scripture has played a significant role in the teachings and healing of prominent Word of Faith advocates. It is sometimes expressed as, *"You can have what you say."* King uncovers similar insights among Puritans, Pietists, and Keswick teachers, and even Baptists such as Spurgeon and F.B. Meyer. A. B. Simpson also uses the popular scripture Romans 4:17, "calling things that are not as though they are" and applies it to our exercise of faith. In the context, it is important to note that it is *God* who is doing this. The primary reference is to the miraculous birth of Isaac from his aged parents but also to the raising of Christ from the dead (vv. 24–25).

The teaching of positive confession has been very contentious. Sometimes the very sensible caution not to speak negatively or to dwell on failure can lead to a legalism that refuses to acknowledge reality. There are indeed situations where God may require of us to place our trust in Him and not express any negativity, but this caution needs to be tempered by common sense.

Kenneth Hagin Jr., in his book *Another Look at Faith* (1996), provides a helpful *reproof* of unbalanced positions. He gives examples of people who are so afraid of negative confession that, in the end, they are simply lying. This correction coming from the son of the acknowledged founder of the Word of Faith movement underscores the significance of avoiding extremes. Critics were quick to judge this teaching and derisively call it the "Name it and claim it" formula of faith. This superficial characterization is applied not only to positive confession but also to prosperity teaching, the fourth of the distinctive Word of Faith teachings we are examining.

4. Prosperity

The "Prosperity Gospel" has been at the forefront of criticism against the Word of Faith movement, but I would argue that it is also a teaching that has a very strong biblical base. It all depends how one defines and expresses "prosperity." The biblical concept *salvation* is broad in its scope. It certainly includes a physical aspect, such as the healing of the body. The Hebrew and Greek words are encompassing. God saves His people from the work of the evil one. This salvation includes spiritual, material, and physical dimensions. Salvation can be deliverance from our enemies and oppressors. The blessed man in the Old Testament sits under his own vine and fig tree and enjoys their produce. He will see his children's children. Psalm 144:12–15 is typical. It refers to the blessing of children, to garners full of every kind of produce, to flocks bearing thousands of offspring, and to cattle producing offspring without blemish or loss. The Lord satisfies our years with good things (Ps 103:5). The list goes on.

In an early article in which he compares the soteriologies of Liberation and Pentecostal theologies, Croatian-born Yale theologian Miroslav Volf shows that these two "strange bedfellows" both emphasize the material dimensions of salvation. In contrast to this emphasis, Volf develops the argument that it is the heritage of classical Protestantism, especially in its Lutheran form, which rather focuses on the "inner man" and the spiritual blessing of the forgiveness of sins. The sole purpose of Jesus' miracles was seen as encouraging faith. Human well-being was not seen as an aspect of salvation itself. This view results in a thoroughgoing spiritualization of the Nazareth manifesto found in Luke 4:18–19. This view would limit the release of captives to those caught up in prisons of addiction and sin; recovery of sight only to those spiritually blind; liberation only to those oppressed by the devil.

While redemption may begin by restoring the relationship between God and human beings, to focus on this core of redemption to the exclusion of its material aspects does violence to the rich heritage of Scripture. Philippians 4:19 says simply, "But my God shall supply all your need according to His riches in glory by Christ Jesus." In this sense, the Church was ripe for the recovery of the dimension of God's blessing of prosperity.

Oral Roberts, who died at the age of 91 (Dec. 15, 2009), is known for his discovery of this insight from Third John verse 2, "Beloved, I pray that in all respects you may prosper and be in good health, just as your soul prospers." Assemblies of God New Testament scholar Gordon Fee cautions that this is more of a salutation than a promise, but nevertheless the juxtaposition of prosperity and health with the blessings of the soul is instructive. To those caught in the throes of poverty, this is indeed liberating. God cares not only about our rescue from sin but also about our bodies and concrete living.

The fact that healing was seen as being "in the atonement" illustrates the inherent holism of Pentecostal soteriology. Unfortunately, that term originally presupposed the rejection of medical means. The material part of the gospel is also evident from the last line of the Nazareth manifesto that is often ignored. Jesus comes to announce the year of Jubilee—the year of God's material favor. The year of Jubilee, every fifty years, was a time of debt cancellation and economic restoration when the land, the major source of wealth in an agricultural society, was returned to its original owners.

Unfortunately, in the heady days of recovering the biblical truth that God desires to bless us materially, several preachers and teachers went overboard. Greed and selfishness entered in.

Charles Farah exposes those who interpreted God's desire that we should prosper in terms of owning Cadillacs, jewelry, furs, etc., in his book *Faith or Presumption: From the Pinnacle of the Temple*. Expressions like "Children of the Lord" and "Heirs of the Most High God" degenerate into "King's Kids" who live like rock stars or spoiled royalty. A most unfortunate book title from this era reads, *How to Write Your Own Ticket with God*. Paul King illustrates that devotional writers of the nineteenth century acknowledged the value of material wealth but also its hazard—forgetting God. George Müller considered the *motive* for wanting to prosper crucial. The apostle Paul states in Philippians 4 that he has learned to be content in whatever circumstances he is in. He knew how to live in prosperity *and* with humble means. Above all, the Scriptures exhort us to generosity. Prosperity should be defined as having your needs met and being able to bless the poor with your surplus.

The word *prosperity* has in fact become thoroughly discredited. In the future, people may prefer to speak of a holistic gospel. The prosperity teaching has had a major influence internationally. In Latin America, it has affected most churches, even Roman Catholicism. It is expressed in Brazil through the influential Universal Church of God. The same can be said of Africa south of the Sahara. Some lapse into hype and overstatement, but gradually a more balanced approach is developing. Nigeria, South Africa, and Kenya have been deeply influenced by prosperity teaching. Trinity Broadcasting Network from Santa Ana, California, and Europe's God TV are the largest disseminators of this message. Many who cannot afford theological seminaries by default receive their religious training through television.

Openness to the supernatural and the access to power through the Holy Spirit are especially attractive in a continent with a long tradition of animist beliefs. There is also a yearning for hope. Africans are very sensitive to divine guidance through dreams. Sometimes up to 50% of converts from traditional African religions to Christianity credit dreams with their conversion. The struggle against extremism has not yet been won globally. While churches that preach a superficial gospel that equates biblical prosperity with luxury and ostentatious life styles grow rapidly, churches that make less extravagant claims outlast them.

There is also evidence that leaders become more balanced over time. For example, Kenneth E. Hagin, who is generally considered to be the Father of the Word of Faith movement, published such a book in 2000 titled *The Midas Touch: a Balanced Approach to Biblical Prosperity.* In this work, he strongly rejects the extremes to which some of his followers have taken his teachings. This publication illustrates the move toward self-correction and balance that has been going on within the faith movement. After some 65 years of ministry, Hagin maintained that in biblical teaching there is a main road of truth between ditches of error on either side of the road. We are to esteem spiritual things more than earthly things and to keep our motives pure. Hagin writes, "In God's economy, prosperity is the means to an end—world evangelism."

Hagin refers interestingly to Gordon Lindsay, founder of Christ for the Nations Institute in Dallas, who was involved in the healing revival of the mid-twentieth century and who alluded to the Catholic practice of venerating holy relics, bones of saints, etc. Lindsay found similar gimmicks among preachers of his day: blessed sawdust on which an angel is supposed to have walked, bottled demons, magic pictures, etc. Hagin approvingly quotes a fellow minister who said, "Being focused on what we receive as a result of our giving corrupts the very attitude of our giving. . . . ." Hagin also denies that the hundredfold return principle refers to financial giving. He credits a revelation from God to noticing that Mark 10 is referring to Christian service and the parable of the sower referring to the disseminating of God's Word. In this example Hagin actually admits his own mistake in previously applying this to financial returns.

This admission further illustrates how the Word of Faith movement is growing into balance. Instead of condemning all prosperity teaching, those who threw the first stones should applaud this more balanced and mature approach, which includes self-correction. Personally, I would prefer to abandon the term "prosperity" and rather speak of the encompassing blessing of God that includes healing, restoration, forgiveness of sins, as well as relational and material blessings.

Perhaps a way forward in the prosperity debate would be to introduce new terminology. I propose that we distinguish between *God's comprehensive blessing* and what has come to be termed the Prosperity Gospel.

Comprehensive blessing would be God's meeting the need of fallen human beings through the atoning death of Christ on the Cross. The Son of God has appeared to defeat the works of the devil (1 John 3:8). This provision is encompassing: rebirth and new life in Christ, forgiveness of sin, sanctification, physical healing, emotional well being, deliverance from the demonic, as well as God's favor in material blessings. The Old Testament calls this holistic vision "shalom," or peace. To the references given above, one can add scriptures such as Deuteronomy 28:1–14, where we find a long list of blessings to those who obey the Lord and live within His covenant of grace. The favor of God includes having ample offspring, increase of livestock, food, protection, good harvests, etc. Verse 11 states, "The Lord will make you abound in prosperity." This is the abundant life of John 10:10, and in Luke 6:38 we are promised, "Give, and it shall be given unto you; good measure, pressed down, and shaken together and running over. . . ." When Paul speaks of God supplying "all your need" in Philippians 4:19, he is addressing a congregation that has responded to Paul's own need in a generous and sacrificial manner.

Scripture gives these prayers and promises within the context of covenantal faithfulness. They address "needs" rather than "wants," and they admonish us to be givers and to help others generously. God's blessings are lavish and concrete and touch every aspect of our lives. The fact that some have misused these scriptures should never prevent us from teaching on them.

Problems start occurring when one approaches this biblical theme with a mindset of guarantees and rational calculation. When one posits a direct and automatic correlation between faith and wealth, one has strayed from comprehensive blessing to the counterfeit, the *Prosperity Gospel*.

This perspective is not new or unique. In the seventeenth and eighteenth centuries, some Puritan believers tried to find "evidence" for their eternal election, proving to others God's blessing on them by their prosperity. In this practical syllogism, they attempted to argue back from their current state of material wealth, bolstered by the proverbial Protestant work ethic, to illustrate that God's favor rested on them and that, therefore, they must be among the number of God's chosen ones. The faulty reasoning behind this view is not hard to pinpoint. Material wealth may result from God's blessing. It may also come from inheritance, exploitation, or a life of crime. God shows His favor in diverse ways. Many recognize Mother Teresa of Calcutta as a woman of exceptional spiritual devotion and love but certainly did not consider her financially prosperous!

We encounter a similar mindset today when Christians make facile judgments about lack of faith being the cause of lack of healing. Some extremists have even suggested that a fatal accident of a child in a plane crash would not have occurred if the head of the household had been faithful in praying for those under his "covering." Such harsh and erroneous judgments have wounded many.

In their recent book *When Helping Hurts,* Steve Corbett and Brian Fikkert claim that "the health and wealth gospel" teaches that "God rewards increasing levels of faith with greater amounts of wealth" (p. 69). I find this statement surprising. I have to say that I have never heard a preacher put it that way, and I suspect that they are fulminating against a bit of a straw man. Nevertheless, such a facile correlation between faith and wealth is distasteful, ludicrous, and unbiblical. That would indeed reduce the gospel to a formula for greed and materialism.

The general public holds a widespread prejudice against the so-called Prosperity Gospel. Many claim that such preachers and most TV evangelists are "just after your money" and that they hoodwink gullible people to support them, while misappropriating the funds to enable their jet-setting and luxurious lifestyles. Obviously, it has become all too easy to demonize those with whom we disagree in our public discourse! The above perception is inaccurate and unbalanced, but those cases to which it does apply are a stumbling block and grievous scandal within Christian ministry. I believe that the process of self-correction of extremes and growth in balance in the Word of Faith movement should make such excesses rare.

However, the tendency for believers to seek to avoid suffering and selfishly think of our own desires first is not rare at all. Compassion for the poor is a biblical mandate to which we need to be exhorted. The very nature of *agape* love denotes sacrifice on behalf of others. At the April 2010 Empowered 21 Global Congress on the Holy Spirit in Tulsa, Oklahoma, the new president of Oral Roberts University, Dr. Mark Rutland, spoke on the nature of *power* in the Full Gospel movement. He challenged us by speaking of the power to serve, to love when we are hated, the power to give rather than to get— even the power to become martyrs. This type of Pentecostal power will provide a powerful antidote against the Prosperity Gospel. We need to identify with the power of both the Cross and the Resurrection but not allow the controversy to mute our proclamation of God's holistic salvation and comprehensive blessing.

Conclusion

In conclusion, I present a synopsis of this chapter. The brief overview of the last twenty years revealed a lack of centralized vision and focus in the Spirit movements of the contemporary scene. These need leaders with discerning minds and courage. Many have been discouraged by the preponderance of moral lapses "in high places." The younger generation desires leaders who can be reliable spiritual role models. One of the most encouraging signs, however, is the passion for contemporary Christian worship, its influence on the youth, and its spreading beyond the traditionally charismatic circles. As worshipers advance to the very throne of heaven, experiencing liminality at the threshold where Jesus Christ Himself in His human nature leads the heavenly throng as worship leader in the sanctuary (Heb 8:1, 2), they understand the reality that lies at the heart of the next two sections of this chapter. Increasingly, our churches need the authentic demonstration and impartation of the charisms of the Spirit and of valid supernatural experience that leads to growth in holiness and change in lifestyle.

Revisiting Spirit Baptism

The doctrine of Spirit baptism is revisited in the second part of this chapter. Much of the current discourse focuses on revising the Classical Pentecostal teaching on glossolalia as the "initial physical evidence of baptism in the Holy Spirit." Strong voices, such as Frank Macchia, Steve Land, and Gordon Anderson, to name but a few, advocate flexibility from *within* the Pentecostal tradition. With the help of Norbert Baumert, I have come to a more nuanced position myself. I no longer simply equate Spirit baptism with the experiential dimension of the Christian life per se, but recognize it as an entrance, among many, to "life in the Spirit" that incorporates an open view of reality as God's creation and that is equally open to all charisms of the Spirit and to a variety of spiritual and supernatural experiences, revelations, and direction. This disposition, or *attitude of faith,* is deeply grounded in a biblical understanding of the nature of reality itself—life before the face of God—which the Protestant Reformers called living "coram Deo." South African philosopher H.W. Rossouw used the terminology "the salvific situation of faith coram Deo" (Afrikaans: die religieuse heilsituasie coram Deo). Rather than a theology of subsequent stages, I develop a tripartite pneumatology incorporating a foundational, teleological, and culminating understanding of the work of the Third Person of the Trinity. This understanding refers respectively to the Spirit as the Agent of the new birth (ontological), as the indwelling and gradually sanctifying Spirit, and as the transforming Spirit whose work culminates in believers through episodic charismatic empowerment and enabling (functional). These latter two more functional aspects of the Spirit's work correlate with what some of the classic devotional writers of the nineteenth and twentieth centuries have termed the *internal* and *external* work of the Spirit. Finally, I suggested a way to combine both of the aspects *event* and *dimension* in an understanding of Spirit baptism.

The Word of Faith: Leading Twenty-first-century Spirit Movements

The last section of this chapter concludes that the *Word of Faith* movement has stepped into the role of the major carrier of the Holy Spirit renewal movements of the twenty-first century. Practical and historical factors are involved here, such as the growth and ebb and flow of various streams of the whole movement and the role of leadership. However, it is theologically appropriate that this stream within contemporary Spirit movements will lead these movements because it is founded on this dynamic understanding of active faith as its doctrinal distinctive. I attempt to show that this perspective has sound biblical roots and is philosophically grounded in an understanding of reality that avoids the perennial polarity of realism and idealism that lies at the very heart of all theoretical thought.

The argumentation leads to this conclusion by probing the pivotal research of Paul King in *Only Believe*. He has shown that the four vintage teachings of the Word of Faith movement (stripped of extreme applications and imbalanced deductions)—namely, claiming the inheritance, exercising the authority, confessing positively, and teaching prosperity (God's encompassing blessing)—are not "strange fire" or aberrations but dimensions of a biblical and historical faith that can be verified in Scripture as well as in church history, especially in the classic faith authors of the nineteenth and twentieth centuries. King shows us that the problems that have occurred in the recent past result from over-emphasis and lack of balance. Through an admirable process of maturing and self-correction, the movement has eliminated most of the difficulties. Public perception of this, as one may expect, has lagged behind, and in theological circles, much has also gone unnoticed. This study concludes, therefore, that the mantle of leadership of the Spirit movements in the twenty-first century, especially globally, rests on a revitalized Word of Faith movement. May its leaders and members rise to the occasion through God's grace, transforming much of the body of Christ through vibrant and sound faith and preparing the Bride for the Coming King, together with the Church universal.

Select Bibliography

Anderson, Allan. *An Introduction to Pentecostalism*. Cambridge, United Kingdom: Cambridge University Press, 2004.

Anderson, Gordon L. "Baptism in the Holy Spirit, Initial Evidence, and a New Model." *Enrichment Journal* (2005:01): 1–10.

Arnold, Clinton E. *3 Crucial Questions about Spiritual Warfare*. Grand Rapids, MI: Baker, 1997.

Badcock, Gary D. *Light of Truth & Fire of Love: A Theology of the Holy Spirit*. Grand Rapids MI: Eerdmans, 1997.

Barron, Bruce. *Heaven on Earth: The Social & Political Agendas of Dominion Theology*. Grand Rapids, MI: Zondervan, 1992.

———. *The Health and Wealth Gospel: What's Going on Today in a Movement that Has Shaped the Faith of Millions*. Downers Grove, IL: InterVarsity, 1987.

Bartleman, Frank. *Azusa Street: The Roots of Modern-day Pentecost*. Plainfield, NJ: Logos International, 1980.

Batten, Jim. "The Two Aspects of the Spirit in the New Testament: A Response to Archie Hui." *Affirmation & Critique* (10:2, Oct. 2005): 103–109.

Baumert, Norbert. *Charisma-Taufe-Geisttaufe: Normativität und Persönliche Berufung*. Würzburg: Echter, 2001.

Bloesch, Donald G. *The Holy Spirit: Works & Gifts*. Downers Grove, IL: InterVarsity, 2000.

Blue, Ken. *Authority to Heal*. Downers Grove, IL: InterVarsity, 1987.

Brand, Chad Owen (Ed.) *Perspectives on Spirit Baptism: Five Views*. Nashville, Tennessee: Broadman & Holman, 2004.

Bruner, Fredrick Dale. *A Theology of the Holy Spirit: The Pentecostal Experience and the New Testament Witness.* Grand Rapids, MI: Eerdmans, 1980.

Burgess, Stanley M. and McGee, Gary B. (Ed.) *Dictionary of Pentecostal and Charismatic Movements.* Grand Rapids, MI: Regency Reference Library, 1988.

Burgess, Stanley M. (Ed). *The New International Dictionary of Pentecostal and Charismatic Movements.* Grand Rapids, MI: Zondervan, 2002.

Cole, Graham A. *He Who Gives Life: The Doctrine of the Holy Spirit.* Wheaton, IL: Crossway, 2007.

Congar, Yves. *I Believe in the Holy Spirit: The Experience of the Spirit* (Volume I). New York, NY: Seabury, 1983.

————.*I Believe in the Holy Spirit: Lord Giver of Life* (Volume II). New York, NY: Seabury, 1983.

————. *I Believe in the Holy Spirit: The River of Life Flows in the East and in the West* (Volume III). New York, NY: Seabury, 1983.

Corbett, Steve and Brian Fikkert. *When Helping Hurts: How to Alleviate Poverty without Hurting the Poor . . . and Yourself.* Chicago: Moody, 2009.

Dayton, Donald W. *Theological Roots of Pentecostalism.* Grand Rapids, MI: Francis Asbury, 1987.

DeArteaga, William. *Quenching the Spirit: Discover the Real Spirit behind the Charismatic Controversy.* (Second Edition) Lake Mary, FL: Creation House, Second Edition, 1996.

Deere, Jack. *Surprised by the Power of the Spirit: A Former Dallas Seminary Professor Discovers that God Speaks & Heals Today.* Grand Rapids, MI: Zondervan Publishing House, 1993.

Dorries, David W. *Spirit-Filled Christology: Merging Theology and Power.* San Diego, CA: Aventine Press, 2006.

Dunn, James D.G. *Baptism in the Holy Spirit.* London: SCM Press, 1970.

Eisenlöffel, Ludwig. *. . . bis alle eins werden: Siebzig Jahre Berliner Erklärung und ihre Folgen.* Erzhausen: Leuchter, 1979.

Ervin, Howard M. *Conversion-Initiation and the Baptism in the Holy Spirit.* Peabody, MA: Hendrickson, 1984.

————. *Healing: Sign of the Kingdom.* Peabody, MA: Hendrickson, 2002.

Farah, Charles. *From the Pinnacle of the Temple: Faith or Presumption?* Plainfield, N.J: Logos International, 1979.

Faupel, D. William. *The Everlasting Gospel: The Significance of Eschatology the Development of Pentecostal Thought.* Sheffield, England: Sheffield Academic Press, 1996.

Foster, K. Neill and King, Paul L. *Binding & Loosing: Exercising Authority over the Dark Powers.* Camp Hill PA: Christian Publications, 1998.

Greig, Gary, Packer, J.I., and Kevin N. Springer, eds. *The Kingdom and the Power: Are Healing and the Spiritual Gifts Used by Jesus and the Early Church Meant for the Church Today? A Biblical Look at How to Bring the Gospel to the World with Power.* Ventura, CA: Regal Books, 1993.

Grossmann, Siegfried. *Charisma: The Gifts of the Spirit.* Wheaton, IL: Key Publishers, 1971.

―――. *There Are Other Gifts than Tongues.* Wheaton, IL: Tyndale House Publishers, 1973.

Grudem, Wayne A. (Ed.). *Are Miraculous Gifts for Today? Four Views.* Grand Rapids, MI: Zondervan, 1996.

Hagin, Kenneth E. *The Midas Touch: A Balanced Approach to Biblical Prosperity.* Tulsa, OK: Faith Library Publications, 2000.

Hagin, Kenneth Jr. *Another Look at Faith.* Tulsa, OK: Faith Library Publications, 1996.

Hamilton, James M. *God's Indwelling Presence: The Holy Spirit in the Old & New Testaments.* Nashville, TN: B&H Publishing Group, 2006.

Hanegraaff, Hank. *Christianity in Crisis.* Eugene, OR: Harvest House, 1993.

Harrell, David Edwin. *All Things Are Possible: The Healing and Charismatic Revivals in Modern America.* Bloomington: Indiana University Press, 1975.

Hart, Larry. "Spirit Baptism: A Dimensional Charismatic Perspective." In *Perspectives on Spirit Baptism: Five Views.* (Ed. by C. O. Brand) Nashville, TN: Broadman & Holman, 2004.

Hayford, Jack. *The Beauty of Spiritual Language: My Journey toward the Heart of God.* Dallas, TX: Word, 1992.

Hayford, Jack W. & Moore, S. David. *The Charismatic Century: The Enduring Impact of the Azusa Street Revival.* New York, NY: Warner Faith, 2006.

Hoffman, Bengt R. *Luther and the Mystics; A Re-examination of Luther's Spiritual Experience and his Relationship to the Mystics.* Minneapolis, MN: Augsburg, 1976.

Hoffman, Pavel. *The Ontological-Functional Work of the Spirit in the Believer: Reflections on the Subsequence of Spirit Baptism* (Unpublished Master's Thesis at Oral Roberts University).

Hollenweger, Walter J. *Pentecostalism: Origins and Developments Worldwide*. Peabody, MA: Hendrickson, 1997.

———.*The Pentecostals*. London: SCM Press, 1972.

Horness, J. "Contemporary Music-driven Worship." In *Exploring the Worship Spectrum: Six Views*. (Ed. by Paul Basden.) Grand Rapids, MI: Zondervan, 2004.

Hui, Archie. "The Pneumatology of Watchman Nee: A New Testament Perspective." *Evangelical Quarterly* (75: 4, 2003): 3–29

Hummel, Charles E. *Fire in the Fireplace: Charismatic Renewal in the Nineties*. Downers Grove, IL: InterVarsity, 1993.

Hunt, Dave and McMahon, T. A. *The Seduction of Christianity: Spiritual Discernment in the Last Days*. Eugene, OR: Harvest House, 1985.

Hunter, Harold D. *Spirit-Baptism: A Pentecostal Alternative*. Lanham, MD: University Press of America, 1983.

Hyatt, Eddie L. *2000 Years of Charismatic Christianity*. Lake Mary, FL: Charisma House, 2002.

Isgrigg, Daniel D. *Pilgrimage into Pentecost: The Pneumatological Legacy of Howard M. Ervin*. Tulsa, OK: Word & Spirit, 2008.

James, William. *The Varieties of Religious Experience: A Study in Human Nature*. New York, NY: Collier, 1961.

Jenkins, Philip. *The Next Christendom: the Coming of Global Christianity*. Oxford, England: Oxford University Press, 2002.

Jüngel, Eberhard. *Unterwegs Zur Sache: Theologische Bemerkungen*. Munich, Germany: Chr. Kaiser, 1972.

Kelsey, Morton. *Healing & Christianity*. Minneapolis, MN: Augsburg, 1995.

King, Paul L. *A Believer with Authority: The Life and Message of John A. MacMillan*. Camp Hill, PA: Christian Publications, 2001.

———. *Moving Mountains: Lessons in Bold Faith from Great Evangelical Leaders*. Grand Rapids, MI: Chosen Books, 2004.

———. *Only Believe: Examining the Origins and Development of Classic and Contemporary Word of Faith Theologies*. Tulsa, OK: Word & Spirit, 2008.

Kraft, Charles H. *Christianity with Power: Your Worldview and Your Experience of the Supernatural*. Ann Arbor, MI: Servant, 1989.

———.*Defeating Dark Angels: Breaking Demonic Oppression in the Believer's Life*. Ann Arbor, MI: Servant Publications, 1992.

Ladd, George Eldon. *Jesus and the Kingdom: The Eschatology of Biblical Realism.* New York: Harper & Row, 1964.

Land, Steven J. *Pentecostal Spirituality: A Passion for the Kingdom.* Sheffield, England: Sheffield Academic Press, 2001.

Lederle, Henry I. *Treasures Old and New: Interpretations of "Spirit-Baptism" in the Charismatic Renewal Movement.* Peabody, MA: Hendrickson, 1988.

———. "Initial Evidence and the Charismatic Movement: An Ecumenical Appraisal." In *Initial Evidence: Historical and Biblical Perspectives on the Pentecostal Doctrine of Spirit Baptism* (Ed. by Gary B. McGee). Peabody, MA: Hendrickson Publishers, 1991.

MacArthur, John F. *Charismatic Chaos.* Grand Rapids, MI: Zondervan, 1992.

Macchia, Frank D. *Baptized in the Spirit: Global Pentecostal Theology.* Grand Rapids, MI: Zondervan, 2006.

MacMillan, John A. *The Authority of the Believer.* Camp Hill, PA: Christian Publications, 1997.

Mathew, Thomson K. *Spirit-Led Ministry in the 21st Century.* Fairfax, VA: Xulon Press, 2004.

McConnell, D.R. *A Different Gospel: A Historical and Biblical Analysis of the Modern Faith Movement.* Peabody, MA: Hendrickson, 1988.

McDonnell, Kilian (Ed.) *Presence Power Praise: Documents on the Charismatic Renewal.* 3 vols. Collegeville, MN: Liturgical Press, 1980.

McDonnell, Kilian and Montague, George T. *Christian Initiation and Baptism in the Holy Spirit: Evidence from the First Eight Centuries* (Second, Revised Edition). Collegeville, MN: Liturgical Press, 1994.

McGee, Gary B., ed. *Initial Evidence: Historical and Biblical Perspectives on the Pentecostal Doctrine of Spirit Baptism.* Peabody, MA: Hendrickson Publishers, 1991.

McIntyre, John. *The Shape of Pneumatology: Studies in the Doctrine of the Holy Spirit.* Edinburgh, Scotland: T&T Clark, 1997.

McKim, Donald K. *Introducing the Reformed Faith.* Louisville, KY: Westminster John Knox, 2001.

Moltmann, Jürgen. *The Spirit of Life: A Universal Affirmation.* Minneapolis MN: Fortress, 1992.

Montague, George T. *The Holy Spirit: Growth of a Biblical Tradition.* New York, NY: Paulist, 1976.

Moody, D. L. *Power from on High: A Vital Message for the Worldwide Church Today.* Tonbridge, England: Sovereign World, 1992.

Moore, S(eth). David. *The Shepherding Movement: Controversy and Charismatic Ecclesiology.* Journal of Pentecostal Theology: Supplement Series, 27. New York: T & T Clark, 2003; Palo Alto, CA: ebrary, 2009.

Nee, Watchman. *The Breaking of the Outer Man and the Release of the Spirit.* Anaheim, CA: Living Stream Ministry, 1997.

———. *The Communion of the Holy Spirit.* Richmond, Virginia: Christian Fellowship Publishers, 1994.

Niebuhr, H. Richard. *Christ and Culture.* New York: Harper and Row, 1956.

O'Connor, Edward D. *The Pentecostal Movement in the Catholic Church.* Notre Dame, IN: Ave Maria, 1971.

Ortiz, Juan Carlos. *Disciple.* Carol Stream, IL: Creation House, 1975.

Palma, Anthony D. "Spirit Baptism: Before and After." *Enrichment Journal* (2005: 01): 1–6.

Paulk, Earl. *Held in the Heavens Until . . . : God's Strategy for Planet Earth.* Atlanta, GA: K Dimension Publishers, 1985.

Phiri, Isaac and Maxwell, Joe. "Gospel Riches: Africa's Rapid Embrace of Prosperity: Pentecostalism Provokes Concern and Hope." *Christianity Today* (51: 7, July 2007): 22–29.

Pinnock, Clark H. *Flame of Love: A Theology of the Holy Spirit.* Downers Grove, IL: InterVarsity, 1996.

Quebedeaux, Richard. *The New Charismatics II: How a Christian Renewal Movement Became Part of the American Religious Mainstream.* San Francisco, CA: Harper & Row, 1983.

Reed, David A. *"In Jesus' Name": The History and Beliefs of Oneness Pentecostals.* Blandford Forum, UK: Deo Publishing, 2007.

Reid, Michael S.B. *Strategic Level Spiritual Warfare: A Modern Mythology?* Fairfax, VA: Xulon Press, 2002.

Riss, Richard (M). "The Latter Rain Movement of 1948." *Pneuma: The Journal of the Society for Pentecostal Studies* (4:1, 1982): 32–45.

———. "The New Order of the Latter Rain: A Look at the Revival Movement on Its 40th Anniversary." *Assemblies of God Heritage* (7:3, Fall 1987): 15–19.

Robeck, Cecil M. *The Azusa Street Mission & Revival: The Birth of the Global Pentecostal Movement.* Nashville, TN: Nelson Reference & Electronic, 2006.

Shelton, James B. *Mighty in Word and Deed: The Role of the Holy Spirit in Luke—Acts.* Peabody, MA: Hendrickson, 1991.

Sherrill, J.L. *They Speak with Other Tongues.* New York: McGraw-Hill, 1964.

Smail, Tom; Andrew Walker and Nigel Wright. *The Love of Power or the Power of Love: A Careful Assessment of the Problems within the Charismatic and Word-of-Faith Movements*. Minneapolis, MN: Bethany House, 1994.

Smail, Thomas A. *Reflected Glory: The Spirit in Christ and Christians*. London: Hodder & Stoughton, 1975.

Smedes, Lewis B. (Ed.) *Ministry and the Miraculous: A Case Study at Fuller Theological Seminary*. Los Angeles, CA: Fuller Seminary Press, 1987.

Sullivan, Francis A. *Charisms and Charismatic Renewal: A Biblical and Theological Study*. Dublin, Ireland: Gill and MacMillan, 1982.

Synan, Vinson. (Ed) *Aspects of Pentecostal-Charismatic Origins*. Plainfield, NJ: Logos International, 1975.

Synan, Vinson. *In the Latter Days: The Outpouring of the Holy Spirit in the Twentieth Century*. Ann Arbor, MI: Servant Books, 1984.

———.*The Century of the Holy Spirit: 100 Years of Pentecostal and Charismatic Renewal*. Nashville, TN: Thomas Nelson, 2001.

———.*The Holiness-Pentecostal Tradition: Charismatic Movements in the Twentieth Century* (Second Edition). Grand Rapids, MI: Eerdmans, 1997.

Turner, Max. *The Holy Spirit and Spiritual Gifts*. Peabody MA: Hendrickson Publishers, 1996.

Twelftree, Graham H. *Jesus the Exorcist: A Contribution to the Study of the Historical Jesus*. Peabody, MA: Hendrickson, 1993.

Van Ruler, Arnold A. *Calvinist Trinitarianism and Theocentric Politics*. Lewiston, NY: Edwin Mellen, 1989.

Vandervelde, George (Ed.) *The Holy Spirit: Renewing and Empowering Presence*. Winfield, British Columbia: Wood Lake Book, 1989.

Volf, Miroslav. "Materiality of Salvation: An Investigation in the Soteriologies of Liberation and Pentecostal Theologies." In *Journal of Ecumenical Studies* (26:3, Summer 1989): 447–467.

Wagner, C. Peter. *Engaging the Enemy: How to Fight & Defeat Territorial Spirits*. Ventura, CA: Regal, 1991.

———.(Ed.). *The New Apostolic Churches*. Ventura, CA: Regal, 1998.

Walker, Andrew. *Restoring the Kingdom: The Radical Christianity of the House Church Movement*. London: Hodder and Stoughton, 1985.

Warfield, Benjamin B. *Counterfeit Miracles*. London: The Banner of Truth Trust, 1972.

Wesley, John. *A Plain Account of Christian Perfection.* In *Selected Prayers, Hymns, Journal Notes, Sermons, Letters and Treatises.* (Ed. By F. Whaling) London, SPCK, 1981.

Williams, J. Rodman. *Renewal Theology: Salvation, the Holy Spirit, and Christian Living.* Grand Rapids, MI: Zondervan, 1990.

Wilson, Mark W. (Ed.) *Spirit and Renewal: Essays in Honor of J. Rodman Williams.* Sheffield, England: Sheffield Academic Press, 1994.

Wimber, John (with Kevin Springer). *Power Healing.* New York: HarperCollins, 1987.

Wright, N.T. *Surprised by Hope: Rethinking Heaven, the Resurrection, and the Mission of the Church.* New York, NY: HarperOne, 2008.

Yong, Amos. *Beyond the Impasse: Toward a Pneumatological Theology of Religions.* Grand Rapids, MI: Baker Academic, 2003.

———.*The Spirit Poured Out on All Flesh: Pentecostalism and the Possibility of Global Theology.* Grand Rapids, MI: Baker Academic, 2005.

Yun, Koo Dong. *Baptism in the Holy Spirit: an Ecumenical Theology of Spirit Baptism.* Lanham, MD: University Press of America, 2003.

Index